Sound in Motion

Sound in Motion

A Performer's Guide
to Greater Musical Expression

David McGill

Indiana University Press

BLOOMINGTON AND INDIANAPOLIS

This book is a publication of

Indiana University Press
601 North Morton Street
Bloomington, IN 47404-3797 USA

http://iupress.indiana.edu

Telephone orders 800-842-6796
Fax orders 812-855-7931
Orders by e-mail iuporder@indiana.edu

© 2007 by David McGill
All rights reserved

The paper used in this publication meets the minimum requirements of American National Standard for Information Sciences—Permanence of Paper for Printed Library Materials, ANSI Z39.48-1984.

MANUFACTURED IN THE UNITED STATES OF AMERICA

Library of Congress Cataloging-in-Publication Data

McGill, David, bassoonist.
Sound in motion : a performer's guide to greater musical expression / David McGill.
p. cm.
Includes bibliographical references (p.   ), discography (p.   ), and index.
ISBN 978-0-253-34921-7 (cloth : alk. paper) — ISBN 978-0-253-21926-8 (pbk. : alk. paper) 1. Instrumental music—Interpretation (Phrasing, dynamics, etc.) 2. Tabuteau, Marcel, 1887–1966. I. Title.
MT170.M34 2007
784.14'3—dc22
2007007695

1 2 3 4 5 12 11 10 09 08 07

IN MEMORIAM
Andrew Bogiages
(1971–1997)
My student and friend

To my teachers

~ JOHN DE LANCIE ~
—whose insightful and incisive teaching forms
the basis for this book.

~ JOHN MINSKER ~
—whose unceasing quest for perfection brought all his
students at Curtis closer to their ideals.

~ SOL SCHOENBACH ~
—whose probing musical mind revealed the logic
behind many seeming musical mysteries.

Contents

Preface

While traveling through Scotland, I encountered a stranger on a train who took an interest in my writing. This young man, after learning my book was about music, remarked that he had once seen an amusing newspaper cartoon that said, "Writing about music is like dancing about architecture."

Although a book about music is flawed from the outset because one art form can only vaguely help to define another—as painting cannot shed much light on the art of acting—music has been, and will continue to be, one of the most written and talked about of human endeavors.

Although I am a bassoonist, this is not a bassoon method. There is one section of the book that relates specifically to wind techniques, but what I have mainly written about is musical thinking. My hope is that this book, written from an orchestral woodwind instrumentalist's perspective, will be of some value to musicians of every stripe.

It is strange that so few performing musicians throughout history have written a thorough analysis of musical phrasing. To the exclusion of performers, it seems largely to have been only within the jurisdiction of theoreticians to write on this subject. Busy performers have usually limited themselves to writing about the technique of playing a given instrument, if they have bothered to write anything at all. Surely many have avoided putting their ideas about musical performance on paper because they feared criticism from the academic community. It is true that once one writes down ideas, one must be prepared to defend and support them upon a solid rational framework. I realize that this commentary will provoke diverse opinions. Once one takes a stand on any issue, one's world is immediately divided into two camps—those who agree and those who disagree. (My mother perceptively pointed out a third—those who don't care!)

At the very least, I hope this book will raise questions in the mind of the reader that may otherwise have remained unexplored.

Acknowledgments

It took me ten years to absorb the musical concepts I was given at the Curtis Institute of Music. It took another ten to put them on paper. With heartfelt thanks I acknowledge my students for reading portions of the book and helping me to make clearer those concepts on the printed page. I thank my former Cleveland Orchestra colleagues and my Chicago Symphony Orchestra colleagues, especially Michael Henoch, for providing me with their invaluable input. I also wish to express gratitude to my friends Fredy Perez, Richard Fleischman, Cole Seaton, Carla Chrisfield, and Curt Maslanka for their support and much-needed words of encouragement.

Thanks to Sarah Underwood, Noé Cantú, and Ken Chin for putting portions of my illegible handwriting into the computer. Thanks to the Chicago Symphony Orchestra's librarians, Mark Swanson, Carole Keller, and Peter Conover, for cheerfully gathering and copying pages of scores and parts for my use. Most of all, thanks are due Jelena Dirks, who got this project moving into the home stretch by putting the great majority of the musical examples into the text; and to Ke Liu for meticulously preparing those examples for publication. Special thanks also go to my sister, Sharon Oliver, who prepared the graphics. My great admiration and heartfelt thanks go to Roderick Branch for his excellent editorial suggestions. Any errors in the text are mine, and mine alone.

Wayne Rapier, of Boston Records, deserves special mention for allowing me to quote freely from the CD *Marcel Tabuteau's Lessons.*

I also owe thanks to my mother, Louise T. McGill. She was never too busy—or so she said—to listen to my newest "creation" and offer her perceptive suggestions, no matter what hour of the day or wee hour of the morning I called.

Most of all, thanks are due those who gave of themselves daily for so many years at the Curtis Institute of Music—my teachers Dr. Sol Schoenbach (1915–99), John de Lancie (1921–2002), and John Minsker (1912–2007), who were kind enough to examine portions of this text to see just how much I had twisted their words.

Part 1

A Style Is Born

Strauss: Also Sprach Zarathustra, *Sunrise*

"... I wish to lavish my knowledge on the earth ..." Zarathustra, "Zarathustra's Preface" by Friedrich Nietzsche.

Truly musical phrasing is musical *thought* in sound. Rationalized phrasing has the potential to reach far deeper into the psyche of the listener than performance based solely on instinct, however good that instinct may be. All musicians can learn to play more expressively through carefully directed thought.

The Beginning

All young performers learn the history of compositional styles (baroque, classical, romantic, etc.), but, apart from a few notable exceptions, they are not taught about the great historical instrumentalists and the various performance styles they embodied. The reason for this is that compositions from various periods exist on paper and can be easily studied, but there is no way to examine concretely the playing of performers who were active before the advent of recording. Their playing has vanished into the air. Despite the existence of a few subjective contemporary reviews and a handful of teaching methods of the distant past, historical performance styles remain an enigma.

American woodwind instrumentalists today are aware of the existence of an American style of woodwind playing, but most are, understandably, blithely unaware of its origin. The roots of a rationalized system of musical phrasing, which led to the creation of this distinctly American woodwind style, can be traced back to one legendary performer and teacher who began to open the eyes of his students in Philadelphia beginning in the 1920s. This well-documented stylistic phenomenon—born less than a century ago and preserved on disc—was largely brought about through the efforts of Marcel Tabuteau. He happened to be an oboist, but his message was universal.

Marcel Tabuteau ca. 1920s. From the collection of David McGill.

Tabuteau and His Influence

All roads in this recent evolution in the history of performance inevitably lead to Marcel Tabuteau (1887–1966), principal oboist of
the Philadelphia Orchestra from 1915 to 1954. In addition to the
oboe, he taught the woodwind classes and, later in his tenure, even
a string class at the Curtis Institute of Music.

In his thirty years of teaching at Curtis, Tabuteau had approximately fifty oboe students. The following is a list of his most notable:

Name	Position
Rhadames Angelucci	Principal, *Minnesota Orchestra*
Perry Bauman	Principal, *Toronto Symphony*
Robert Bloom	Principal, *NBC Symphony*, English Horn, *Philadelphia Orchestra*
William Criss	Principal, *Metropolitan Opera*/top Los Angeles film studio player
John de Lancie	Principal, *Philadelphia Orchestra, Pittsburgh Symphony*
Alfred Genovese	Principal, *Boston Symphony, Metropolitan Opera, Baltimore Symphony*
Harold Gomberg	Principal, *New York Philharmonic, Toronto Symphony, Saint Louis Symphony*
Ralph Gomberg	Principal, *Boston Symphony*
Felix Kraus	English Horn/Second, *Cleveland Orchestra*
Marc Lifschey	Principal, *Cleveland Orchestra, Metropolitan Opera, San Francisco Symphony, Buffalo Philharmonic, National Symphony*
John Mack	Principal, *Cleveland Orchestra, National Symphony, New Orleans Symphony*
Arno Mariotti	Principal, *Detroit Symphony, Pittsburgh Symphony*
John Minsker	English Horn, *Philadelphia Orchestra, Detroit Symphony*
Charles Morris	Second/Assistant Principal, *Philadelphia Orchestra*
Louis Rosenblatt	English Horn, *Philadelphia Orchestra*
Martha Scherer-Alfee	English Horn, *Buffalo Philharmonic*
Harry Shulman	Principal, *NBC Symphony, Pittsburgh Symphony, ABC Orchestra*
Laila Storch	Principal, *Houston Symphony/Oboe, Soni Ventorum Woodwind Quintet*
J. Laurence Thorstenberg	English Horn, *Boston Symphony, Chicago Symphony*

Most teachers hope for one or two students in a lifetime who will go on to enjoy great careers. This list of nineteen is nearly half of all those Marcel Tabuteau taught at Curtis.

However, Tabuteau's influence spread far beyond his oboe progeny to affect the other instrumentalists who attended his woodwind and string classes. Apart from this legion of students, there were many other musicians who were indirectly influenced by his teachings through their own musical contacts. Consequently, they may not have realized the debt they owed him. Hundreds more were also to gain from simply hearing him play. Many of his Philadelphia Orchestra colleagues readily admitted to his influence on their playing and thinking. Musicians in other orchestras have stated that Tabuteau inspired them as well from afar. Even now, nearly every American woodwind player has somehow been affected by the high standard he and his students set.

There is probably no teacher of any musical instrument who, through the success of his or her students, ever held such a grip on the musical style of a country as Marcel Tabuteau did in mid-twentieth-century America. A great many of the young musicians Tabuteau worked with passed along his concepts to new generations of musicians who never had direct contact with him. Through this dissemination of his teachings, Tabuteau ultimately affected playing and musical thinking in America profoundly. He exerted a greater impact than any other single musician at that crucial time when no national style existed within the United States.

The Times

At the turn of the twentieth century, there was a vacuum in the American musical scene into which poured many of Europe's finest musicians—Hungarian and Russian string players; German brass players; French woodwind players. They were welcomed openly as ambassadors of culture by the upper echelons of American society, which wished to emulate Europe in all things artistic. It is notable that in the first years of the twentieth century, due to the substantial influx of well-trained musical immigrants into America's musical centers, the languages spoken in the Philadelphia Orchestra's and Boston Symphony's rehearsals were German and French, respectively. Americans did not resent this situation. At that time, they understood as a matter of course that the language of high culture was foreign.

In the field of classical music, America did not yet have the pedagogical musical tradition that could produce the type of outstanding players found in profusion in the capitals of Europe. Conductors of young American ensembles wooed recent graduates from top European music conservatories to take the massive step of pursuing their artistic goals across the Atlantic. Thus it was that in 1905, eighteen-year-old Marcel Tabuteau—his *premier prix* from the Paris Conservatoire freshly in hand—accepted the challenge of making his fortune in the "land of opportunity."

For the next half-century, with a monumental single-mindedness of purpose, Marcel Tabuteau forged a musical dynasty of immense proportions before returning to his native France, leaving behind a legacy that still grows to this day.

Thanks to Tabuteau's efforts, by the time he retired in 1954, the first-desk woodwind players of most American symphony orchestras were homegrown.

His Message

Undeniably, Tabuteau had a sweeping impact on the oboe world, most recognizable in the hybrid tone he developed. At the beginning of his career, as the newly appointed English hornist of the New York Symphony Society, he began to experiment with tone quality after hearing the orchestra's German principal oboist. By fusing the flexibility of his native French style with the tonal richness of the German style, he created a new oboe sonority, now known as the Tabuteau or American oboe sound. His further development of the long-scrape reed—referred to as the American style reed—also helped him arrive at this ideal. Another feature of this style is the controlled use of a narrow vibrato that does not compromise the pitch of the note being played.

John de Lancie, Tabuteau's student and successor as principal oboist of the Philadelphia Orchestra, and oboe and woodwind instructor at the Curtis Institute of Music, put it well when describing Tabuteau's effect on the oboists of his day: "There may be other areas of endeavor where people can say that so-and-so had as great an influence, but I can't imagine anybody having had *more* of an influence, whether it be in painting or in poetry or in literature. . . . *His influence was total. Everybody wanted to play and sound like Tabuteau.*"[1]

Marcel Tabuteau's most important contribution to the world of music was his development of a universally applicable, systematic approach to musical phrasing. By virtue of this phrasing system, his influence extended far beyond his oboe students. Many master musicians on such diverse instruments as piano, violin, tuba, and even timpani testified that they learned from listening to or participating in his woodwind and string classes at Curtis.

Marcel Tabuteau was interviewed for a segment of the Philadelphia Woodwind Quintet's 1959 television series, *200 Years of Woodwinds*. The interview touches on the universality of Tabuteau's teaching method. With a sly smile Tabuteau says, "I must confess to you that when a *horn* player thanks me for the little fun we had together, I am very proud of it." Composer Samuel Barber (also a Curtis graduate), who was the show's next guest in the series, recalled, "I remember so well, going to the woodwind classes." When asked if his musical ideas were influenced by listening to Tabuteau's classes, Barber stated, "Oh, I'm sure—Yes! I'm sure that they were, because [in the] first place, those were *extraordinary* sessions and I'm glad that you got Mr. Tabuteau—that wonderful artist—on film, so that the public can see what you all went through. . . . It was not only listening to the woodwinds that was . . . so important for a composer's ear, . . . but also the wonderful musicianship which I think he's transmitted to you all: *the phrasing*." John de Lancie recalled, "Sam Barber told me on several occasions that everything he learned about music, he learned from Tabuteau and [the piano pedagogue] Isabelle Vengerova."

Tabuteau's precise teaching allowed his students to delve deeply into the function of every note, with profound musical results. The purpose of this academic approach was to communicate fully the emotional content of the music through the recognition and definition of the music's natural contours. This way of playing speaks with clarity and a convincing grammatical precision. With thought, every musician who studied with him could profitably apply Tabuteau's methods to his or her own music making. And most of them did.

Those present at a 1997 reunion of Curtis graduates, from 1937 and before, vividly recalled his teaching. The Institute's director, Gary Graffman, wrote of the occasion:

> Much of the discussion centered around memories of the renowned oboist, Marcel Tabuteau—funny anecdotes, naturally, but also descriptions of his unique teaching methods. Tabuteau's influence as a musician was, and still is, remarkable. It is remarkable that his way of thinking about music is perpetuated years

after his death, but it is particularly amazing, I think, because Tabuteau influenced not only oboists and wind players, but [also] musicians in all disciplines. What can an oboist teach a pianist? Well, performers of all kinds still remember Tabuteau's "phrase-making" seminars.

And, as if to prove this point yet again, one of our newest alumni, a violist, commented that during his years at Curtis scarcely a lesson went by without his teacher [Karen Tuttle] telling him something that Tabuteau—an oboist, remember!—had told her! This tradition has now continued for over 60 years.[2]

Marcel Tabuteau changed the lives of those around him. Through his playing and teaching, he defined the "natural" in music. His phrasing existed in harmony with the music's structure and his teaching explained how to achieve this result. This was his *raison d'être*.

Through it all, the search for forward motion was Tabuteau's primary objective.

Part 2

What Is Music?

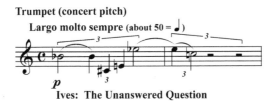

Trumpet (concert pitch)

Largo molto sempre (about 50 = ♩)

Ives: The Unanswered Question

The answer to this question is elusive. A kind of answer exists, but it is not like those we are trained to look for in grade school, such as $2 + 2 = 4$. Such a profound question can only begin to be answered piece by piece. And often, one special piece holds the key to a fuller understanding of a great mystery.

In Voltaire's *Candide*, the title character roams the earth encountering adventure after senseless adventure in search of the answer to the question "What is the meaning of life?" In the end, he finds that the simple tending to a plot of earth holds life's greatest pleasure and meaning. Through his novella, Voltaire concludes that what is important in life is work and that *work is its own reward* because it cultivates personal growth. If we thoughtfully apply this working mentality to our own lives, it can have an immediately tangible day-to-day impact upon how we think about the process of living life and reaching our goals.

Similarly, there is one facet of the answer to our question about music that can help us reach our musical goals. Marcel Tabuteau's message of forward motion gives us the key part of the answer to that question and allows us to direct our thinking toward the process of making music. Like Voltaire's answer about the meaning of life—tending to the growth of one's own garden—this musical revelation holds concrete consequences for us as performers. The note-by-note search for forward motion profoundly affects how we approach making music.

In the pages to come, I have tried to define the borders around the essence of what music is, as Voltaire illustrated the meaning of life in *Candide*, by setting aside what lies outside those borders. A methodical process of elimination more clearly delineates the limits of the question. By first identifying those issues popularly associated with music making, which, in reality, are unrelated to the essence of musical performance, one can then focus on the true elements necessary to achieve meaningful musical expression.

Fun?

Clarinet in D
Immer sehr lebhaft

mf lustig   *sfz*
Strauss: Till Eulenspiegel

I remember a conversation with a fellow student at the Curtis Institute who, after a year of study there, announced she was leaving the school and quitting music. I asked her why she was renouncing her dream, and she answered, "I've learned how difficult it is; it's not *fun* anymore."

On hearing that one's profession is that of a musician, members of the public often exclaim, "Oh, that must be fun!" Musicians usually reply, "Oh yes, it is." But on reflection, I suspect many professionals feel a little differently. An amateur who assumes that a professional musician is having fun in concert may have had his or her last experience with musical performance in the high school marching band or in the neighbor's garage, where pressure to meet critical standards was minimal. Most professional musicians have also, at one time or another, been asked, "Do you get paid for that?" The sense that music is purely an idle pursuit that gives exactly the same pleasure to listener as to performer is deeply ingrained in the public mind. However, professional music making is very different from listening to music passively as a diversion from the pressures of life. It is not without joy, but it is not exactly fun. The very act of playing an instrument can cause physical pain and mental strain for the performer. In order to uphold the highest standard at all times, performers cannot simply allow the music to wash over them without thought, because live music making does not afford the performer the luxury of a second chance. This is the single greatest pressure the performer feels.

In English, we "play" our instruments. In Spanish, the verb used is "tocar" (to touch), and in Italian it is "suonare" (to sound). Both of these words seem a bit more appropriate than "play" when describing what musicians do with their instruments. That English word's association with the diversion of childish play has seemed to permeate the public's perception of what we, as trained professionals, do on our instruments: *play* as opposed to *work*. By the way, both "tocar" and "suonare" hold other equally telling connotations; we "touch" our instruments, through "sound," in a way that will hopefully "touch" the listener.

There is no shame in admitting that a career in music is not mere fun. It is extremely difficult work. The "fun page" of any local newspaper aptly displays what fun can be—puzzles, games, and cartoons. "Fun" is simply too base a word to describe what performing means to serious musicians. When invested with all the effort it deserves, music can be deeply fulfilling and can touch our most profound emotions. Music can and often does communicate a sense of fun to the listener, but this carefree feeling is transmitted through the strict discipline and diligence exercised by the musicians on stage. John de Lancie said quite candidly, "I never played, in my life, for fun. Playing was always hard work. I don't say that I didn't enjoy it, but it was never something that came easily to me."[1]

The linguistic difference between the words "fun" and "enjoyment" also adds to the confusion. One experiences joy in music's execution on a deeper level than the fun one feels when making faces in the mirror. The word "enjoy" implies an appreciation that involves an active thoughtfulness. The word "fun," on the other hand, holds a connotation of disengaged mental idleness. While listening to music, there is nothing wrong with adopting a state of mental passivity, from time to time, in order to relieve the tensions we all feel in life, but the abandonment of one's intellectual capacity is clearly not a part of performing classical music. Audience members often believe that because they feel a relaxed pleasure in music's performance, the performers are feeling exactly the same way. But it is discipline, risk taking, intense concentration, and the struggle and search for beauty that provide whatever satisfaction—or, more often, dissatisfaction—the discerning musician experiences before, during, and after the concert experience. In concert, pleasure is the audience's rightful dividend, but the professional musician is engaged in a higher quest.

The public should neither be concerned with nor aware of the countless difficulties that confront professional musicians in live performance. If they are, the musician has not done his or her job well. Serious pursuits—Olympic competition for the athletes; ballet as experienced by the dancers; operatic or symphonic performances as produced by the musicians—are stress-inducing events that stretch the limits of human endurance and ability. Even so, the sensation felt by a classical musician during certain concerts may verge on a sort of ecstasy, such is the intensity of the truly musical experience. The word "fun" utterly fails to describe the depth of that feeling.

Composer Gian-Carlo Menotti once related a story in which the Italian tenor Enrico Caruso (1873–1921) commented on the public's reaction to his art: "When somebody asked Caruso what people liked so much in his voice, he said, 'It's the fear in my voice.'" Menotti noted that the same quality could be felt in the performances of the Greek American soprano Maria Callas (1923–77): "She always gave a sense that perhaps she would not be able to finish an aria. It was sort of like watching Callas fighting against Callas. It was sort of a bullfight in which she finally killed the monster and she was acclaimed as the victorious heroine of the moment."[2] Conductor Carlo Maria Giulini said of her performances, "It was a kind of victory through a hard fight."[3]

Maria Callas herself remarked, "Music is very difficult. . . . It's really not as easy as the public thinks. There's a lot to it—lots of devotion, dedication [and] respect for the composer. . . . It's a whole *science*, a whole *art*." She went on: "I still work, because, you see, we go by very little [with printed music] and you have to search. . . . It's like reading a book. Many times you read a book but you have to read between the lines too. . . . We have to read what the composer would have wanted: a thousand colors, expressions. It's really not as easy as all that, *if* one really cares that much—and I do. *I do*."[4]

Magic?

Dukas: The Sorcerer's Apprentice

Most of us who enter our first year of musical study at a college or conservatory believe that music is a magical thing. We hope that from deep within ourselves, a supernatural feeling will arise to carry us on wings to the desired musical result without our having to expend mental energy thinking about our performance. It is only natural that we carry such mental baggage because as audience members, as children, we had been transported by music without active thought. Mistakenly, we expect to be transported in the same passive way once we become adult performers up on the stage.

We must abandon that long-ingrained misconception in order to progress from the comfort of the untrained listener to the discomfort of the trained professional. A true professional is driven by a sense of accountability; driven to do justice to the music by carefully analyzing it in order to discover what is correct in its performance. John de Lancie said, "Whenever you play anything—even at home—if there was a puff of smoke and Beethoven or even your teacher or mine were to appear and ask you, 'Why did you just play that phrase *that* way?' . . . you should be able to clearly justify and explain what you're doing."

A professional magician on stage knows the tricks of the trade that make the audience suspend its disbelief; he knows there is no magic. When we musicians let go of our belief in the magic of it all, we are then—and only then—freed to become the magician who, through stagecraft, creates marvelous illusions. The magic occurs in the mind of the listener, not in what the performer does on stage.

There is little substance to playing that relies upon whims to create musical "magic," as if to say, "I just think it sounds good this way." If no deeper study of the music's structure has gone into the realization of one's music making, it doesn't take long for those who are educated to see through it as mere posturing. Only after the music has been rationalized can the well-informed musician communicate what is really in the music, not just what he or she may wish were in it.

Feeling?

Schumann: Piano Concerto in A minor

Musicians love music. That love is born of profound feelings and fuels the years of practice necessary to realize the dream of becoming a professional. However, a professional musician who is simply content to feel the music during performance without understanding its structure is not really qualified to interpret the classics for discerning listeners.

Feelings can, in fact, be detrimental. I have had many bad days in performance when I felt sick, tired, or even bored. I have had feelings of nervousness and tension due to the difficulty of the composition. These feelings have no place in the music.

I have also sometimes had to play music in concert that was anything but the kind of music I love. At these times, one must sublimate one's true feelings and play the music as though the composition were from one's own pen. Musicians must also often present the same concert again and again and give the audience the impression that it is the first time, every time, regardless of one's personal feelings.

Then there have been those marvelous concerts where I have found the performance to be so moving that I felt I was almost unable to play. The tears that have welled up in my eyes at these times have not had a beneficial effect on my concentration or my eyesight!

We perform in the "moment of ecstasy," so to speak, but, as professionals, we must retain some sense of separation from that exultation so as not to lose composure or control over our instruments. Attractive though the romantic notion is of the musician experiencing rapturous paroxysms or pangs of pain during performance, the musician must remove himself or herself from that subjective state of mind.

Professional musicians are not paid to simply feel the music in a public act of exhibitionism and then, by virtue of this, to mesmerize the audience into feeling exactly the same way. Even so, many audience members do believe that they are listening in on the performer's feelings in concert. If the listener leaves the concert convinced that he or she has felt the performer's feelings, the truth remains that that listener is capable of feeling only his or her own emotions. Those evoked by the music will be different for everyone. Performers present the music—the audience feels it. Of course, any sensitive musician will always feel something in performance, and this is as it should be. But good, bad, or indifferent, those feelings are incidental.

Marcel Tabuteau said, "I have always been in favor to play as I think. Of course, the ideal combination would be to play with *thinking* and *intelligent feeling*."[1] In his concept of music making, even the emotional act of feeling is tempered with intelligence. Laila Storch, a student of Tabuteau's at Curtis in the 1940s, told a story about Tabuteau's mental approach to playing. After he had demonstrated the opening oboe solo from Schumann's Piano Concerto in one of her lessons, she marveled at his seemingly heartfelt expression. Tabuteau gruffly said to her, "You think this is *feeling?*—NO!" Then he proceeded to demonstrate, note by note, what he had been doing to create the impression of deep emotional involvement.

Tabuteau believed what he said: "If you think beautifully, you play beautiful [*sic*]. I believe to play as you think more than to play as you feel because how about the day you are not feeling so well?"[2] This is the key. Even if the goldfish died—or worse—on the day of a performance, a musician must still go out and give the music its due. Rather than simply feeling your way around the music, successful communication of the music's content depends on having a plan for natural phrasing formulated through analysis of the music's natural structure—phrase by phrase.

Great feeling does not make a great performer. Each and every audience member has the same capacity for feeling emotion as deeply as the musician on the stage. A truly great performer must have far more at his or her disposal in concert.

Talent?

Hanon: The Virtuoso Pianist, In Sixty Exercises, Part I, #1

"Genius does what it must. Talent does what it can."
—Chinese fortune cookie.

Most musicians feel it is possible to teach technique. Yet many of those same musicians also feel it is practically impossible to teach someone to be expressive; how often has one heard the phrase "You've either got it or you don't"?

What those musicians mean is that many people are born "unmusical."

Does one have to be born musical? The musical expression exhibited by a performer is often summed up by the word "talent." People generally concede that a musician must practice to get the notes, but conversely believe that expression just comes to the "talented." Perhaps it is simply easier to believe that a supernatural gift from beyond is responsible for one's expressive capabilities. To accept the fact that intellectual effort is involved in expressive art seems to be a difficult concept to swallow. Many prefer to believe that something that provides so much pleasure could not possibly require so much thought.

Talents are generally believed to be traits that only a chosen few exhibit. To say that one has the talent of great physical dexterity, a discerning ear, or a sharp eye is very different from saying expression itself is a talent. Is it not plausible that we are all born with the ability to express feelings? Even small children cry when they fall down, or laugh when they are amused. Expression is in all of us.

Undoubtedly, some people are more demonstrative than others, but nearly all people seem to be able to communicate their shifting emotional states. The aptitudes involving movement, hearing, and seeing, mentioned above, are inborn—they *are* talents—and improving technical proficiency within the areas mapped out by these talents is not the only possibility for development. Expressive growth is also possible if one is willing to put forth the required *mental* effort.

Meaningful expression in musical performance results when inborn talents are coupled with another innate endowment—a probing intelligence. Intelligence is a talent, but the element that one mines from within the music—through intelligent thought—is the *expression*. There is a critical difference between feeling the music, as audience members do, and unleashing the expression within a composition, which is what performers should do.

How can the intellect guide a musician toward appropriate expression in performance? I believe the common usage of the word "talent" (as when describing expression) more accurately refers to applied intelligence. I also believe that intelligence is synonymous with awareness. And it is an undeniable fact that one can be brought to awareness, as a child is made aware of the traffic in the street outside his or her home. Because of this awareness, the child then learns to look both ways before crossing the street. Behavior can be modified. Similarly, in music, one can be taught to be aware of the musical traffic that fills the page so as to avoid musical accidents. Once one gains this knowledge, phrasing choices appropriate to the musical situation become clear. The music is played more expressively—more true to itself. Therefore, it is not unreasonable to conclude that one can be taught to be musical.

The "Blessed" Ones

Musical performance is not a blank canvas upon which we performers paint whatever comes to mind—although it is possible to do this and get by for an entire career. After years of reinforcement from proud relatives, easily impressed amateurs, and audience members, the young musician can become brainwashed by the idea that he or she is one of that rare breed who is blessed with expressive talent. But the possibility of producing great art dies when one believes his or her talent alone will carry the day—"I just do what feels right at the moment—I *feel* the music." This way of blindly feeling one's way through a musical performance, at the expense of studying the music's structure, may indeed be expressive, but expressive of what? The unquestioning belief in one's spur-of-the-moment impulses can, by its very nature, yield only a hit-and-miss result. On reflection, it seems the very height of egotism to trust one's gut reactions so implicitly.

Every performer would secretly like to believe he or she is another Mozart. Exasperatingly, Mozart is often portrayed as a genius who simply dictated what was in his head without thinking. However, it was precisely because he *was* thinking—*always thinking*—that he had those wonderfully intelligent things in his head to dictate at all. Genius is the opposite of thoughtlessness. The word "intelligence" connotes thoughtfulness. The word "talent," on the other hand, connotes a lack of thought. At the bottom line, intelligence remains the necessary element that makes communication of any idea worthwhile—whether written, spoken, sung, or played. Talent is a handy word to be bandied about among those discussing their children at afternoon tea, but meaningful expression in musical performance is no accident of nature.

"You're So Lucky"

Those who have done their homework are actually demeaned when one proffers the compliment: "You were just born with talent." This is not a compliment to those who have worked for years at honing the ability to express emotion intelligently through music. It pigeonholes them into the category of those who "have it" and thus do not have to work like "the rest of us." Furthermore, the idea of work held by those who hold this belief seems only to mean busy work, such as études and finger exercises. They do not seem to classify the long hours of thought necessary to cull emotional meaning from the notes as work at all. A casual listener can be quickly fooled into thinking one is witnessing talent, that is, "expressiveness," by cascades of notes and gratuitous choreography. It takes more thought to appreciate the subtle, deeper aspects at the core of intelligent musicianship. Many people do not want to know that it takes work—both physical *and mental*—to play an instrument musically.

And, unfortunately, many of those people are musicians themselves.

What Is "It"?

So if musical talent is really what so many think it is—namely, expression—why study at all if you are one of the ones who has it? Won't everything you do be wonderful by nature? Conversely, why study if you are one of the ones who does not have it? If nature has placed a cap on your abilities, why engage in a futile search for expression?

I believe we continue that search because, ultimately, we know it is possible to grow. Musical expression is not just the possession of a chosen few. By virtue of our innate intelligence and human capacity to express and feel our emotions, we are all born with the potential to be musically expressive—to varying degrees, of course, but whatever one's starting point, the level can be raised with proper guidance.

Philip Farkas (1914–92), who served as principal Horn of the Chicago Symphony, Boston Symphony, and Cleveland Orchestra, wrote: "Can musicianship be improved or developed through study? The answer must be, 'yes'! The musicianship which is inborn in all of us is but a seed which must be nurtured in many ways in order to flower. . . . It is man's nature to be musical."[1]

Depth of expression is not a talent. The real talent that leads to musical expression is intelligence. The development of expression is the development of the intellect.

Selflessness?

G.P.

Art forms fall into two main categories: binary and ternary. Binary art forms, such as painting and sculpture, involve the creator and the viewer. Music, being a ternary art form, involves at least three participants—composer, *performer*, and listener. By virtue of this, it is possible to make music in endless ways because the "middle man"—the performer—may change an infinite number of times. Unlike a painting, a musical composition takes on different hues with each interpretation. Without the indispensable intermediary of the performer, music would remain inert—embedded in the page. Composer (creative artist) and performer (*re*-creative artist), like playwright and actor, work in tandem. In performance, one's existence is necessary for the existence of the other.

Many mediocre compositions have been given intelligent, musical performances, just as mediocre plays have been masterfully realized by fine actors. By the same token, many musical masterpieces have been marred by uninformed performance. In concert, the quality of the playing is as important as the quality of the composition.

We should not buy into the "selfless performer" attitude put forth by some musicians. These well-intentioned performers say, "We are nothing; we are only serving the composer." Do these musicians feel that as long as the correct notes are played in the correct time, in tune, and with the composer's prescribed dynamics that the job has been done? Even they must feel they have more to give than those basic things—that the music demands more than a paint-by-number philosophy.

In those painting kits many of us dabbled with as children, we first had to learn what number corresponds to what color paint and then fill in the blanks accordingly. But if one stops there, the final picture is disjointed. It can hardly be considered art. With written music, the composer gives us instructions similar to those in a paint-by-number kit; there is only so much that can be written down. The blend of colors, the intensity given to each note, and a thousand other details are left to the performer to interpret. Exposing these hidden details completes the picture. Knowledge of the music's structure helps the player provide those details.

Each composer realizes that the music he or she writes is dead until the performer breathes life into the corpse of the score and re-animates the ideas behind the notes. After all, how can terror or ecstasy be reduced to quarter notes, C-sharps, and sixteenth rests? The sensitive performer imbues these poor symbols with human emotions the composer can only hint at. Likewise, in the world of architecture, the draftsman's blueprint scarcely resembles the finished sitting room complete with wallpaper and throw pillows. The details provided by the homeowner turn a house into a home, just as the musical details supplied by the performer turn notes into music.

The British American conductor Leopold Stokowski (1882–1977) said,

> The best the composer can do when within him he hears in his soul a great melody—we'll say—is to put it on paper. But that paper—we call it music, but that's not music—that's only paper. It's black marks on paper. Somehow it is our privilege and our necessity to try to realize what was in the soul of the composer in his inner hearing and to make that alive again. This is very difficult. One must realize that our system of notation is extremely limited. . . . Some believe that one should merely mechanically reproduce the marks on the paper but I don't believe in that. We must defend the composer against the mechanical conception of life, which is becoming more and more strong today. . . . Our duty is to give to the listener that inspiration that the composer had.[1]

One only serves the music fully by giving of one's self completely through study, not by feigning false modesty, by abdicating responsibility, or by exercising blind faith in one's feelings. Players do serve the composer, but not by negating their intelligence.

Professionalism

Tenor
Mässig

Walther: zu kün - den wa - - - gen   ein   Meis - - - ter - sin - - - ger möcht ich   sein!
"... I dare proclaim it; a mastersinger would I be!"
Wagner: Die Meistersinger, Act I, scene iii

"Fun," "magic," "feeling," "talent," and "selflessness"—these are not the crucial elements necessary to perform classical music well, although there are facets of them that are involved in music making. Admittedly, one can and often does experience fun, sense magic, feel emotion, express one's talent, and give one's self over to the composition. But the truly necessary ingredient in meaningful musical performance is the professionalism of the players and their dedication to seeking musical truth. Otherwise, performing can easily descend to the level of a crude act of public self-indulgence. Waiting for inspiration to strike in order to make one's playing interesting runs the risk of obscuring the music's natural features by imposing an arbitrary interpretation on it. Professionalism resides on a higher plane. Showmanship and artistry are not the same.

Analysis

Analysis is not a dirty word. Self-respecting musicians must analyze music in order to find a plan for one's phrasing. The music's surface elements are flexible things (dynamics, ornaments, instrumentation, etc.), but the underlying grammatical structure (consonance, dissonance, meter, harmony, skeletal structure, etc.) is not. Musical grammar is absolute. Identifying and showing the music's "grammatical structure," while playing, is the performer's duty. But simply knowing that structure is not enough; it must be *expressed* in performance.

Completing the Picture

In the mid-nineteenth century, the infant art of photography developed a means to capture three dimensions. By peering through a goggle-like instrument, called a stereoscope, at two photographic images, one was miraculously transported into a single three-dimensional world.

From the collection of David McGill.

At first glance, the images seem to be exactly alike, yet each is taken from a slightly different perspective. Similarly, the musical instructions given by the composer (analogous to the image on the left) must be complemented by the educated interpretation of the performer (the image on the right) for the music to achieve a deeper dimension through a fusion of the two images. However, if a musician's interpretation of the composer's message is distorted by thoughtless playing, the listener cannot combine the two opposing musical "images" together in the mind and will not be able to absorb the complete aural "picture" in all its depth.

John de Lancie said: "The printed music is the photographic 'negative,' which is processed by your mind into a 'positive' image." This statement vividly expresses the truth that what we see on the page is the opposite of what music really is. Notes are represented as separated dots on the page and must be metamorphosed into a seamless line. Notes are also mute markings that must be translated into sound. Yet each feature in the printed music has its own counterpart in living sound just as every detail in a photographic negative is reflected in its positive image.

Giving the Music Its Due

The composer has often spent months, sometimes years, writing and rewriting a given composition. Nearly twenty years passed before Brahms was convinced that his First Symphony was ready to send into the world. Sibelius spent seven years writing and rewriting his Fifth Symphony. He said that his quest was for what would be "ultimately and *forever* right." Performers, in good conscience, should strive for the same.

In preparing a work for performance, one should be able to identify the function of each note (appoggiatura, passing tone, neighbor tone, etc.). This is the first step toward revealing the music's grammatical structure. Once one knows the function of a note, it will never change. The grammatical functions of the individual notes having been determined, identifying the skeletal structure of the music, often obscured beneath hordes of ornamental notes, is the next step. When this underlying framework is understood, then the phrasing and articulation of music become clear in almost every instance. Defining this grammatical structure leads one to communicate the music's true meaning.

The same principle is true when delivering a speech in a foreign language. It is not enough to simply pronounce the words phonetically; their meaning is communicated only if they are understood and phrased grammatically. Imagine an opera singer who does not understand the words he or she sings. Likewise, an instrumentalist who concentrates only on technical development without learning the basics of musical grammar is just as poorly prepared to communicate musical emotion.

Music is a human creation that can and should be understood by professionals. The term "professional" means more than simply "someone who is paid for what he or she does." A real professional possesses a thorough knowledge of his or her profession and does not simply demonstrate a feeling for it. After all, doesn't a professional "profess *to know*" rather than "profess *to feel*"?

Often, musicians feel they do not want to cloud their minds with knowledge of the music's structure for fear that a dry, expressionless performance will result ("paralysis by analysis"). The old cliché coined by George Bernard Shaw, "Those who *can*—do; those who *can't*—teach," vividly illustrates this widely held prejudice. Music theory teachers have long given the impression that in order to know about the building blocks of music one must first kill it and then perform a musical autopsy, leaving only a corpse behind. But performers need to realize that musicians start with a corpse. Only by analyzing these sparse musical remains can we then begin to resuscitate the music note by note.

Music making is more than showing what you can do. It is the art of showing what the composer has done, by reanimating and communicating his or her message to the listener through the heart *and* the mind. This is what a professional musician should do.

Motion

Paganini: Moto Perpetuo

My woodwind instructor, John de Lancie, began his first freshman class each year at the Curtis Institute of Music by asking: "What is music?" This bombshell brought forth many timid responses such as "tone," "pitch," "dynamics," "phrasing," "line," and "sound." Once a student hit upon "sound," de Lancie explained that sound itself is indeed an essential element. But then shouldn't street noises or rustling leaves be considered music? To some, they are "music to the ears," but they are not structured, ordered sound as in musical composition. To further steer our thinking, de Lancie used the analogy of an animal sitting in a faraway field. He asked us, "How could you tell if this animal is alive?" The obvious response came forth: "If it moves." With that, Mr. de Lancie followed with this definition: *"Music is sound in motion."*

Music must move to be alive. This concrete explanation gave us something to ponder. From that revelatory moment, the search was on to find the motion within the sounds we made on our instruments. But, how to find it?

Mr. de Lancie went on to say that a technique Marcel Tabuteau, his teacher, called "note grouping" could help us find the music's inner motion—its life. Understanding note grouping is the key; it is the essential first step one must take toward understanding what music is.

Part 3

Note Grouping

Oboe

(Allegro moderato)

Bach: Cantata #56, Aria: *"Endlich wird mein Joch wieder von mir weichen müssen"*
"At last my yoke must be lifted from me"

To be understood, an idea must be communicated in a clear and logical way. Marcel Tabuteau hit upon the root of musical communication through the development of his ideas about note grouping. These concepts helped countless numbers of musicians understand what notes can do when their meaning is defined. Understanding note grouping unleashes the forward motion, the expression, the *music* within each note. Changing pitches alone is not enough to create motion in music. The power to communicate resides in forward motion thoughtfully applied to the notes.

Music is not notes. Music is what the notes *do*.

Sound Writing (?)

Piano I
  Solemn, fateful

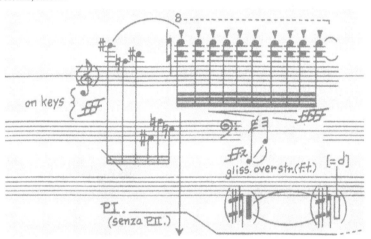

**Crumb: Music for a Summer Evening - *Makrokosmos III*,
III - The Advent: *Hymn for the Nativity of the Star Child***

The written word developed long after spoken language. In the Western languages, writers substitute symbols—the letters of the alphabet—for the sounds in the words themselves.

Music was also not originally written down. It sprang forth as *song* that expressed emotion that could not be adequately expressed through words alone. In order for composers to communicate these emotional musical thoughts to performers, symbols were invented to represent music's individual components. Written music is far removed from that pure and unified form in the composer's mind.

Is the farmer singing in the field more musical than the highly trained professional musician? Sadly, this is often the case because the paper gets in the way of the professional's performance. The farmer is not concerned with written notes. Only pure music—pure expression—is present in his song; it is not tainted by the false language of written musical notation.

The Un-Missing Link

In the English language, we have two words that define the difference between speaking, which is in the air, and writing, which is on the page. But unfortunately, when we refer to *music*, we have only that one word, which means both *heard* and *printed* music. Often, musicians absentmindedly believe that what we see on the page is music, when what we look at is only a crude attempt at defining musical thought on paper.

How would patrons in a concert hall react if they were simply given sheets of printed music by the ushers and told, "Here's the music—hope you enjoy it!" before sitting in front of an empty stage for two hours? Real music exists only when it is in the air. The paper contains only the composer's instructions for *how to make music*. Likewise, a printed recipe for chocolate cake is not nearly as tasty as the cake itself.

Music flows from the composer's mind, through the performer's mind, into the listener's mind. The paper in the middle is only a communication link—like a telephone. And the telephone is most assuredly not the conversation.

Learning to Read

Written language is an artificial, external science developed to allow us to put permanently on paper that which would otherwise vanish into the air—speech. Only after four or five years of learning the basics of language by rote from infancy do we then begin learning the unnatural deconstructive process of reading and writing. We first learn the sounds of individual letters—A as in apple, B as in boy, C as in cat—and we begin to connect the sounds we make to those letters on the page. The process of learning written language goes on for a very long time (usually a minimum of twelve years of schooling) and encompasses the complex rules governing pronunciation, grammar, and spelling, along with their many exceptions.

Musicians also learn their musical ABCs, but do it much more quickly—usually within the first two or three years of study and, most crucially, they usually learn how to *play and read* simultaneously from the beginning. Therefore, in early musical training, musicians unfortunately tend to mix what they hear with what they see. This can detrimentally affect one's playing for the rest of one's life.[1]

As young instrumentalists, we learn the key signatures, rhythmical note values, the major and minor scales, and the fingerings for our instruments. From that point, for the next few years, we usually jump into reading as much music as possible without really knowing what to do musically.

Sadly, most young musicians are not taught that there are musical principles that can guide one's phrasing choices. They are most often led to believe that in order to be a good musician, all one needs to do is get control of the instrument, learn how to read music, and then just *feel* it. Because of this lack of understanding, many musicians have very little to say about the music itself in performance. They make guesses at how best to express emotion. But there is a better way to make music than by simply groping for "what feels good."

After learning how to read music, musicians must be reeducated into a higher state of understanding. Just as there are grammatical rules that structure our sentences in the most communicative way, there are also musical rules that allow musical tones to speak more clearly.

A Picture Is Worth a Thousand Words

The sounds in spoken language are not actually the things they represent, just as musical sounds are mere representations of deeper feelings and thoughts. In both cases we are two steps removed from the reality being expressed.

In written language, printed words represent (1) spoken sounds that, in turn, represent (2) feelings, ideas, or things.

In written music, printed notes represent (1) musical sounds that, in turn, represent (2) feelings, ideas, or things.

In performed speech (acting), as well as in performed music, the process is even more complex.

In theatrical performance, the playwright has ideas and emotions that he or she then (1) translates in his or her mind into a narrative. Then, the playwright (2) writes that story in the form of words. Next, the actor (3) reads and studies those words and (4) speaks the words in performance in a way that (5) attempts to inspire within the listener the ideas and emotions of the playwright.

In musical performance, the composer has ideas and emotions that he or she then (1) translates in his or her mind into a musical narrative. Then, the composer (2) writes those musical ideas in the form of notes. Next, the performing musician (3) reads and studies those notes and (4) makes musical sounds in performance in a way that (5) attempts to inspire within the listener the ideas and emotions of the composer.

This five-step communicative process involves three individuals (creator, re-creator, and listener). This book focuses on steps 3 and 4—the realization of a way of musical performance, through study, that attempts to inspire within the listener the ideas and emotions of the composer.

Passing on the Message

Children play a game called "Telephone" in which a whispered story is passed from ear to ear. The last person to receive the message then speaks aloud the story that he or she has heard. Finally, the original storyteller recounts the original story. To their amusement, all the players are usually amazed at how the story has changed in the telling.

This same phenomenon occurs, to a degree, with music. The means of communication between composer and performer (i.e., written musical notation) is highly flawed, and the communication between performer and listener (i.e., live musical performance) is often garbled by misunderstanding by one or the other of these two parties. The warped result of this failed communication can be very different from the composer's original intent. But in musical performance, this miscommunication is much less amusing an occurrence than that in the children's game.

This is the way of much so-called tradition—repeating what one has been told second- and thirdhand without questioning whether what has been passed down has remained unscathed in the telling.

In music, the relationships of the notes to one another are the only immutable traditions.

What Is Note Grouping?

Vivaldi: The Four Seasons, *Winter*

When we read a written text aloud, we speak by joining groups of letters together as words. Likewise, when we play written music we should join groups of notes together to form musical "words."

We do not speak to another person by spelling out every word letter by letter.

"H-O-W-A-R-E-Y-O-U-T-O-D-A-Y"

Even if the letters in the above phrase were written with sixteenth-note stems above them, four to a beat, their meaning would still be obscured (example 1).

Example 1

The words do not correspond to the groups delineated by the beams. However, when notes that perform various musical functions are placed above the letters (example 2), the words can be deciphered to form an intelligible grammatical phrase.

Example 2

Fortunately, letters are separated into their proper word groupings on the page so that, while reading, detective work is not usually
needed to determine their meaning.

With printed music, however, detective work is very often
needed. Musicians are constantly confronted with sequences of
notes printed together in groups of two, three, or four to the beat.
This simplistic mathematical subdivision almost never corresponds
to the musical meaning of the notes.

Once the words in the above example are understood and spoken, the extra dimension of expression is introduced: the words are
inflected in a way that *reflects their meaning*. In fact, the question
mark at the end of this grammatical phrase can be placed there only
after one has understood the words. By the same token, only after
the note groupings within musical phrases are clear in the musician's
mind can they be inflected in a meaningful way that communicates.

The old American novelty song *Mairzy Doats*[1] is a good example of the humor to be found in incorrect letter grouping.

Example 3

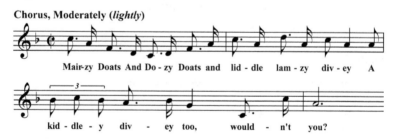

Translation: "Mares eat oats and does eat oats and little lambs eat ivy.
A kid'll eat ivy too, wouldn't you?"

English speakers immediately acknowledge and accept this linguistic joke when it is pointed out because they are immersed in the
fine nuances of their language from birth. But in music, musicians
can be conditioned into thinking that something should sound a

certain way because they have always seen it that way on the page and heard it played in a way that reflects that visual representation. Unfortunately, because of years of this visual conditioning, musicians are often reluctant to acknowledge or accept corrected note groupings even after those groupings are pointed out to them.

Just as the incorrect letter grouping delineated by the beams in example 1 camouflages the meaning of the words, the flaws within our system of musical notation often camouflage musical meaning.

So how do we overcome the visual obstructions in printed music in order to find correct groupings? There are many factors that can dictate those groups. First, we must examine the most basic type of note grouping in order to understand how forward motion is created.

Basic Grouping

Violin I
I - Allegro con brio

ff

Beethoven: Symphony #5

Marcel Tabuteau used numbers to explain how to create forward motion. However, before analyzing his usage of numbers, it helps to examine how a young player might innocently count a series of notes (examples 4 and 5).

Example 4

1 - 2,   1 - 2,   1 - 2,   1 - 2,   1 - 2,   1 - 2,   1 - 2,   1 - 2

Example 5

1 - 2 - 3 - 4,   1 - 2 - 3 - 4,   1 - 2 - 3 - 4,   1 - 2 - 3 - 4

This is a perfectly logical numbering because there are two eighths and four sixteenth notes in each beat. But by thinking of eighths and sixteenths in this conventional way—mentally placing "1" on the first note of each beat and then simply counting up—the played result often *dynamically* sounds like examples 6 and 7.

Example 6

2 - 1,   2 - 1,   2 - 1,   2 - 1,   2 - 1,   2 - 1,   2 - 1,   2 - 1,
>   >   >   >   >   >   >   >

Example 7

4 - 3 - 2 - 1,   4 - 3 - 2 - 1,   4 - 3 - 2 - 1,   4 - 3 - 2 - 1
>   >   >   >

Students do this because when one counts objects rapidly aloud, there is a natural trailing away of the voice.

"1–2–3–4–5"

However, playing as one counts is not the most musical way to phrase.

The numbers in examples 6 and 7 reflect the actual volume of each spoken number in examples 4 and 5. This is one way that Tabuteau used numbers: to show the relative volume or intensity of each note.

Go back and speak examples 4 and 5 a couple of times and you will hear the accents caused by thinking in this numerically correct but unmusical way. Then speak examples 6 and 7 where the numbers accurately reflect the accented progression heard in examples 4 and 5. Note that the volume of each note is the exact opposite of the numbers originally assigned to them. With this numbering, there is no progression from one beat into the next—*no forward motion.*

In order to create forward motion, Marcel Tabuteau used numbers to explain basic musical grouping of sixteenths as shown in example 8. He always began with the number "1," which indicated an un-accented beginning.

Example 8

1,   1 - 2 - 3 - 4,   1 - 2 - 3 - 4,   1 - 2 - 3 - 4,   1 - 2 - 3 - 4

The first note of the bar is the starting point. The remaining notes of each beat then lead forward to the next beat. The arrival of each beat is prepared. This eliminates the unmusical accents noted in examples 6 and 7. In example 8, the motion flows from one beat into the next.

In addition to numbers, Tabuteau often used the words "up" and "down" to convey the same point. For "1, 1-2-3-4" he would substitute "down, up-up-up-down." This is similar to the bowing on string instruments. Up bows have a slight natural crescendo because of the approach of the greater weight at the frog of the bow. Down bows have a natural diminuendo.

In example 8, an additional sixteenth note has been added at the end. The reason for this is that in Tabuteau's number system the last grouping is not complete until a final arrival note has been stated or, at least, implied. This is because musical note grouping is closely related to language, where we speak in upbeat word groups that culminate in a downbeat feel. A sentence such as "Oh, I wish to be in love with you forever more" is nothing more than a series of four-syllable verbal groupings strung together.

Example 9

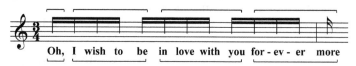

When thinking like this while playing, a normal speech-like progression is achieved. There is an arrival point to each four-note group.

This example shows that one's thinking dramatically affects one's playing in a tangible way. Tabuteau hit on a basic musical truth by mapping out this principle of basic grouping: *Use the inner notes of each beat to lead to the next beat* or *use the inner beats of a bar of music to lead to the next downbeat.*

Example 10

Example 11

There are many exceptions to this principle, but as when learning the ABCs, one must start at the beginning.

Punchiness

Vivaldi wrote many concertos—all of which have extended sequences of sixteenth notes. Judging by performances of those concertos it often seems *de rigueur* to accent the first note of each printed group of four sixteenths. The remaining three then wither away from the beginning of each beat, as illustrated in example 12.

Example 12

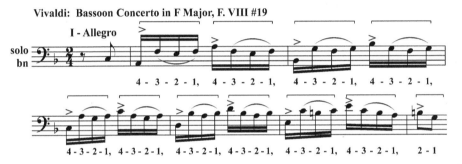

Vivaldi: Bassoon Concerto in F Major, F. VIII #19

To a sensitive listener, the cumulative effect of playing in this way throughout an entire movement is one of unrelieved punchiness.

But when the three inner sixteenths of each beat are made to function as pick-ups, the cumulative effect is one of surging momentum, as illustrated in example 13.

Example 13

This method of grouping sixteenths provides a three-to-one ratio of "ups" to "downs." It changes the psychological effect the music has on the listener. Instead of feeling jabbed by unprepared, accented beats, the listener will be drawn into the music, pulled forward by the natural momentum of proper note grouping. Like climbing a ladder hand over hand, each note group reaches toward the next beat—linking them together. Forward motion is created. The music lives.

The Big Question

After learning basic grouping, many students ask, "Do all of the inner notes *always* lead to the next beat?" The short answer is "No." But basic grouping does work a great deal of the time. Various considerations dictate other types of groups. But first, it is necessary to understand that there is also a harmonic component to note grouping.

Harmonic Grouping

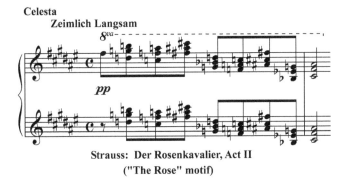

Celesta
Zeimlich Langsam

pp

Strauss: Der Rosenkavalier, Act II
("The Rose" motif)

Note grouping links chords together, emphasizes their functions, and creates forward motion.

The plagal "Amen" in church music (IV-I) is a good example of a simple harmonic grouping. The word "Amen" itself contains an upbeat and a downbeat—an "up" and a "down" inflection. These two halves form one unit—one word (example 14). This is the basic formula for what a note group is—*a two-part musical germ consisting of an "up" and a "down" inflection.*

Example 14

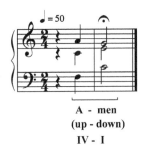

A - men
(up - down)
IV - I

The harmonies of the two syllables here are linked into one unit that contains motion from one harmony into the next.

Both the "up" and the "down" can also have many notes.

Example 15

Sentence structure clearly illustrates the concept of harmonic grouping.

A complete sentence requires two basic parts: subject and verb. If we state a subject alone—for example, the word "I"—a listener will naturally know something is missing and likely reply, "You *what*?" If we add a verb—"I *go*"—a short but nevertheless complete sentence has been communicated. A simple chord progression, as in example 16, can be applied to this sentence to show its relative musical completeness.

Example 16

In this same way, a single chord played alone will create a sense of anticipation within the listener, as he or she waits for another chord to follow.

Our earlier sentence, and its underlying chord structure, can be continued by adding an object: "I go to *school*."

Example 17

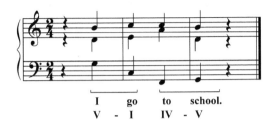

I   go   to   school.
V - I   IV - V

And it can continue to be lengthened with many more groupings, ad infinitum.

Example 18

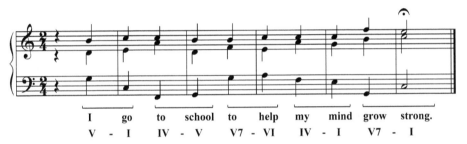

I go to school to help my mind grow strong.
V - I   IV - V   V7 - VI   IV - I   V7 - I

The entire sentence is merely a series of individual "up/down" word groups linked together. The "up" always reaches culmination on a "down." Each word group, as each harmonic group, should be able to stand on its own, having more or less a feeling of completeness in itself. Each group also communicates a specific idea or emotion that contributes to the meaning of the entire sentence or musical phrase.

These harmonic groupings connect like puzzle pieces. Harmonic groupings help create the forward motion needed to turn dead printed notes into living, evolving, musical sound.

Rhythmic Grouping

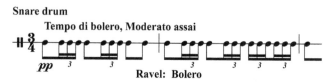

Snare drum

Tempo di bolero, Moderato assai

Ravel: Bolero

"Faulty musical . . . rhythm is the result of carelessness, thoughtlessness or poor instruction and certainly is not the result of some deficiency of nature." Philip Farkas (*The Art of Musicianship*, 27).

In his class at Curtis, John de Lancie taught how a subdivided rhythm within a beat is not defined in the mind until the following beat is sounded. As illustration, he asked a student to "count off five seconds." That sounded simple enough. The student would respond deliberately with "1-2-3-4-5." Silence from Mr. de Lancie. Then, "No—you try." "1-2-3-4-5." "No." Then came the explanation: "If you want to define five seconds you have to start with *zero*, or end with *six*." Holding his hands up, he demonstrated his point:

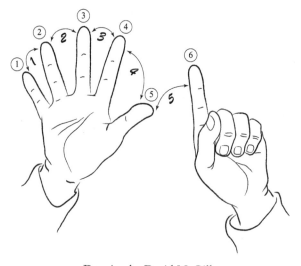

Drawing by David McGill.

If you start with "one" and end with "five" only *four* seconds have been defined.

Unfortunately, most of us can momentarily forget the difference between counting things (1, 2, 3, 4 kittens) and counting measurements (time, distance, and quantities).

Applying the principle of measurement to musical subdivision, de Lancie reasoned that a triplet, being a measure of time, could not be clearly defined as such if played out of the context of a beat pattern and without the next beat.

Example 19

That figure could imply this to the ear:

Example 20

But a triplet rhythm is better defined for those listening if one adds a stronger arrival note on the following beat.

Example 21

As when defining five seconds by counting from one to six, so too a triplet is not defined until a fourth note is played, or at least firmly implied. This concept sets the stage for greater understanding of rhythmic note grouping.

Mixed Patterns and Odd Divisions

There is practically no more awkward sound than that of a young player wrestling with musical phrases that contain mixed subdivi-

sions of the beat. The following technique immediately yields positive results in such a situation.

When a string of eighths evolves into triplets, the player should
first realize that the first triplet note is sounded in exactly the same
metrical time as the previous eighths.

Example 22

The difference between this first triplet note and the previous
eighths is that it is *prematurely interrupted* during its expected
eighth-note length by the early arrival of the second triplet note.
The first triplet note is only then defined as *having had* a triplet
note value, instead of having been an eighth note. However, in
music we do not look back to what *has been*. Music moves forward
in time.

Therefore, the first note of a change of rhythm strikes the listener the same as whatever the previous rhythmic pattern was, because that rhythm has been established in the mind.

Think of the numbers in example 23 when changing from
eighths to triplets.

Example 23

And not:

Example 24

In example 25 the listener perceives a duple rhythm only after
the second eighth note of the second bar has sounded. The first one

psychologically remains a triplet note because a triplet rhythm has been established in the previous beat.

Example 25

Brahms: Symphony #1
I - Allegro
Correct:

bassi

Incorrect:

When grouped incorrectly, as marked below example 25, the first beat of the second measure is most often involuntarily accented. This robs the second beat, an accented dotted quarter note, of its impact.

The placement of the second note following a change of rhythm is crucial, whether triplets follow eighths or vice versa. If the second note of the second bar in example 25 is treated as a pick-up to the next beat, rhythmical accuracy is assured.

In Ravel's *Bolero* (example 26) there is a trouble spot that is often distorted rhythmically in performance. Yet grouping from the second note of each beat effortlessly evens out the troublesome rhythm.

Example 26

Ravel: Bolero
Tempo di bolero, Moderato assai

bn

In all music, if you think of where the next beat will arrive, instead of where the last beat has sounded, your solid rhythm will be the envy of your colleagues.

Although studying and practicing the music is an exhaustive process, in performance it should sound as though we are playing every note for the first time, without knowledge of what the next one will be. The legendary conductor George Szell said, "The music must sound completely spontaneous—however—as a result of meticulous planning."[1]

While playing, think of the printed music as being hidden by a piece of paper. As you mentally slide that cover sheet away, imagine playing the notes as they are revealed, not anticipating how many notes will subdivide each upcoming beat. In this way, changing rhythms will be linked together without the seams showing, and with no accenting of the beats.

Example 27

Tchaikovsky: Concerto for Violin and Orchestra
II - Canzonetta, Andante
1 - 2, 1 - 2, 1 - 2 - 3, 1 - 2 - 3 - 4

Mentally group quintuplets as illustrated in example 28.

Example 28

1, 1- 2 - 3 - 4 - 5, 1 - 2 - 3 - 4 - 5

With a septuplet, Marcel Tabuteau used the French *"sept,"* (pronounced *set*) instead of the two-syllable English word "seven," for obvious reasons.

Example 29

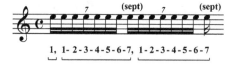

1, 1- 2 - 3 - 4 - 5 - 6 - 7, 1 - 2 - 3 - 4 - 5 - 6 - 7

This rhythmic concept is related to basic grouping and has the same effect of creating forward motion. Furthermore, thinking in this way has the effect of smoothing out the rhythmic instability and accenting that so often occurs when playing odd subdivisions.

The following exercise, example 30, proves the ease with which rhythmical changes can be accomplished by thinking in this way. First practice speaking the numbers and then add the pitches.

Example 30

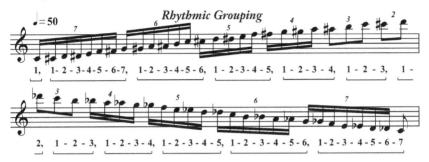

Any combination of rhythmical subdivisions will become easier to perform when this simple system of anticipating each upcoming beat is applied.

Example 31

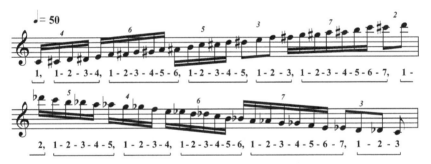

The end of the flute cadenza from the fourth movement of Bartók's *Concerto for Orchestra* (example 32) is one instance where application of this way of thinking can eliminate any hint of unmusical accenting of the beats.

Example 32

Applying this principle to the opening bassoon solo of Stravinsky's *Rite of Spring* (example 33) can eradicate all trace of rhythmical uncertainty.

Example 33

These numbers do not refer to phrasing or dynamics. Here, they only help to keep the rhythmic subdivision of the beat accurate. Numbers signifying phrasing would be quite different.[2]

The natural feel of this method of rhythmic grouping suggests that Marcel Tabuteau simply defined, with his system, what was already within the human mind, much as the rules of grammar define standard language usage. But in performance, the natural is all too often obscured by peripheral considerations, including the primitive nature of printed musical notation.

Off Beats or Upbeats?

When playing off beats in fast music, one should group many beats together in larger units—two or four beats in one gesture. Do not feel every small beat. More important, think of those larger groupings as *upbeats* to the next bar and not as off beats from the preceding beats (example 34). In this way, you will be astounded that you can finally play a long sequence of rapid off beats without suddenly finding yourself playing on the beat!

Example 34

In Flamenco music there is often an excited accompaniment of hand clapping where one person claps on, and another off, the beat (example 35). This occurs extremely rapidly, yet the performer who performs the off beat line is completely relaxed. This relaxation is possible only because the musician thinks forward, treating all the off beats as *upbeats*. Surprisingly little effort is required to accomplish this.

Example 35

Also, in a typical waltz accompaniment, think of the two so-called off beats as upbeats. They will then be placed exactly, with no rushing.

Example 36

A tricky woodwind passage in Bizet's youthful Symphony in C can be played much more smoothly if the players are not concerned with playing off the beat (example 37).

Example 37

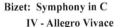

The sixteenth-note bar is the "up" bar and the half-note bar is the "down" bar in this musical note group. Do not make any pulsation—physical (head bobbing!) or mental—on the sixteenth rest, and the figure will be played on time. An accent on the first sixteenth is also avoided by thinking forward in this way. You should feel only one inflection—an arrival impulse on the half note.

Any time you encounter this kind of figure (quick notes following a sixteenth rest in a fast tempo), the tendency is to begin the fig-

ure late because of the common fascination with the rest on the
beat. Negate the importance of the rest and aim ahead to the first
upcoming strong beat later in the figure to avoid the conductor habitually yelling, "LATE!"

Ties and Rests

When there is a tie followed by quicker note values, do not think of
those notes as "coming off" the tie. Play them as upbeats leading to
the next beat. This avoids lateness and prevents an accent from occurring on the first note after the tie.

In a figure such as that in example 38, many players place a
strong mental impulse on the fourth beat of the bar, causing the sixteenths to be played late. But if you aim mentally for the following
downbeat, the sixteenths occur where they should.

Example 38

Conversely, in a figure such as in example 39, where a long note
is followed by a rest *and* quick pick-ups to the next bar, the little
notes will often be played too early if the long note is not sustained
dynamically. If the dynamic dies away during the long note, it is
more difficult to feel the inner beats. The notes following the rest
are likely to be anticipated.

Example 39

However, the little notes must still act as upbeats instead of notes played "after" the fourth beat. Here, simply sustaining the dynamic during the long note has an impact on the rhythm.

Attitude

Of course, rushing is not good rhythm, and dragging is equally bad. As the great pianist Leon Fleisher said, "Playing rhythmically means to play as late as possible *without* being late."

Motivic Grouping

Soprano
Lebhaft

Brünhilde: Ho jo - to-ho ___ !   Ho jo - to - ho ___ !
Wagner: Die Walküre, Act III - *Ride of the Valkyries*

A motif (or motive) is a short rhythmic or melodic musical idea that occurs throughout a composition. It can be manipulated in many ways—inverted, divided, expanded, contracted, and so forth.

Although a motif is clearly identifiable most of the time, tradition can dictate distorted ways of playing that can obscure a motif's true shape.

"Ride of the Valkyries"—Which Way Did They Go?

The Ring of the Nibelung, Richard Wagner's massive, fifteen-hour, integrated four-opera cycle, is filled with motifs. He used them to identify musically each character and mood. The sword, the ring, and love itself each have their own motivic themes.

"Ride of the Valkyries" from *Die Walküre* (second of the four operas) introduces one of the most famous melodies in all of classical music. In performance it is normally phrased as shown in example 40.

Brass players usually take a breath on the bar lines and make a crescendo to the highest note of each bar (beat two). Countless performances, recordings, and even television commercials evidence the universality of this way of phrasing. In a famous Warner Bros. cartoon titled "What's Opera, Doc?" (1957), Elmer Fudd sings, "Kill da wabbit" (Kill the rabbit) under the three beats of each bar, underscoring the traditional bar-by-bar grouping. But is this the right way—the musical way—it should be played?

Example 40

Wagner: Die Walküre, Act III - *Ride of the Valkyries*

Example 41

By inflecting the line in this traditional way, three differently constructed note groupings emerge:

However, these groupings do not follow the shape of the free-standing motif that heralds the Valkyries (the illegitimate warmongering daughters of the deity Wotan). The motif, which underpins this melody, stands alone as in examples 42 and 43, and appears this way many times during the course of the *Ring*.

Example 42

Wagner: Seigfried, Act III, scene iii

Example 43

Wagner: Götterdämmerung, *Prologue*

The larger phrase heard in "Ride" is simply this rising motif
stated four times:

Example 44

The only change Wagner makes between the first statement of
the motif and its subsequent repetitions here is his lengthening of
the pick-up in order to connect the four statements into one long
phrase. If Wagner had not lengthened the pick-up notes, the theme
would appear as in example 45.

Example 45

If written this way, it would not be remotely possible for orchestral players to breathe on the bar lines.
    If the motif consisted of the first full bar, with its final descend-
ing interval, as traditionally played—

Example 46

—then it would be supported by appearances of that sort in the
score. This does occur roughly twenty-four times in the last three
operas of the *Ring*.

Example 47

Wagner: Götterdämmerung, Act III, scene iii
    Sehr breit, und langsamer als zuvor

However, the version of the motif ending on the uppermost note appears at least 132 times. This is more than a 5-to-1 ratio. Which is the rule and which is its exception? In keeping with standard motivic manipulation, there are also a handful of variations of this motif that do not clearly fit either mold.

If Wagner's motif is grouped in the traditional way, then Wagner would more logically have written the longer phrase in the "Ride" with a short pick-up added to each bar (as well as a final downward note in the last bar) in order to provide a sense of motivic symmetry:

Example 48

Regarding the meter itself, in 9/8 time (as in all meters) the *first* beat of the bar is traditionally the strongest. Not surprisingly, Wagner has highlighted its greater weight by placing an accent on the first note of each bar, contradicting the common practice of accenting the second beat.

Example 49

Famed English music critic and Wagner scholar Ernest Newman (1868–1959) bemoaned that, in concert, two common performance errors usually mar this phrase: performers tend to swallow the last note of each bar and overlook Wagner's accent on the first beat in favor of an unwritten emphasis on the second.[1]

By lengthening the first pick-up note and removing the sixteenth notes, we can analyze the unornamented structure of the phrase more clearly (example 50).

Example 50

This skeletal structure consists of an upbeat, an arrival, and a resolution.

Replacing all the notes as written and setting words to the motif also illustrates its proper phrasing (example 51).

Example 51

> "They're getting a - way.   They're getting a - way.   They're getting a - way.   They're getting a - way."

Of course, these are not the composer's lyrics. If only Wagner *had* set words to this motif . . .

It so happens that he did. But Wagner set this melody to words only once in the entire *Ring*. In Act 3, scene 1 of *Die Walküre*, immediately following the end of what would be the concert version of the "Ride," Siegrune sings:

Example 52

> **(zu den Andern)**
>
> sop
>
> Siegrune: In   brün - stigem Ritt   jagt   Brünn - hilde   hier!
>   In   fe - verish ride   flies   Brünn - hilde   here!

Then she stops; no word or descending interval occurs on the third beat of the last bar. Siegrune states two grammatically coherent German clauses that cannot be parsed in any other way without destroying their meaning. Incontrovertibly, the motif was intended by the composer to be grouped in this way.

Examined methodically, it is clear that Wagner's motivic treatment here is firmly based in the natural construction of German syntax, and is also strongly supported by repetition of the freestanding motif throughout the *Ring*. Yet tradition, bar line breathing, and even an animated cartoon have twisted Wagner's straightforward use of motivic repetition.

I have never heard the longer phrase from the "Ride" played in a way that shows its true motivic construction. Perhaps this analysis will stimulate some reexamination of this, as well as other similarly timeworn traditions.

Defining Motifs

In many instances, the shape of a motivic pattern becomes clear only when the end of the last grouping in a sequence is identified. The "Ride" illustrates this technique ideally because the phrase ends on the upper note of the motif, indicating that the preceding upper notes should also be interpreted as endings of note groups.

Example 53

(Phrase ends on upper note of figure. Look back to find other upper notes to find endings of previous note groups.)

Rhythmical Motifs

The principal theme of the first movement of Beethoven's Fifth Symphony (example 54) perfectly illustrates basic grouping and also demonstrates the concept of motivic grouping. Beethoven made his intended note groupings clear by voicing the theme among different instrumental groups.

Example 54

If this theme had been written for a single instrument, this phrase could easily fall into accented punchiness in performance, as illustrated in example 55.

Example 55

Similarly, we can surmise that if this phrase had been written for one wind instrument seventy-five years earlier, when baroque composers did not specify articulations as clearly as Beethoven did, the following traditional woodwind articulation could have been employed, obscuring the motif's shape (example 56).

Example 56

Happily, through meticulous scoring, Beethoven assured that this can never happen. Beethoven's motif from the first two bars (example 57) remains recognizable throughout the movement.

Example 57

The first movement of Beethoven's Seventh Symphony demonstrates that recognizing a motif's true structure can also clarify its rhythmical integrity. Often, when a student encounters this rhythm—

Example 58

—the teacher advises the student to mentally superimpose the word "Amsterdam" over the notes while playing. However, this technique creates an unnatural space between the beats and encourages the student to play the last note of each beat weakly. The rhythm can then easily degenerate into a strongly accented duple rhythm.

Example 59

This, in effect, changes the meter from 6/8 to 2/4 time.

The dividing point between motivic groupings then becomes the beats themselves. There is no forward motion. Furthermore, the three-part subdivision of the beat is destroyed. This transformation of the beat from triple to duple in this symphony is commonly heard, even in recordings of great orchestras with great conductors.

This movement prompted Richard Wagner to declare Beethoven's Seventh Symphony to be "the apotheosis of the dance." But its waltz-like lilt is conveyed only when the motif is recognized as beginning on the sixteenth note and not on the dotted eighth at the beginning of each beat. In developing this motivic rhythm, Beethoven throws it around the various sections of the orchestra (example 60).

Example 60

This grouping should occur throughout the movement—even as Beethoven plays with the structure of the motif (example 61).

Example 61

Grouping the motif in this way ensures steady rhythm and preserves the lilt Wagner so eloquently noted, especially when Beethoven repeats this motif incessantly.

In addition, in the principal theme at the beginning of the movement, Beethoven clearly reinforces the sixteenth note's role as the first note of the motif by first stating it after a long note.

Example 62

In example 62, the staccatos Beethoven places over the last two notes of each bar show the proper grouping. Note that there are no staccatos on the repeated A's in the middle of the third bar (marked with arrows in example 63). These notes form the end of the previous note group and should be played noticeably longer than the staccato notes that follow. Then, those staccato notes provide renewed vigor in leading to the appoggiatura on the fourth bar.

Example 63

In concert, the string passage in example 64 (mm. 267–272) is particularly tricky to render correctly.

Example 64

It almost always degenerates into a strict duple rhythm:

Example 65

String players can avoid this pitfall by thinking of the waltzlike subdivisions within each beat, "6-1, 3-4, 6-1," and so on. Practicing this phrase without the sixteenth note reinforces the proper rhythm. Mentally superimposing the word "long" on the eighth-note pick-up joins it with the following beat.

Example 66

The same rhythmical problem is often heard in the final variant of the main theme played *ff* by the French horns at the end of the movement. It can often sound as though written in a militaristic 2/4 time.

Example 67

Internalizing the proper waltz grouping rectifies this common rhythmical error and restores the correct feeling of 6/8 time.

Example 68

Individual Dialogue

There are many compositions that contain phrases in which implied counterpoint written for a single instrument creates the effect of a dialogue between two separate voices. These moments of "dialogue" should be well defined by the performer in order for the audience to perceive the polyphonic nature of the writing.

In example 69, players often wrongly play the last note of each beat as a resolution, simply because it shares a beam with the previous notes.

Example 69

The musical grouping that defines the dialogue is:

Example 70

Clearly defining the musical conversation by phrasing each voice as though performed by different players results in a much more interesting presentation.

The second movement of Shostakovich's First Symphony also provides an example of two-part motivic phrase construction. The first motivic idea (weaker voice) is slurred and the second (main voice) is detached. Giving each voice its own character brings the dialogue to life and solidifies the rhythm.

Example 71

This theme occurs again later in the movement at a much slower pace. Because of this slower tempo, the bassoonist should take extra care as to how the sixteenths are placed. Thinking, "1, 1-2," during the two sixteenths and the slurred eighth keeps the sixteenths rhythmically rigid and gives them a feeling of motion toward the eighth (example 72). This also keeps the second sixteenth from being swallowed.

Example 72

Imagining that the two voices are played by different sections of the orchestra can add further variety and color to one's playing.

Example 73

Motif vs. Function

One phrase in Wagner's overture to *Die Meistersinger* provides another interesting note grouping challenge (example 74).

Example 74

In the second bar, the second sixteenth of beats two, three, and four is a lower neighbor. This understandably leads one to conclude that it should be grouped with the main consonant pitch that surrounds it. But Wagner has already set a motivic pattern in the first bar—three sixteenths leading to the next beat. Once that pattern is established in the ear, the motif of four rising notes reigns supreme, holding dominion over the principle of the neighbor tone.

If motivic phrasing options are considered carefully, performers can reach conclusions that clarify the composer's often obscure treatment of a motif.

Far from squelching one's natural creativity, reasoning illuminates one's choices.

Range and Scaling

Flute, Glockenspiel, Piano
Andantino

Saint-Saëns: **Carnival of the Animals, VII-** *Aquarium*

Woodwind instruments, the double reeds in particular, suffer from a constricted dynamic range, especially as compared to brass instruments. Even the string instruments have a wider range of contrast. At any rate, all musicians wish to expand their dynamic range—or at least create the illusion that their range is wider than it actually is.

If you think of the dynamic range of your instrument as being numbered from 1 to 25, then there is a far wider spectrum of color available than the comparatively limited palette given by the eight most common dynamic indications: *ppp–pp–p–mp–mf–f–ff–fff*.

Even 1 to 25 can seem somewhat limiting, but this numbering is much better than the conventional dynamics already mentioned. Thinking with numbers opens your mind to the myriad of dynamic nuances possible within the living line of music and allows you to scale inflections with precision.

Limitations and Illusion

A fish in a fishbowl is only able to travel so far in any given direction without running into the glass. Likewise, woodwinds can only go for a short distance dynamically before reaching their limit. John de Lancie often reminded the students in his woodwind class of this fact: "You have to make a *super-human effort* to make contrast." And he was not just referring to the loud end of the spectrum.

Regardless of your instrument, if you were to play the figure in example 75 with each note a little louder than the last, you would soon reach your absolute upward dynamic limit.

Example 75

In order to create the illusion of continual forward motion and growth without forcing, instrumentalists should learn to master a subtle forward and back stepping of dynamic as in example 76. This must be done delicately to avoid producing a seasick quality.

Example 76

This controlled manipulation of the wind allows for sustained, scaled growth.

Another method involves gently backing away from the arrival of each beat. This can be put to especially effective use on figures in a slower tempo.

Example 77

Inevitably, when a student first tries to apply this concept, over-grouping results, and example 77 winds up sounding like example 78.

Example 78

This understandable exaggeration evens out with time and practice.

The Tabuteau Number System

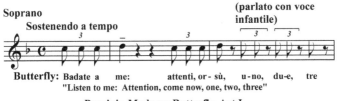

Puccini: Madama Butterfly, Act I

Skeptics have voiced the opinion that using numbers to teach musicianship must be, by definition, unmusical. They have understandably associated numbers with mathematics and, after all, what could be drier and more unemotional than arithmetic? However, Marcel Tabuteau showed that thinking with numbers from time to time not only creates forward motion but can also help define one's phrasing. This system makes music making more, not less, expressive.

There is much conjecture about the number system Tabuteau used. The confusion arises for two reasons. First, it evolved throughout his teaching career. He incorporated numbers into his teaching more as the years went on. His earliest students had almost no exposure to it; his later ones were exposed to it almost constantly. Therefore, if one had heard about Tabuteau's number system from one of his students from the 1920s, it would most probably be a different view than that expressed by one who had studied with him in the 1950s or 1960s. Second, and by far the factor that causes the most speculation, is the fact that Tabuteau used numbers in four distinct ways.

Scale and Scaling Numbers

The most basic way Marcel Tabuteau used numbers was in teaching his students how to play a long tone, deliberately scaling the intensity up and down by thinking of numbers as they played:

Example 79

He also required his students to perfect playing their scales in a special way that reinforced musical thinking. He would first have them play a progression from scale degrees one to five slowly, breathing after five, then returning down to one. Aside from signifying scale degrees, these numbers also signified the relative volume and intensity of each note.

Example 80

He often had them play this progression as in example 81, with an inner undulation, as if bowing up and down on a string instrument.

Example 81

down, up-down, up-down, up-down, up-down

Then the progression would grow—this time up to nine and back.

Example 82

The scale would sometimes progress up to thirteen or even sev-
enteen, always with a breath after the uppermost note before beginning the descent.

To reinforce the musical logic of breathing after a downbeat,
Tabuteau would demonstrate the stilted effect created by breathing on
the bar line—a very popular but mostly unmusical habit (example 83).

Example 83

In this instance, breathing on the bar line is akin to the breath-
less speech of an excited child who takes a breath before his or her
spoken statement is fin-"*gasp*"-ished. Breathing after the first beat
of the bar sounds sophisticated next to this.

This scale exercise prepared Tabuteau's students for more intricate uses of numbers.

Motion Numbers

Tabuteau's use of numbers to show forward motion within small
note values such as sixteenth notes (example 84) is his best-known
number usage.

Example 84

Basic grouping.

Tabuteau also often repeated numbers in such a way as to

heighten internal motion within figures that contain repeated pitches (example 85).

Example 85

1, 1 - 2, 2 - 3, 3 - 4, 4 - 5

This numbering cannot work well in extremely fast tempos for obvious reasons. The numbering in example 86 works a bit better for faster repeated pitches (note the slight backtracking at each downbeat):

Example 86

1, 1 - 2 - 3 - 2, 2 - 3 - 4 - 3, 3 - 4 - 5 - 4, 4 - 5 - 6 - 5

Slightly lifting off the downbeats in this way creates an elegant lightness.

Repeat the number progressions in examples 85 and 86 verbally a few times, and you will be convinced of the forward motion and intensity achieved by Tabuteau's use of number repetition and subtle backtracking.

Rhythmic Numbers

As explained in *Rhythmic Grouping*, Tabuteau also used numbers to help in the accurate realization of odd subdivisions of the beat.

Example 87

1, 1 - 2 - 3 - 4 - 5, 1 - 2 - 3 - 4 - 5

Phrasing Numbers

The fourth way Marcel Tabuteau used numbers shows the overall shape of musical phrasing. The previous ways are actually parts of this more intricate use. Scale numbers show volume, internal numbers create forward impetus, and rhythmic numbers create steadiness, but with this fourth usage, these functions are put to the service of intelligent, architecturally coherent phrasing.

The reason Tabuteau used numbers instead of descriptive words to help explain phrasing to his students is that numbers are infinitely more precise than poetic language. When a teacher says to a student, "Play it like you are looking at the sunset"—admittedly a pretty picture—how does this translate into musical inflections? Phrasing can paint the picture, to be sure, but it is much more difficult for the picture to paint phrasing for the student. Numbers are one tool that helps the student immensely in understanding how to paint that picture. After the numbers are understood by the student, then the teacher can usefully incorporate poetic language into the lessons.

A few months before his death, Tabuteau was given a tape recorder so he could record his teaching concepts. The resulting tapes were edited and released in the 1960s as a double LP, *The Art of the Oboe*. Contained within this treasure-trove recording (re-released on CD as *Marcel Tabuteau's Lessons*) are a number of "number" examples directly from Tabuteau's mouth.[1]

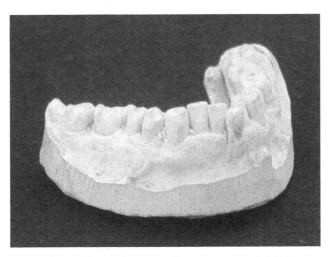

Photo 18.01. Tabuteau's mouth. Photo courtesy of Felix Kraus.

Many of Tabuteau's students pointed out that he used only *consecutive* numbers when explaining phrasing, in order to create a sense of line. This is different from his usage of numbers in explain-

ing complex rhythmic patterns, where the number sequence would
repeat itself.

Example 88

1,   1- 2 - 3 - 4 - 5,   1 - 2 - 3 - 4 - 5

There is a jump downward from 5 to 1 when the pattern repeats. This numerical jump does not literally indicate musical
phrasing or volume. It merely evens out rhythmic subdivision and
assures forward motion.

Generally when Tabuteau repeated a number (as in the first part
of example 88: "1, *1-2-3-4-5*"), that repetition signified a separation
of note groups in the mind. Only if the numbers were sequential
were they a part of the same mental grouping. Bear this in mind as
you study the following excerpts.

Although low numbers (1, 2, 3, 4, 5) are used in the following
examples, those numbers do not necessarily signify the lowest part
of one's dynamic range. They simply serve as reference points that
allow a quick understanding of the proportionate phrasing being
defined. They are also convenient because they are one-syllable
words that are easy to sing using one number per note. These low
numbers are another source of confusion about the multifaceted
Tabuteau number system.

In the oboe solo from the second movement of Rimsky-
Korsakov's *Scheherazade* (example 89), take special notice of
Tabuteau's use of repeated numbers to create inner intensity.

Example 89

1, 1 - 2   2, 2 - 3   3, 3 - 4 - 3   1, 1 - 2   2, 2 - 3, 3 - 2

This number pattern keeps the inner sixteenth notes from
being swallowed.[2] Here, he delineates many small groups, but one
can also see larger groups formed by connecting the smaller groups

together. A sense of overall proportion is communicated when thinking these numbers while playing. The brackets underneath show the layers of phrasing outlined by these numbers.

When describing the groupings for example 90, a phrase from Delibes' ballet *Sylvia*,[3] Tabuteau diverges for a moment to make a comparison between note grouping and the makeup of the human body. "You see, we have three or four groups, after that it is the equivalent of the first phalange of one finger; second!; the third!; between all the phalanges and the wrist; from the wrist to the elbow; from the elbow to the shoulder! You know, we have all those groups to make one straight arm!"[4]

Example 90

These numbers in example 90 indicate growing intensity as the notes fall to the B-natural on the fourth beat. The numbering of the final group (4-3) indicates that the chromatic passing tone (B-flat) is to be brought out even more than the last note (A), which is simply a chord tone.

Tabuteau also reminds the listener that expression is more than a manipulation of dynamic: "Remember, the progression of numbers is not exactly a crescendo or a diminuendo. It is, rather, a scaling of *color*. To understand this point, think of the bowing distribution on the violin in the space between the fingerboard and the bridge." The tone produced by playing over the fingerboard is mellower. As the bow approaches the bridge it grows progressively brighter. Thus, the heady concept of tone coloration on a woodwind instrument such as the oboe is made understandable through Tabuteau's simple genius as a teacher. By reminding the listener that the numbers he uses do not simply define volume but rather a color intensity, he drives home the point that intensity may rise while the dynamic actually fades, and vice versa.

Proportion

Some hypothesize that Tabuteau's French sense of logic was the catalyst for the development of his number system in which he applied concrete or exact methods to abstract or inexact studies: 1 is always less than 2; 7 is always greater than 6. Instead of nebulous, albeit poetic talk, Tabuteau's use of numbers made one aware of just how much more or less a given note is in comparison to all the other notes within that phrase. Each note's relative intensity and/or volume is defined. The shape of musical phrasing then has a concreteness in the mind that it would otherwise lack. With the inner confidence this provides, one can then take wing in a meaningful way while performing.[5]

Laila Storch said that Tabuteau "projected a feeling of form into the ether, into the air—but not just dry form, I mean living, vital, pulsing form—so that you could hear it. And it was done by extremely slow and painstaking work. That's the other thing; it wasn't just a flash of [inspiration]. It was slow practice and clear articulation and knowing where each note went and where it fit into the pattern."

By developing this system, pinpoint precision in the analysis and teaching of musical phrasing was at Tabuteau's disposal. He was able to define the most ephemeral art by using the most basic tool. Sculptors, after all, use the primitive implements of hammer and chisel to create the smoothest curves and the most intricate designs.

This number system is a teaching tool of inestimable value. However, after learning how to use Tabuteau's numbers, one must progress beyond them to a state where one's phrasing comes more naturally. It is worth noting that several of Tabuteau's students recalled hearing him say, "These numbers are for *stupid* people!" and "Numbers are for lesser days" when inspiration comes less easily. Nevertheless, his system worked to get his students to strictly analyze what they were doing.

The most important element of musical phrasing can be summed up in a single word: proportion. This is exactly what Marcel Tabuteau's number system assures.

Why Does Grouping
Sound Natural?

Violin I
I - Allegro ma non troppo

Beethoven: Symphony #6 (*Pastorale*)

The relationship between music and speech is not the only reason note grouping sounds natural. A host of natural phenomena also relate to it.

The "up/down" grouping in music is similar to the "in/out" in breathing. A breath is not only composed of the inhalation. It is a completed action only when followed by an exhalation. Marcel Tabuteau said, "Like us, music must inhale and exhale to be alive."[1]

Grouping can also be likened to walking. One foot is raised up and then falls down to the floor as a single step. The footfall is simply the natural consequence of the "up" action.

When we lift up something heavy and then set it down elsewhere, there is tension and release. These opposing elements are essential to keep music moving forward.

The up/down or anticipation/culmination groups are at the heart of what makes or breaks a performance. When audience members are involved by anticipating what is to come, then the performance has lifted them out of themselves and put them into the musical thought of the composer. The listener is drawn forward by the "up" and allowed to relax on the "down" only to be lifted again immediately by the next "up" inflection.

The world of nature also provides examples of this up/down cohesion.

The movement of ocean waves is a perfect example. All the energy is contained within the surge of the surf up to the shore. When the wave falls down on the coastline, its energy is released—again, tension and release. A single wave consists of both its arrival and departure. Like a breath or a step, it, too, is binary in its time structure.

Perhaps the most persuasive example of nature's relationship to note grouping is Newton's third law of motion: *For every action there is an equal and opposite reaction.* For every up there is a down—even if one of the two is not explicitly printed in the music. What goes up must come down.

All these natural actions show that it is not the downbeats that should be constantly emphasized, as is often the case; it is rather the upbeats that should most often have the greater inner intensity. The "up" is most important because it is in action. The "down" moves forward only as a result of the energy expended on the "up" inflection. The greater the tension on the "up," the more emphatically the "down" can be played.

The physical symmetry present in nature also relates to the two-halved concept of note grouping. Our bodies have two symmetrical halves that make a whole, as do the bodies of virtually every living creature. Even the individual leaves on the trees are made up of two roughly equal halves.

What about the First Note?

As seen so far, the first note of a phrase—if it falls on a beat—frequently forms a separate unit unto itself. But this seemingly lonely on-beat note really functions as the second half of an implied grouping with the silent upbeat that precedes it. When a conductor starts a performance that begins on a downbeat, he or she gives a preparatory upbeat, after all.

The first note of a phrase or composition that begins on a downbeat can also be thought of as a stepping-stone from which to begin the musical journey forward, a standing position prior to taking the first step. It provides a "curtain up" scenario from which the musical drama can begin to move forward.

Grouping and Motion

In order for music making to make sense in large-scale phrasing, it must make sense at the smallest level of note grouping. Just as the smallest groups of words in any sentence form more or less complete subphrases, each musical grouping must also be able to stand on its own as a separate component that has a feeling of rightness. Any journey must be taken one step at a time. So too each musical journey is simply a series of small forward-moving steps.

Groupings are the basic components of music—two-part unified entities with intrinsic motion that flows from one half of *itself* into the other, uniting those halves into a single, inseparable unit: the nucleus of musical life. With proper note grouping, the music is poured from one note into the next. Each note is only a vessel that holds the music for a short time.

Building your musical performance with these basic units allows your playing to have a deeply cohesive flow. You will have built your performance from the bottom up, as all structures that are meant to last are built.

In *Marcel Tabuteau's Lessons,* Tabuteau asks the listener's indulgence after giving numerous examples of up/down groupings: "You will excuse me with my 'up' and 'down,' but to me it is very important."

Part 4

The Larger Picture

Trumpet in C
Allegro giusto

Mussorgsky/Ravel: **Pictures at an Exhibition,** *Promenade*

The note groupings explained so far are equivalent to the words in a sentence. But only after the functions of the notes within those groupings are understood can the line and skeletal framework that support the musical "words" be discovered. At this point, one's phrasing finally becomes architecturally relevant.

In language and in music both aspects are important—the minuscule and the grand. Both have the potential to heighten or negate the listener's ability to "get the idea" and feel the emotion behind the words or notes.

Sound Connection

Cellos
Andante maestoso

Tchaikovsky: Nutcracker, #14 - *Pas de Deux*

Printed music is only a pale likeness of the true sound of performed music as it sails through the air. Played music has everything to do with what one hears and nothing to do with what one sees. It is telling that the ancient Greek philosopher Aristotle believed that the eyes are the organs of temptation and the ears are the organs of instruction.

Shapes

Although printed notes are written as round separated dots with spaces between them, do not be tempted to play them in a round, separated way. If they are not slurred, sometimes players play them as they see them—separated from each other and with fading tone—instead of full value, connected to what has gone before and to what follows. Often, one hears the following kind of playing (example 91):

Example 91

Mussorgsky/Ravel: Pictures at an Exhibition, X - *Great Gate of Kiev*
Allegro alla breve. Maestoso, Con grandezza

tbns

Playing such as this destroys the line of music. Each note dies. Sometimes this type of playing is justified by the remark, "Well, that's what a piano does." However, pianists spend much time developing techniques to disguise their instrument's inability to sustain. The piano is a percussion instrument, after all. All instrumentalists are better served by emulating the human voice in song.

Yet, as with all concepts of musical playing, this too has its exceptions. It is sometimes appropriate to shorten or taper certain quicker notes, especially in music before Beethoven. Almost any allegro movement of a jocular character, from any classical or baroque work, requires this kind of shortening of quarters and eighths from time to time. Composers before 1800 did not generally specify where they wanted notes to be played staccato. Some used the wedge (∨) to mark short notes at times, but its use was not universal. It was initially used in France by, among others, Couperin. Its use became widespread by the second half of the eighteenth century—notably, by Mozart—but it gradually died out during the early part of the nineteenth. Johannes Brahms seems to have been one of the last to use it consistently. After the wedge went out of favor, the dot became the standard marking for staccato, although for a time both markings were used. Now, the wedge is interpreted to mean the note should be played with a stronger attack than a note marked with a staccato.

In general, however, the separate round shapes of the notes on the page bear no relation to the sounds we should most often produce on stage.

Beams

The beams that connect notes together can lead to unnatural grouping and breathing. Groups of two, four, or eight eighth notes connected by a common beam can lead one to hammer out each beamed group, beat, or bar. But in almost every case, beams do not indicate phrasing. For the most part, they exist for one reason only: rhythmical subdivision. And that reason is completely unrelated to musical phrasing.

There are a few composers who occasionally used beams to indicate phrasing. Brahms sometimes beamed certain notes together against the beats—but with the musical content—to show his intended groupings.

Example 92

Brahms: Symphony #4

Berlioz breaks the beams of the sextuplets in the timpani part at the beginning of the fourth movement of his *Symphonie Fantastique.* His grouping shows the timpanist that, rather than trailing away, the last five notes of each beat should lead to the next.

Example 93

Berlioz also breaks the beams in the bassoon part of the same movement. The resulting note groups follow the contour and changing range of the notes.

Example 94

However, when playing the vast majority of music where the composer has not shown the groupings through beaming, one must decipher the groupings, simply because of the unfortunate fact that if note groups were beamed together in a musical way, sight-reading would become nearly impossible.

In his book *Note Grouping,* James Thurmond uses the following example (95) from Wagner's overture to *Die Meistersinger* to illustrate this point:[1]

Example 95

The incorrect groupings delineated by the beams (a) are easily readable but unmusical. The correct ones (b) are musical but unreadable.

Still, we must try to see through unnatural metrical groupings to get at the musical meaning behind the notes.

Bar Lines

Bar lines encourage unnatural breaths to occur. Wind players often breathe on the bar line simply because what they see—namely that dividing line between the bars—leads them to believe that an aural separation is permissible. Marcel Tabuteau said very plainly, "Remember, a breath should *never* be taken between an 'up' and 'down' inflection,"[2] which, for the most part, means, "Do not breathe on the bar line." Donald Peck, longtime principal flutist of the Chicago Symphony (and a student in Tabuteau's wind class), put it succinctly: "The bar line is a door—not a wall."

Example 96 illustrates the musical clumsiness of bar line breathing. The F-sharp is obviously a leading tone to the G that follows, yet the awkward breath indicated is commonly heard in performance.

Example 96

Mozart: Quartet in F for Oboe and Strings
III - Rondo. Allegro (ma non troppo)

It is far more musical to breathe after the high E-flat.

The correlation between printed music and printed text further illustrates this point. If you were an actor rehearsing a play and the director asked you to "go back and pick it up at line 191," you would return to that line and begin reading where the next sentence begins—not where the line of text itself begins. This is because the separations between each line of printed text are not natural punctuation points any more than the bar lines in music are. However, since we are so well attuned to the connection between the written word and its spoken counterpart, we disregard those meaningless separations.

As an example of the stilted effect breathing on the bar line can cause, read this paragraph aloud, taking a breath at the end of each printed line of text. The absurdity of this quickly becomes apparent. Only if the sentence being read happens to end at the end of the line of printed text does it then make sense to take a breath at that point. In music, if you catch yourself breathing on a bar line when the musical structure does not support it, try to find a better place to breathe within the bar, even if a slur must be broken. (Now you may go back and reread this paragraph without breathing at the ends of the lines of text so you can more fully absorb its meaning!)

There are rare instances where bar line breathing is permissible, indeed, appropriate. In the adagio of Mozart's *Sinfonia Concertante* for winds and orchestra, there is a figure where the solo oboe has a suspension that resolves on the last beat of the bar (example 97). This occurs four bars in succession. Here, punctuating between the bars defines the resolution. Breathing on the bar line would not disrupt or distort the music. In his 1940 recording of this work Marcel Tabuteau does not breathe after each bar, but he does make slight punctuations at each point of harmonic resolution. He also appropriately emphasizes the dissonant suspension in the middle of the bar.

Example 97

Mozart: Sinfonia Concertante for Oboe, Clarinet, Horn and Bassoon

In example 98, from Jean Françaix's *L'horloge de flore* for oboe and orchestra, the phrasing also goes bar by bar.

Example 98

This bar-by-bar phrasing, as well as that illustrated in example 97, is an exception. It is the musical content—and not the bar line—that dictates where motifs, groupings, and phrases begin or end.

Slurs

Sometimes slurs are indications of phrasing, but just as often they simply show where an articulation in wind or string playing occurs. The functions of the notes and the motivic structure define whether a slur serves either an *articulation* or a *phrasing* function.

PIANO TECHNIQUE ON ALL INSTRUMENTS?

Most conductors are pianists, and many of them approach musical interpretation largely in terms of pianistic technique. For example, in example 99 a pianist really has no way of making a readily noticeable difference between the legato *articulated* notes in the first part of the example and the legato *slurred* ones in the second. Each note will still have an attack as the hammer strikes the string whether a slur is imagined in the mind of the pianist or not.

Example 99

Some conductors see a series of legato notes with no slur, and think those notes should be played with spaces simply because that is the only way a noticeable difference of articulation could be made on the piano. But in the first part of example 99, wind or string players would smoothly rearticulate the notes with the tongue or bow while sustaining and, in the second part, would simply change the fingering while the movement of the wind or bow continues.

CLIPPING

Some conductors advise orchestras that slurs are phrasing marks. When they see a series of two-note slurred groups, they ask the orchestra to "phrase" more. What they mean is: "*Clip* the second note under the slur." This request occurs most often in music of the baroque and classical eras. Is this a subconscious manifestation of keyboard technique imposed upon the sustaining instruments of the orchestra?

Many composers indicate where they want the notes to be clipped.

Stylistically, the works of Franz Joseph Haydn (1732–1809) lead from the baroque into the classical era. In the second movement of his "Surprise" Symphony he writes clipped notes followed immediately by staccatos (example 100).

Example 100

In example 101, Mozart has not shortened the resolution of the last appoggiatura at the beginning of the eighth bar. Only the resolutions of the *upward*-resolving appoggiaturas in bars 2, 3, and 6 have been clipped.

Example 101

Mozart makes a clear contrast regarding note length in the fourth bar of example 102.

Example 102

Mozart: Piano Concerto #25 in C Major
III - Finale. Allegretto

vln I

In the introduction of his Quintet for Piano and Winds, all of the winds clip the figure in example 103.

Example 103

Mozart: Quintet for Piano and Winds (K.452)

I - Largo

ob

In the third movement of the same piece (example 104), there is a falling sequence of two-note slurs (A = appoggiatura / R = resolution).

Example 104

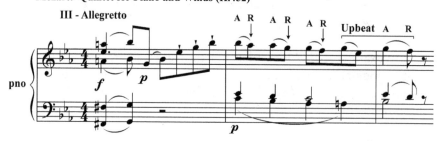

Mozart: Quintet for Piano and Winds (K.452)

III - Allegretto

A R   A R   A R   Upbeat A   R

pno

Mozart has neither written rests between the two-note slurs— as he did in the introduction of the same work—nor has he placed staccato wedges on them, as he did on the last three notes of the preceding bar. Of course, it is appropriate to lighten up the volume on the second note of a two-note slur when that note is the resolution of a dissonance (as in the first three groups here). However, lightening the dynamic should not be confused with clipping the note's length.

The fourth two-note slur in the second bar of example 104 deserves special consideration. Playing this last slurred group of the bar as a pick-up to the next bar is supported harmonically by the raised A-natural in the bass, which functions as a leading tone to the dominant chord that follows. Furthermore, the intervals formed between that A-natural in the left hand and the G and E-flat in the right are a seventh and a tritone, respectively. As dissonances, they both seek resolution. The tritone is certainly not the resolution of the seventh. The harmonic tension created by both these dissonant intervals finally resolves itself on the *second* beat of the following bar, after the downbeat appoggiatura. The single slur over the entire bar in the left hand also implies a longer line, lending supporting evidence against clipping the resolutions of the first three two-note slurs. These clues lead to an evolved decision—one far more informed than "I just feel it this way" or the highly presumptuous "That's the way they did it then."

If the second eighth note of a slurred group of two is a dissonant anticipation of the following note (and therefore not a resolution), it should strongly lead into that next note in order to resolve. And if the second note happens to be a dissonant passing tone, it should also lead onward toward harmonic resolution on the following note (see example 105).

Example 105

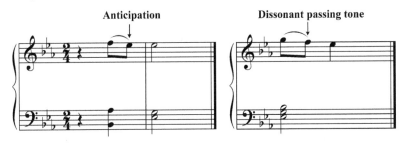

The previous Haydn and Mozart examples illustrate that some composers wrote where they wanted the second note shortened in slurred two-note groups. Other composers were not so specific. However, when no indication is present, there is no *de facto* reason to clip the second note because it is "in the style" to do so. Without first taking the harmonic factors of consonance and dissonance into account (not to mention the printed duration of the note!), one cannot reach a reasoned answer to the question of whether or not to clip. At the very least, if one opts to clip, one should admit that it is an addition to—or, more correctly, a *subtraction from*—the printed score.

Consider this advice from C. P. E. Bach—a musical giant who bridged the gap between the baroque and classical eras: "Broken seconds are played by alternate fingers. . . . Alternation is better for this kind of passage, usually slurred, than a *repeated* finger which causes an excessive detaching of the notes."[3] Bach's illustration follows:

Example 106

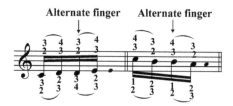

This master, the son of Johann Sebastian Bach, was concerned enough about "*excessive detaching of the notes*" in figures such as this that he specifically warned against "clipping" the second note of those slurred two-note groups so often encountered in baroque and classical compositions.

MANY SLURS — ONE PHRASE

The point where two slurs meet does not automatically signify a dividing point between phrases. Instead of an ending and a beginning at every new slur, those moments are most often simply articulation points within a much longer phrase.

Example 107

In example 107, the slurs are definitely not phrase markings. The beginning of each new slur simply calls for a bow change that provides a clear articulation of the first note under the new slur. Only the last slur, which goes over the bar line, should be considered a purely phrasing slur.

Sometimes slurs must be broken as a matter of survival in wind or string playing (as when one is about to run out of air or bow). Choosing a musically appropriate point at which to perpetrate this "crime" is paramount. Breathing or changing bows between note groups is usually best.

The breath marked in example 108 is perfectly musical and is actually helpful in delineating the repeated B at the end of this phrase. Additionally, the bar-by-bar slurs here obviously do not indicate phrasing.

Example 108

Reshaping the Notes

If one thinks "geometrically" from time to time with rectangular and/or triangular shapes in mind, as in example 109, better phrasing can result.

Example 109

It has been said that music, particularly slow music, is elongated speech. The line of the music must be consciously sustained so as to resemble how one uses the breath in normal-speed conversation.

Think of written notes as tubes that funnel the music forward from pitch to pitch (example 110).

Example 110

This helps one avoid the musically unhealthy habit of playing notes as they appear on the page, namely, as separated dots.

Evolution?

Finally, it is worth noting that the earliest written systems of musical notation often used square, rectangular, or diamond-shaped note heads that were either joined together or so closely spaced that they were practically joined in a visual attempt to show the sound connection that should exist between the notes.

Leaf from an early Chorale (anonymous), ca. 1550.
From the collection of David McGill.

The system of musical notation we use today is best in that it is easier to sight-read. The earlier system was better in another important respect: it was visually one step closer to singing.

Modern disjointed notation has had the detrimental effect of leading children who are just learning to read music down the wrong path, by subliminally influencing them to play in an unvocal, disjointed way. To a greater or lesser degree, many adult musicians carry this ingrained habit into their professional careers.

This is the hurdle musicians must overcome: to read and perform the separated hieroglyphics of today's musical notation in a way that approximates linear singing.

Type and Function

Flute/Violin I
Allegro con brio

Rossini: Barber of Seville, *Overture*

"Each note has a reason to exist." —Maria Callas
(interview with Edward Downes, 1967).

Musical "parts of speech" all have their effect on musical perfor-mance. The functions of musical notes are not just theoretical top-ics dreamed up to keep music theory professors off the streets. They hold meaningful expressions of emotion. Music becomes much more expressive when the inherent functions of the notes are not only understood, but also demonstrated by the performer.

The functions of the notes can define where note groupings begin and end, and also where the inflection occurs within a note group. Notes are notations of pitch and duration—that is why they are called "notes"—but pitch alone is of comparatively little importance. It is the relationship of one pitch with another that is all-important.

The first step for identifying a note type is determining whether that note is in or out of the prevailing chord. If one does nothing more than this, one is well on the way to achieving an emo-tionally moving performance.

Chord Tones

If you are a single-line instrumentalist practicing a concerto, or-chestral part, chamber piece, or sonata that has an accompaniment, you are playing only a part of that composition. Without knowing the relationship of your line to the other parts, it is impossible to realize your part as the composer envisioned. Use a score and your ears to determine the functions of the notes, bearing in mind that context determines function.

The first step is to compare your line with the bass line, if you are not already the bass. Then check the other lines to see how they interact with yours. However, the bass line is preeminent, having the greatest effect upon phrasing because of its innate harmonic weight.

When determining where a grouping begins or ends, remember that forward motion is the prime goal. If there is doubt in your mind as to whether a note is an "up" or "down" inflection, opt for "up." Most of the time, you will be right.

Unlike dissonant non-chord tones, chord tones have no inherent harmonic tension, so it is the shapes they form that create musical interest. In example 111, three sixteenths at the beginning of each beat fall. The last note of each beat then serves as a pick-up to the next. This is different from basic grouping which, in this instance, would not fit the shape of the figures at all.

Example 111

Once the shapes outlined are recognized, it is easy to see which grouping fits best. The correct mental grouping also clarifies this phrase's inner rhythmic structure.

Example 112

There are also groupings of the following kinds:

Example 113

Example 114

Keep the eyes open for patterns and communicate them to the listener.

THE SEVENTH

The seventh of a chord is a special case. It is technically a dissonance, but composers treat it in much the same way as any other consonant chord tone. Like consonant tones, sevenths can be leapt to and from. And unlike many other dissonant notes, their resolution does not always occur on the next, or nearly the next, note. The resolution is often postponed or even negated altogether.

Example 115

Neighbor Tones

Neighbor tones belong to the note they embellish. A neighbor tone (N) is almost always surrounded by its main pitch.

Example 116

In example 117, one must lighten up on the third sixteenth of each beat in order to clearly group the lower neighbor tone with its main pitch. This also helps bring out the single pick-up given to each upcoming beat. The numbers below the notes indicate intensity and relative volume.

Example 117

Because of the functions of the notes here, basic grouping would be grossly out of place (example 118).

Example 118

Sometimes, there are figures that contain both upper (U) and lower (L) neighbors. The two middle notes of each beat in example 119 are the neighbors and the two outer notes are the main pitch.

Example 119

When this type of figure occurs, it could be interpreted that the first and third notes of each beat are appoggiaturas (A) with resolutions (R) following (example 120).

Example 120

However, unless the underlying harmony changes on every eighth, there can be no support for such a conclusion.

This figure can also be misconstrued to be a series of rising broken thirds, with one incongruous rising interval of a fourth (example 121).

Example 121

But if the underlying harmony changes only on each beat or remains constant throughout the bar, the logical deduction is that this
figure is simply a rising arpeggio of quarter notes ornamented with
upper and lower neighbor tones. Removing the neighbor tones reveals this skeletal structure. That underlying framework can then be
grouped as in example 122.

Example 122

This grouping still works well when the upper and lower neighbors are returned to their former positions, tucked away within each
beat (example 123).

Example 123

The greatest benefit of interpreting this type of figure in this
way is that it achieves great musical fluidity by removing mental
clutter.

Although dissonant, a seventh in a chord can still be ornamented with upper or lower neighbors (example 124).

Example 124

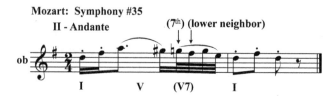

Whether leapt to or from, or ornamented, the seventh creates tension that seeks resolution. Therefore, if time permits, a seventh should usually be lightly emphasized dynamically.

INCOMPLETE UPPER AND LOWER NEIGHBOR TONES

There are times when a composer writes a neighbor tone figure without the first statement of the main consonant pitch, thus beginning the note group on the dissonant upper or lower neighbor itself. When this occurs, the dissonant tone is referred to as an incomplete upper or lower neighbor because, in effect, the first of its surrounding consonant pitches is missing (example 125).

Example 125

Unlike a complete upper or lower neighbor, which calls for no particular emphasis because the main consonant pitch has been established in the ear, the incomplete lower or upper neighbor requires emphasis because of its unprepared dissonance.

Passing Tones

Passing tones belong to the notes they pass to. Do not think of them as passing from the previous note. They lead forward, connecting one harmony to another (example 126) or taking the musical line from one chord tone to another within the same chord.

Example 126

Passing tones become very important in one's phrasing once one is aware of them and highlights them. They have an inherently

energetic presence and yearn for arrival on the next main note. Play
them with an extra measure of inner intensity by using a bit more
bow or wind speed. Do not simply allow them to sound as you move
your fingers.

CHROMATIC PASSING TONES

Chromatic passing tones deserve even greater emphasis than dia-
tonic passing tones. They often create a half-step dissonance with
the underpinning harmony. Chromatic passing tones strongly cry
out to resolve their inner tension on the resolving tone, even if the
resolution is a seventh, as in example 127.

Example 127

Because of the two slurs in example 127, some oboists make a
space after the G-sharp in an attempt to phrase by the slurs. However, this slur-by-slur phrasing negates the inner tension generated
by the chromatic passing tone. Sing example 127 with the word
"long" on the G-sharp to vividly illustrate this point. The beginning of the second slur is simply an articulation point that gives a
slight and appropriate emphasis to the seventh.

Sometimes a chromatic passing tone (C) occurs between an appoggiatura (A) and its resolution:

Example 128

Even though the first note in example 128 is an appoggiatura,
the second is much more dissonant because it is only a half-step

away from the underpinning harmony. It should be highlighted slightly more than the preceding whole-step appoggiatura. It is a surprising event for the ear when the note after an appoggiatura is even more dissonant than the appoggiatura itself.

PASSING SCALES

Unavoidably, some of the notes within scalewise passages are dissonant and they fall on strong beats. This does not, however, imply a need to stress them. Example 129 illustrates how not to play a long passing scale.

Example 129

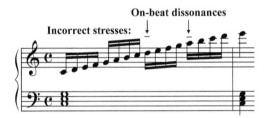

No dissonant function is implied here, because the harmony does not change during the scale. All the scale tones serve but one purpose: to take the musical line to the next arrival point. The scale should be played smoothly.

If the harmony does change during a scale, a case can be made for lightly emphasizing the moment of harmonic change.

Example 130

Showing one or the other of the harmonic changes in example 130 is preferable to showing both. The diminished chord on the third beat is more unexpected than the conventional V7 that follows, even though the scalewise A on the fourth beat is dissonant. Therefore, if one opts to show one of these harmonic changes, the first is the best choice.

There are also passing scales that serve as "linking" groups. They usually fill in the beats between more or less complete phrases or note groups. Instead of leading forward as passing tones do, they sometimes simply float away from the main line of the music, just as a wisp of smoke evaporates (example 131).

Example 131

GAPS AND DIRECTION

Gaps in scalewise patterns can also indicate where groupings start and end.

Example 132

Changes in direction also give clues about the size and shape of note groups.

Example 133

Be especially sensitive to the up and down direction of the notes in any phrase.

Appoggiaturas

In the baroque and classical eras, "appoggiatura" signified any single grace note, whether consonant or dissonant, the length of which was usually subtracted from the following note.

Example 134

Because the vast majority of those grace notes were dissonant, "appoggiatura" later came to mean a dissonant on-beat pitch (by this time written out with normal-sized notes) that resolves to a consonance by step.

Some theoreticians have written that a true appoggiatura must be approached by leap and resolved *downward only*, as in example 135.

Example 135

Still others have written that a dissonant on-beat tone that occurs within a scale pattern should be referred to as an "accented passing tone" rather than as an appoggiatura (example 136).

Example 136

However, throughout this text, I adhere to a simpler, more widely held, and more comprehensive definition of the appoggiatura: a non-chord tone that usually sounds on a beat and then resolves either upward or downward stepwise to a chord tone, regardless of how it is approached (stepwise, by leap, with an anticipation or a rest).

The word "appoggiatura" is derived from the Italian *appoggiare*, which means "to lean upon." Accordingly, an appoggiatura should be stressed by leaning upon it dynamically. It is almost always immediately followed stepwise by its resolution.

Example 137

Occasionally there are ornamental tones between the appoggiatura and its resolution (example 138).

Example 138

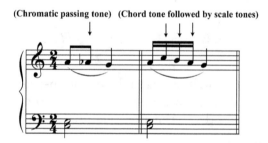

Appoggiaturas almost always occur on the beat, but example 139 illustrates the exception to the rule by having the appoggiaturas fall on the middle of the beats. Here, both upper and lower appoggiaturas are to be found (they could also be named "incomplete upper and lower neighbors"—such is the inexact nature of music theory terminology). Upper appoggiaturas are sometimes referred to as strong (S) and lower appoggiaturas as weak (W).

Example 139

These so-called strong and weak appoggiaturas do not always have to be played strongly or weakly, although when playing many appoggiaturas in a row, approaching them in this way can add variety.

In the clarinet solo in the second movement of his First Symphony, Brahms juxtaposes whole-step (W) and half-step (H) appoggiaturas. These dissonances are followed by a consonant upward leap of a fifth (5).

Example 140

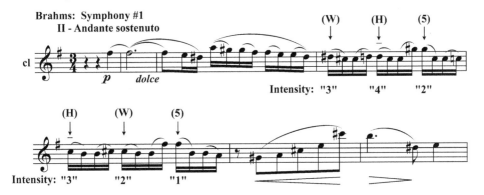

One may opt to show the difference between half-step and whole-step appoggiaturas by playing those of a half step with slightly more intensity and volume and/or lengthening them slightly (as shown with a dash in example 140). Barring the cloistered world of microtonal music, there is no greater dissonant interval than that of a half step. Inarguably, half-step appoggiaturas create much greater tension than whole-step appoggiaturas.

In the fifth bar Brahms reverses the whole-step/half-step pattern of appoggiaturas set in the fourth bar. In both bars, performers usually emphasize the consonant high notes with great relish, but it is the dissonant appoggiaturas that create harmonic tension. Skeletally, the third, fourth, and fifth bars of this phrase outline a descending line. The high notes that diverge from that line should be reined in so as not to disturb it. They represent a sort of musical shrug of the shoulders. During that descending line Brahms does not write a hairpin to and from those high notes, but saves the crescendo for the end of the phrase. In this way, the listener is carried gently downward during the appoggiatura bars and then lifted unexpectedly to the culminating high notes.

Performers must pay great attention to the resolution of an appoggiatura, especially when it ends a phrase. It must be kept alive by supporting the sound and using a subtle vibrato until the end of the note.[1] If an appoggiatura is resolved without vibrato, a dead quality results. Final notes, whether resolutions or not, must be kept alive unless a quality of deadness is consciously desired.

One of the marks of distinction between professional and amateur musicians is the degree of care exercised with regard to the final note of every phrase. The way one leaves the last note of a phrase has a profound effect on the listener. Laila Storch remembered that Marcel Tabuteau described the resolution of an appoggiatura as "the fragrance of the flower" left behind after the flower itself is gone.

This description brings to mind soprano Maria Callas. Her recordings provide hundreds of potent examples of how appoggiaturas and their gentle, living resolutions should be performed. Instrumentalists can emulate her expertise if they imagine singing a two-syllable word with a sudden vowel change on the last syllable. In French, "I love you" is "Je t'aime," and in Italian, "Io t'amo." In both those phrases, the final syllable (the last letter) is barely a whisper. When sung, that syllable is often written to be sustained, but at a much lower level than the syllable immediately before it. When performing appoggiaturas and their resolutions think geometrically, with those foreign phrases in mind, and the result will speak clearly. The geometrical shapes under example 141 attempt to show what the volume of each note should do.

Example 141

Think of the words written below example 142, and imagine singing each syllable with the same emphases they would receive as if they were spoken (A = appoggiatura / R = resolution).

Example 142

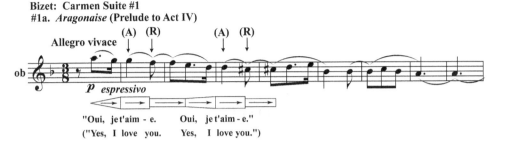

Bizet: Carmen Suite #1
#1a. *Aragonaise* (Prelude to Act IV)

"Oui, je t'aim - e.   Oui, je t'aim - e."
("Yes, I love you.   Yes, I love you.")

To be effective, most appoggiaturas should be sustained at their beginning dynamic for their entire duration, without fading away—unless the composer has so directed. An appoggiatura, after all, is dissonant until its resolution. Unfortunately, there is great temptation to make a diminuendo during an appoggiatura's metrical value as the player anticipates the lower volume of the resolution. But the resolution should be suddenly softer at its beginning because the harmonic tension created by the appoggiatura is eliminated at that very moment—neither sooner nor later. The resolution should then be held at its beginning (lower) dynamic for most of its duration, followed by a quick, final taper at the very end of the note—if it is the last note of a phrase.

An exception to this sustaining principle occurs when the appoggiatura is unusually long in duration. In this instance, a diminuendo can effectively occur throughout both the appoggiatura and its resolution without unduly dissipating the harmonic tension between the appoggiatura and the underlying chord (or chords). However, the resolution should still begin one level softer than the end of the appoggiatura note (example 143).

Example 143

Adagio

Often, a diminuendo is marked under a fairly short appoggiatura and its resolution, but literally observing this marking usually results in a weak or flabby quality on these short appoggiaturas.

DOUBLE FUNCTION

The clarinet solo at the beginning of the third movement of Mozart's *Gran Partita* (K.361) has a note that can be justifiably interpreted to have two functions even though the underlying harmony is constant throughout its duration.

Example 144

Mozart: Serenade in B flat Major for Thirteen Instruments (*Gran Partita*)
III - Largo

This note serves as the resolution of the appoggiatura and, if mentally subdivided during its "life," its second half can also serve as a pick-up to the next note group (example 145).

Example 145

(resolution) (pick-up)

Clarinetist Harold Wright plays it this way in his 1980 recording (Boston Records). He shows both functions clearly. This is a matter of interpretation, but there is time and justification for showing both functions.

Of course, very long notes can have more than one function because the underlying harmonies have time to change and evolve.

APPOGGIATURA ON THE SEVENTH

Even though the seventh is a dissonant note, it is still a chord tone. Therefore, just as all the other notes within a chord can have their appoggiaturas, the seventh can also be ornamented with one, as in example 146. This is one of the few instances in harmonic music where one can resolve to a dissonance with a liberated conscience.

Example 146

Beethoven: Leonore Overture #3

7th in first bassoon   7th in second bassoon

Suspensions

Almost everything said about appoggiaturas applies equally to suspensions. The chief difference between appoggiaturas and suspensions is that the dissonant part of a suspension is always preceded by, in essence, a tied anticipation. The change of harmony that occurs during a suspension can be highlighted in one of two basic ways: one can give either more or less volume, coupled with more or less vibrato (intensity).

The recordings of oboist John de Lancie provide superlative examples to study. In his 1962 recording of Marcello's Concerto for Oboe in C minor, he lifts off a 2–1 suspension in the middle of the second movement by simultaneously lightening the dynamic while intensifying the vibrato, achieving a striking effect.

Example 147

Marcello: Concerto for Oboe in C minor

II - Adagio

Of course, the suspension, being dissonant, still has more sound than its resolution. No matter how much one lightens the dynamic on a suspension (if one chooses to do so) the resolution that follows must still be softer.

Repetitions

A harmonic progression of whole notes has a placid feeling.

Example 148

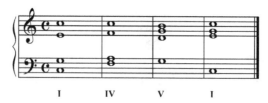

But if that same progression is chopped up into smaller note values, a heightened sense of forward motion occurs. Be aware that the repetitions (R) in example 149 begin on the *second* note. The first note of each bar is merely the statement (S) of a new pitch or harmony. The inner repetitions then actively lead to the first note of each upcoming chord change, forming a harmonic grouping.

Example 149

In the theme of the second movement of Haydn's "Surprise" Symphony, the second statement of each pitch (the second eighth of each beat) links to each subsequent beat. Treating those repetitions as upbeats gives the phrase buoyancy.

Example 150

Unfortunately, the note repetitions in this phrase are often played as rebounds with the first statement of pitch receiving a slight, unintentional accent and the second statement of the pitch leading nowhere. Tired-sounding phrasing results.

Example 151

But the very insistence of pitch repetition should propel the second statement of each pitch urgently forward to the next beat.

However, this forward motion does not necessarily indicate a crescendo. For example, while driving, one does not need to accelerate from 50 to 55 miles per hour in order to simply sustain the rate of forward motion. One only has to keep moving at 50 miles an hour. But if one allows the speed to drop—*50–49–48*—then the feeling of sustained motion is lost.

Sustained forward motion is what music needs in order to live. Repetitions move the line forward. A crucial point about the very nature of music is that it exists in the realm of time. Therefore, it can never move backward because time itself cannot do so.

Rebounds

A rebound note occurs on a weak beat or part of a beat and follows a stronger arrival note. It should be played softer than the arrival. A rebound serves as the weaker final syllable of a multisyllabic musical word.

Example 152

Mozart: Piano Concerto #25 in C Major
I - Allegro maestoso

In slow tempos, a rebound must still have a forward moving impulse during its "life," much like the living resolution of an appoggiatura.

There are also rebounds of a different pitch from the notes that precede them.

Example 153

And there are countless rebounds of the following sort:

Example 154

Like a bouncing ball, each rebound note, when there are multiple rebounds, as in example 154, should bounce with less energy than the previous one. However, they should still have a sense of forward motion.

Escape Tones

A note that is out of the chord but which does not resolve into the chord by step on the next note is likely to be an escape tone.

An escape tone is approached by step and followed by a leap opposite to the direction of the line. It is neither in the chord, nor is it a dissonance that must be resolved by step, nor should it be emphasized simply because it is dissonant.

An escape tone creates the impression that the line has taken a wrong turn and then suddenly skips back on track. Unlike other dissonances, in general an escape tone should be played lighter—as though not sure of itself.

In slow melodies, lingering on the escape tone is often quite effective.

Example 155

Anticipations

An anticipation functions as an upbeat and anticipates the same pitch as its metrically stronger arrival note which follows. The anticipation should strongly lead to that arrival tone.

Example 156

Syncopations

Most music students can give fair definitions for many musical terms. But when it comes to defining a syncopation, there seems to be some difficulty. When I have asked students, "What is a syncopation?" I am usually met with a blank look followed by a long pause. Then comes the usual response, "Well, I can't tell you exactly, but I know one when I see one."

C. P. E. Bach, in the section on accompaniment in his book *Essay on the True Art of Playing Keyboard Instruments* (1753), put it succinctly in addressing syncopated notes: "Chordal tones are either anticipated or retarded by syncopations." Of course, nonchordal tones can also be syncopated.

A syncopation is a form of rhythmic ornamentation. As it is helpful to practice ornamented passages without their ornaments, rearranging the printed rhythm to eliminate an anticipated or retarded syncopation also helps to define its meaning. Slide the syncopation (as if on an abacus) to another rhythmical position within the bar. With most syncopations it can be quickly deduced that the only place the syncopated note can be slid without displacing any other note, and without creating another syncopation, is onto the *following* beat, as in example 158 (unless preceded by a rest, in which case it could be slid forward).

Example 157

Example 158

This simplification reveals that the unornamented position of these particular syncopations is on the following beat. Therefore, an *anticipated* syncopation is a note that is sounded before its metrically proper or simple time. It interrupts before it is expected to sound. The beginnings of the syncopated notes in example 157 arrive metrically just as would any other non-syncopated quarters, that is, on the second beat. Only when they do not change to another pitch on the *next beat* are they belatedly perceived as having arrived too early. Therefore, the element of surprise occurs on the *third* beat, and not where the *sforzando* is marked. Because of this, a syncopation's duration should be emphasized by sustaining the tone, even if sustained at a *pp* dynamic.

Anticipated syncopations usually serve a rhythmic function and they are far more common than retarded syncopations. Retarded syncopations, on the other hand, are related to suspensions because their second half is often dissonant. Unlike example 158, in order to reduce the phrase in example 159 to its unsyncopated, unornamented state, all the retarded syncopations must be slid *forward*—not back, as shown in example 160.

Example 159

Example 160

As rewritten one half beat earlier without syncopations and, thus, without dissonances:

Here, it is clear that those syncopations marked with arrows really function as suspensions because of their dissonance with the underlying harmony. These kinds of retarded syncopations (or, rather, simple suspensions) do not need any hint of accent at their beginning, as purely rhythmic anticipated syncopations might warrant. However, they can sound well with a subtle stress placed on the dissonant *middle* part of the note. Of course, they must not all be stressed equally. The melodic structure, line, and harmony dictate that some should stand out while others are inflected more subtly.

SYNCOPATIONS IN PERFORMANCE

Very often, syncopations are played with accents followed by an immediate diminuendo throughout the remainder of the note. This leaves the impression that a syncopation is a rebound off the preceding beat. However, as demonstrated, a syncopation relates far more to the following beat and should be performed in a way that leads the music forward. The beginning of a syncopation is a pickup to its "home" beat (H), but there is no need to give an accent on that home beat contained inside the syncopation. Simply sustain without fading away.

Example 161

Tchaikovsky: Concerto for Violin in D Major
I - Allegro moderato. Moderato assai

As with all musical principles, this too has its exceptions. Sometimes, during a sequence of falling syncopations—particularly in short note values in a quick tempo—it is musical to give a small accent and pull away after the beginning of each syncopated note. This creates a coy or flirtatious effect. Of course, the momentary mood of the passage must demand this kind of lightness.

Example 162

Mozart: Bassoon Concerto in B flat Major
I - Allegro

In example 162 the syncopated quarters fall playfully, losing intensity. This prepares the ear for the energetic and more serious upbeats that follow. Those upbeats actively lead to the trilled appoggiatura on the next downbeat.

Often in a melodic line there will be syncopations that have both rhythmic and melodic functions. The melodic syncopations in example 163 should be noticeably brought out, while the ones that serve a purely rhythmical function should be played in a more subdued way.

Example 163

Mozart: Piano Concerto #20 in D minor
I - Allegro

The rhythmic syncopations in the first two bars should be played with subtle accents—the melodic ones more smoothly, and with fuller tone.

Syncopations in 6/8 time are often not played rhythmically correctly. In example 164, the syncopations are sometimes played too early.

Example 164

An early placement occurs if the syncopations are thought of as coming after the first large beat of the bar. But if thought of as sounding before the second large beat of the bar, they are placed correctly. Although it may seem like a mental game, thinking to the next beat has an immediately beneficial effect upon one's rhythmical accuracy.

Putting It Together

In any given musical phrase, every note could be labeled by its type. In fact, it is a worthwhile endeavor to do just this from time to time. When understood, every note's function can then have its natural effect upon phrasing.

Skeletal Structure

Arban: The Carnival of Venice, Var. VIII

Just as each mountain in a mountain range is covered with stones, trees, houses, and so on, musical phrases are adorned with ornaments, which, when removed, reveal the true shape of the musical "horizon." This underlying skeletal melody is a kind of *cantus firmus* that supports the ornamental tones.

Boiling It Down

To find the skeletal structure of music, start by eliminating the most obvious ornaments—such as grace notes, trills, and turns—then eliminate upper and lower neighbor tones, appoggiaturas, arpeggiations, and passing tones. What remains after boiling the notes down to this point is basically the skeletal structure with a few larger ornamental figures.

With the following example, this deconstruction proceeds as follows:

Example 165

Mozart: Marriage of Figaro, *Overture*

First take away the neighbor tones.

Example 166

Then remove the scalewise passing tones.

Example 167

Finally, eliminate the ornamental chord tones.

Example 168

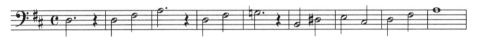

Most often, skeletal tones move with the harmonic structure. They are important because they signal harmonic change.

When practicing complicated passages, it is beneficial to break them down in this manner and then reconstruct them. One's playing will then reflect the music's harmonic structure, instead of being only skin-deep.

Ornamental tones can often appear far above or below the skeletal structure. The farther these notes stray from the skeletal ones, the softer they should be played. Skeletal tones are magnetic. They exert a gravitational pull. The closer one approaches them *pitchwise and metrically*, the stronger their pull becomes.

In example 169, all the tones within each bar are chord tones. The lower tones that occur on each downbeat are the skeletal ones because they coincide with harmonic movement.

Example 169

However, simply playing the non-skeletal tones more softly than the skeletal tones is not enough. The natural ebb and flow of meter should also be taken into account in regard to the non-skeletal tones. Since the skeletal tones occur on the first beat of each bar, which is normally the strongest beat, the notes on beat three are *metrically* the farthest away from any given skeletal note. Therefore, they should be the softest notes within each bar. Any notes between beats one and three recede dynamically to this softer metrical position, and any notes after beat three grow dynamically toward the next skeletal downbeat tone.

When example 169 is ornamented with sixteenth notes, as in example 170, the concept becomes even clearer.

Example 170

In example 170, the harmony is static throughout each bar. This phrase would sound unmusical if played with a crescendo to the third beat, rather than a diminuendo, despite the fact that the highest pitch occurs on beat three. A crescendo to the third beat would undermine the harmonic movement that occurs on the downbeat of each bar and would destroy the gentle ebb and flow that results when the melodic line is phrased with, rather than against, the harmonic movement. But if the underlying harmony or the melodic line itself included a dissonance or some other unexpected harmonic event on the third beat, then that beat would be the focal point and, as such, should be emphasized as an exception.

In John de Lancie's 1962 recording of Marcello's Oboe Concerto in C minor, he plays the highest notes of the phrase in example 171 the softest because they are the farthest from the skeletal tones. Although he decreases their dynamic, he sustains them with intensity, thus avoiding breaking the musical line. Unless the character of a phrase is flippant, this kind of variation in volume should be executed subtly, to avoid creating a swooping effect.

Example 171

De Lancie shows that Marcello composed a line consisting of a progression of repeated D-flats. By highlighting this skeletal structure, instead of the surface elements (the smaller rising notes), de Lancie clearly leads the line to the third D-flat, an appoggiatura.

In example 172, the high note that begins each descending scale is often accented in performance. However, it is the last note of each of those scales that is the skeletal tone. Each note in the descending scales should lead magnetically toward that last note. Skeletal tones most often coincide with changing harmonies and this is exactly what occurs here. Phrasing that has the support of harmonic movement is far more potent than phrasing that ignores harmonic movement.

Example 172

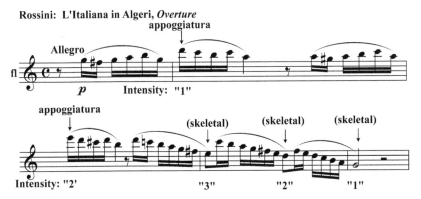

The intensity levels shown above indicate that even though the composer drops the skeletal tones to a lower octave on the E in the third full bar (C["1"]–D["2"]–E["3"]–D["2"]–G["1"]), the E is still the highest point of intensity. Sometimes the phrasing of a melody becomes clearer when all the skeletal tones are mentally condensed into a single octave.

This is the basic rule: In order to preserve the integrity of a composition's skeletal structure, the highest and lowest tones that diverge from it must be held in consciously by the performer.

Example 173 is an episode from the first movement of Mozart's Bassoon Concerto in B-flat Major (K.191).

Example 173

Sometimes, picking out the first note of each beat can bring one a step closer to finding the skeletal structure. The phrasing numbers in example 174 reflect the rise and fall of the line in example 173.

Example 174

But this is not the bedrock of the skeleton, which remains hidden unless the arpeggiations are removed. Only the rising notes at the beginning of every other bar form the true, completely unornamented skeletal structure.

Example 175

The lowest notes in example 174 are farthest away metrically from the skeletal tones shown in example 175 since they occur on the downbeat of a weak bar. Just as there are strong and weak beats within bars, there are also strong and weak bars within phrases.

As mapping the surface of the earth from space reveals forms invisible from a position on the earth itself, one must take a step back in musical analysis in order to see large structures more clearly. This bird's-eye view of the musical terrain uncovers the big picture and helps one avoid being distracted by purely ornamental elements.

There is one other key to finding skeletal notes within complicated figures. If there are many pitches within a single beat (e.g., moving thirty-second notes), look for repeated pitches. Often, the note that is stated the greatest number of times is the skeletal pitch.

Example 176

Only after the skeletal tone has been determined in example 176 does it become clear that the first note of each beat in this figure is an appoggiatura, and that it should be emphasized as a dissonance.

Phenomenology

The Romanian conductor Sergiu Celibidache (1912–1996) made his American debut with the Symphony Orchestra of the Curtis Institute of Music in February 1984. During his extraordinary residency, he delivered a series of lectures on the esoteric subject of "Phenomenology." This imposing word simply means the study of natural phenomena. Celibidache used phenomenology to show that the rate of vibration inherent in each pitch can influence musical phrasing.

Why should a higher skeletal note almost always be higher in volume and intensity than a lower one? There is a physical reason for this: the higher the note, the greater its rate of vibration; therefore, the higher its innate intensity.

Between one octave and another, there exists a two-to-one ratio of vibration.

$$a' = 440 \text{ vibrations per second}$$
$$a = 220 \text{ vibrations per second}$$

The upper octave vibrates at twice the rate of speed, twice the frequency, of the lower one. The notes in between also have their relationships to one another.[1]

Example 177

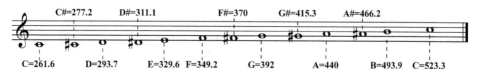

This becomes tangible when one considers singing. A high note is accompanied by a corresponding tightening of the throat muscles.[2] Even a half-step rise from an easily reached pitch can be felt by them. Conversely, a half-step drop is felt as a relief.

This concept is applicable to *skeletal* tones only. Otherwise, every leap upward would jut out and every leap downward would drop in volume; the music would have no sense of line at all and would sound as if the performer were constantly adjusting the volume on a stereo system, creating a nauseating effect. Only the skeletal tones should reflect the phenomenon of rising and falling pitch vibration.

Once one becomes accustomed to looking at music in this way, it becomes clear that composers very often manipulate the skeletal structure. As previously mentioned, when there are confounding passages, it often helps to condense the skeletal tones of any given phrase into one octave for study of that passage. Then the correct relationships between the skeletal tones can usually be seen clearly.

Definition

The notes that make up the skeletal structure of music should be given a little more volume and/or intensity than the surrounding pitches. But this "bone structure" should be apparent only to a certain degree. The volume of each skeletal tone should be prepared by the preceding notes. If skeletal notes are overdefined with too much unprepared, accented emphasis, the phrasing can be too "bony." If the skeletal structure is underdefined, as when all the notes are played nearly the same volume, the phrasing can be too fat—too smooth. What do we admire in an attractive face? Bone structure: high cheekbones, defined chin, regal nose. In the same manner, a defined skeletal structure defines the shape of a musical line and increases its appeal.

As performers, our task is to find where the musical joints are—not simply to feel where they might be. Joints of the human body do, after all, have a fixed position! In music, changing harmonies and motivic groupings dictate where those musical "joints" are. And they, too, are fixed.

The building of one's phrasing must expand to encompass not only the relationship of one note to the next, but also one harmony with the next, each phrase to the previous and following phrases, each section of a movement with every other. Then, like members of the same family, each movement also has its relationship to every other movement. This integrated approach to musical understanding appeals to our innate sense of logic and proportion.

The Final Cadence

Very often, as one approaches a final cadence, the music projects a sense of grand culmination. Although the skeletal line may move downward, the volume and intensity very often move upward. With cadences, the phenomenology of the rise and fall of the skeletal structure often goes right out the window. Many final cadences are gentle, to be sure, but strong cadences generally have an irresistible potency independent of and often contrary to the direction of the magnetic pull of the skeletal structure.

What Is Phrasing?

Strauss: Don Juan

A cartoon from the Philadelphia *Sunday Bulletin*, July 30, 1950:
"Marcel TABUTEAU, solo oboist, Philadelphia Orchestra, since
1915 is regarded as GREATEST MASTER OF PHRASING in the
WORLD! . . . his hobby is French cooking."
From the collection of David McGill.

Phrasing. The art of dividing a melody into groups of connected sounds so as to bring out its greatest musical effect, including also the placing of accent—cres. and decres., rall. and accel., rubato, etc.,—and in pianoforte music, the varieties of touch. In vocal music, it refers chiefly to the breathing places; in violin music, to the bowing. —Clarke, *Pronouncing Dictionary of Musical Terms*, 1896

Phrasing. 1. The bringing-out into proper relief the phrases (whether motives, figures, subjects, or passages).—2. The signs of notation devised to further the above end. —Baker, *Pronouncing Pocket-Manual of Musical Terms*, 1933

Phrasing.—carries a melodic connotation—can be used as a term for musical units of various lengths. Usually applied to the subdivision of a melodic line. —Grove, *Grove Dictionary of Music and Musicians*, ed. Sadie, 1980

Musicians talk about phrasing. But what is it? In his woodwind class, John de Lancie said that phrasing is "the art of defining—*while playing*—the grammatical structure of the music." He elaborated: "Everybody talks about music being the international language. So when you play to other musicians . . . you should play in such a fashion so [they] . . . could be taking dictation and would have no problem understanding what you're doing."[1]

Musical phrasing, like verbal phrasing, does have a grammar. Grammar is not a matter of interpretation. It is absolute. Like parts of speech, all notes have their functions. Phrasing begins with understanding those functions and concludes with bringing those functions into "proper relief" in performance. How much to highlight each function is a matter for interpretation. However, interpretation is only relevant *after* the grammar is understood.

GRAMMAR	→	INTERPRETATION
Appoggiatura		*How much* to bring out
Rise and fall of skeletal structure		*How much* to bring out
Motif		*How much* to bring out

Interpretation is integral to musical performance, but, as with language, before becoming an interpreter one must first understand the words and phrases of the language being translated.

The Relationship to Speaking

A phrase is a collection of note groupings, just as a sentence is a collection of words. In a sentence, there is always one word that is most important as well as one syllable within that word that is the strongest. If a speaker makes all the words nearly equal in intonation and inflection, his speech becomes monotonous. The same is true for music. Each musical phrase has a high point that relates to the high points of the previous and following phrases.

John de Lancie demonstrated how verbal inflection of the high point in a sentence changes the underlying meaning of what one says. For example:

"I saw Linda with David."

With different inflections this sentence can mean five entirely different things. If I say:

"*I* saw Linda with David."

—This means somebody has questioned *who* saw.

"I *saw* Linda with David."

—This is an answer to the question, "Did you *really* see them?"

"I saw *Linda* with David."

—This means everybody understands that David was seen but they weren't sure *who* was with David.

"I saw Linda *with* David."

—This means people are questioning whether the *two* of them were together.

"I saw Linda with *David.*"

—This means there is little extraordinary about having seen Linda but there is something noteworthy about with whom.

Thus, one can take a simple little sentence and by changing the inflection—changing the *impulse*—one can make it mean *five* different things. "This is the responsibility you have as a player," said de Lancie, "to make sure that everybody understands *what you're saying.*"[2]

Phrasing that Breathes

In *The Art of Musicianship,*[3] Philip Farkas recalled an incident with George Szell and the cello section of the Cleveland Orchestra:

At a time when the famous conductor, George Szell, was head of the Cleveland Orchestra and I was its first-horn player, I asked him, in a friendly discussion, if he felt that he was a great conductor as a result of being the magnificent piano virtuoso which he certainly was. His answer was quite surprising. The piano was a great help in studying scores, but his study of the horn in his youth was the factor to which he gave the most credit for his success as a conductor. Any of the wind instruments, he said, would have accomplished the same thing. It was the necessity of studying phrasing in order to breathe at musically correct moments which developed his understanding to such a high degree.

On one occasion, when we were rehearsing Brahms' *Second Symphony*, he became angry at the 'cello section for the way they phrased the opening theme of the second movement. They had played it with the phrases absolutely connected together in one long unbroken line, in the following manner:

Example 178

Upon hearing this he exploded, "Don't you 'cellists ever breathe? After all, the human voice learned to sing long before stringed instruments were invented. And singers must breathe. The audience also breathes. Play it again but this time humanize this long passage. Play it as though you, too, had to breathe while phrasing. Form it into bite-size phrases which the audience can assimilate comfortably while they, too, continue to breathe."

The 'cello section then played the phrase like this:

Example 179

The music immediately became more understandable. It was now phrased in the same manner that we wind players would have *had* to phrase it. Consequently, we, as just listeners, felt more comfortable. I'm sure that the audience that evening felt this same reaction.

Of course, sensitive musicians seek to communicate long phrases, but all phrases, long or short, are made up of smaller units that must be defined *while* playing. Allowing the music to breathe at musically appropriate points, usually between note groups, is paramount.

Parenthetically, wind players should free themselves from the guilt they experience at those rare instances when they must break a slur in order to breathe. Having to breathe is no sin.

Construction

There are two kinds of phrasing: *performed* phrasing and *compositional* phrasing. Performers must understand the structure of compositional phrasing. If not, one's performed phrasing could lack the proper architectural shape and might conflict with the composer's message.

Composers often utilize the classic phrase construction: 2 bars + 2 bars + 4 bars.

Example 180

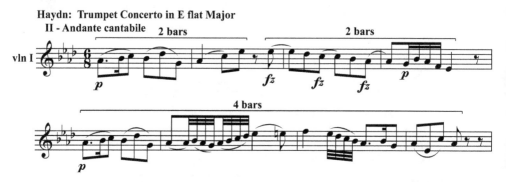

Haydn: Trumpet Concerto in E flat Major
II - Andante cantabile

Within each of these phrasing units there is one note that is most important—the highest point of intensity. When each of the high points is scaled in relation to the others, an architectural form emerges.

There is also the 2 + 2 + 2 + 2 form, as well as 4 + 4.

Most phrases can be grouped into larger 8-bar units. Of course, there are phrases of 16, 24, 32, or even more bars, but they are always made up of subsections.

Then there are phrases of unusual and asymmetrical shape.

Example 181

Mozart: Symphony #39
I - Allegro

Usually these asymmetrical phrases are made up of smaller sections.

Example 182

Mozart: Marriage of Figaro, *Overture*

The five-bar phrase used by Brahms in his *Variations on a Theme by Haydn* is possibly the most famous example of this asymmetrical structure.

Example 183

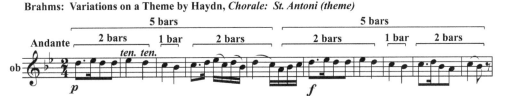

Brahms: Variations on a Theme by Haydn, *Chorale: St. Antoni (theme)*

As in 5/8 bars we most often think of divisions of $3 + 2$ or $2 + 3$, so too, five-bar phrases usually have a $2 + 3$ or $3 + 2$ construction. In example 183, however, Brahms uses a theme that has an extra bar at its center, a $2 + 1 + 2$ construction.

Regarding 5/8 bars themselves, it is the functions of the notes within them that determine how the notes should be grouped. If all the notes are eighths with the first two notes of the bar being an appoggiatura and its resolution, this situation usually dictates a $2 + 3$ grouping as in example 184.

Example 184

The following figure denotes a $1 + 4$ grouping:

Example 185

The opposite (4 + 1) is sometimes found.

Example 186

Here is a 3 + 2 pattern:

Example 187

One will even encounter a relative of the Brahms *Variations* structure (2 + 1 + 2) from time to time.

Example 188

Look for patterns determined by the direction or function of the notes in all time signatures. You will then be able to make sense of otherwise bewildering musical passages and your phrasing will reflect the shape of those figures.

The Goal

With an understanding of classic phrase construction one can see how modern music sprang from older forms. Play modern compositions as if they were classics and the classics as though the ink were still wet on the page.

Phrasing is the crucial element of life the performer adds to the music, whatever its vintage. A kaleidoscopic variety of colors, intensities, and inflections holds the interest of the listener and highlights the composer's message. In essence, musical phrasing is the *absence* of *sameness*.

Repetition

Hal - le - lu - jah!   Hal-le-lu - jah!   Hal - le - lu - jah!   Hal - le - lu - jah!
Handel: Messiah, Second Part, XLII - Chorus: *"Hallelujah!"*

As young musicians, when sight-reading a piece of music that has very few dynamic indications (e.g., a baroque or classical composition), we impatiently try to play up to tempo. With "getting the notes" as our preoccupation, we tend to slip into a comfortable, rather loud dynamic. Once a phrase repetition is spotted coming up, the only practical direction left to go dynamically is down. This saccharine "echo" habit remains with us as we mature. Yet the echo contradicts what we would do in daily life outside of music.

Defining human nature's approach to repetition helps one understand the meaning of musical repetition.

If you were to ask a child to clean up his or her room only to find later that the child had not done so, you would very likely ask again—most assuredly with *more* emphasis, not less. It is human nature to utter any statement more emphatically upon its restatement. Composers often do just the opposite by writing a lower dynamic on the repetition of a phrase. But that echo is a special effect precisely because it contradicts human nature. When no lessening of dynamic is specifically designated by the composer, raising the dynamic level a notch, along with the intensity, is almost always convincing and warranted when a repeated phrase or motif occurs.

In example 189, the flute plays a kind of individual dialogue with itself that contains motivic repetition.

Example 189

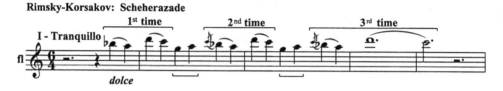

Rimsky-Korsakov: Scheherazade

There is a main and a secondary voice. The two-note figure (G–A) is subservient to the main idea, which contains an appoggiatura on the downbeat. The lower figure also occurs on the weaker beats of the bar and should be played on a lower dynamic level while the repetitions of the upper, main idea grow in intensity upon each repetition. Rimsky-Korsakov also develops the upper idea. The second statement of it begins with an added grace note. The third has the appoggiatura expanded to six times its original length. The lower idea remains the same. Although Rimsky-Korsakov does not write a crescendo during this phrase, the insistent nature of human repetition demands greater urgency each time the main figure is played.

Example 190 contains another individual dialogue.

Example 190

Bach: Brandenburg Concerto #3

These phrasing numbers reflect the insistence of the neighbor tone idea that begins this phrase, and also show the falling structure of the lower idea.

Often, context reveals whether it is better to play a repetition softer or louder than the original statement of a motif or phrase. As mentioned, when an entire phrase is repeated, it usually makes more sense and has greater impact if it is repeated more strongly. This becomes doubly important if what comes after the repetition is *lower* in dynamic. However, if the following musical material is of a *higher* dynamic, it is often better to widen that difference by playing the repeated phrase more softly than its first statement so as not to spoil the contrast of the upcoming higher dynamic level.

When playing a phrase made up of motivic repetitions, it is sometimes desirable to shape it as though it were a long tone (crescendo/diminuendo).

Example 191

Tchaikovsky: Romeo and Juliet Overture-Fantasy

This creates a well-proportioned phrase. Here, the suggested high point occurs where Tchaikovsky changes the motif.

When an entire section of a piece is repeated (such as an exposition in sonata form), it is often effective to emphasize all its dynamics more strongly the second time around—the loud elements louder and the soft elements softer. This provides a compelling reason to have made the repeat. However, grotesque exaggeration—especially of the louder elements—should be avoided. Always leave the impression that no matter how loudly you play, there is more that you could give. Hornist Philip Farkas wrote, "The sound of a solo instrument playing *fortissimo*, except for some unusual dramatic effect, is seldom enjoyable to the listener."[1]

Sequences

Sequences are also a type of repetition. When sequences of phrases rise or fall, the level of intensity and dynamic should also rise or fall.

In example 192, a phrase is first stated and then repeated one step lower upon each restatement.

Example 192

Vivaldi: Concerto for Bassoon in D minor, F. VIII #5
III - Allegro molto

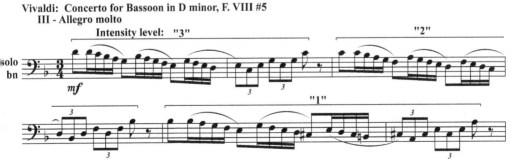

By lowering the volume slightly on each repetition, the phrasing corresponds with the decreasing speed of the vibrations of the notes (see the section "Phenomenology" in the chapter titled "Skeletal Structure"). One way of reinforcing this concept mentally is to imagine that one could add up all the vibrations of all the pitches within the first phrase and then compare that total to the total of all the vibrations in subsequent sequential repetitions of that phrase. The lower the total, the lower the intensity.

Example 193 contains a similar idea from Rossini.

Example 193

Rossini: La Gazza Ladra, *Overture*

As ever, numerous exceptions to this principle can be found. Sometimes the composer interlaces falling sequences.

Example 194

Vivaldi: Concerto for Bassoon in D minor, F. VIII #5

Most melodic sequences containing descending fifths can be effectively highlighted as above.

The Difference

Conductor Sergiu Celibidache said that a repeat in music is not actually a repeat of the same thing. Although the same musical material is repeated, when we hear it a second time, *we* are different because we have heard that material before. Therefore, we approach the repetition differently, just as one would approach a friend differently from a stranger.

What Is Line?

Soprano
Andante sostenuto molto
Con molto sentimento

Wally: Eb - ben?... Ne andrò lon - ta - na
"Well? I shall go far away ..."
Catalani: La Wally, Act I

"Music is written vertically but it's got to sound horizontal." —John de Lancie (University of Toronto master class, 1992).

Language and Line

Line is probably the single most misunderstood facet of musical performance. One thing is certain—musical performance without attention to line is not related to language; the spoken line is the template for the musical line.

John de Lancie explained line in this way: "As I speak, listen to my vocal cords. Within each phrase or sentence I speak, their vibration is essentially unbroken. The consonants of my speech only articulate the well-connected vowels that form the line of the tone." If one were to vocalize only the vowels in the previous sentence, that would clearly illustrate what line is. The breath does not stop and start at each word or syllable as the tongue, lips, and teeth articulate them during speech. Similarly, one should not stop and start the wind or the bow on each note as one plays, separating each mu-si-cal syl-la-ble. No-bo-dy—talks—like—that, unless they are ill or impaired.

Regarding the shape of the spoken line, there is normally a

smooth progression toward an important word, an arrival at the point of the statement, and then a similarly smooth tapering. Words flow one into the other, forming the line of speech. Musical line is exactly the same. As you read this book, be aware of which word in each sentence is its apex. Phrase as you read, making a line to and from that one crucial word.

Inflecting the Line

Groupings can be clearly delineated without disrupting the musical line, just as clearly enunciated words do not disrupt the spoken line. Enunciating musical groupings usually involves playing the first or last notes of those groups a little softer than their inner notes while still playing the central important note with fullness.

However, there are instances in music where an inner note, even an arrival note, should be played more softly than the rest of the notes in that group. The key to playing a given note softer without losing the line is that the lighter note must not wane in intensity or dynamic at any point during its value—its "life." Although it is softer than the surrounding notes, its beginning dynamic remains constant throughout its duration.

There are many examples of this soft sustaining of lighter notes in violinist Fritz Kreisler's recordings.

Example 195

Kreisler: Rondino on a theme of Beethoven

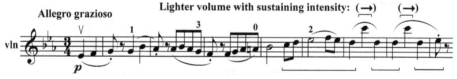

The high notes on beat two of the seventh and eighth bars in example 195 do not swoop away from the line in his playing. Kreisler keeps the line by sustaining the high note at its lower volume throughout its length while also keeping it alive with vibrato.

If the lighter note does fade during its life, the resulting inflection sounds flippant—especially if the note is very short. This type of choppy inflection is a rarely used special effect reserved for salon music or moments in the classical repertoire which are meant to create a humorous or lighthearted effect. It is somewhat related to the momentary use of harmonics on string instruments. Sometimes, when a note far above the others appears, that note can be played very lightly, with a mischievous feeling. This coy inflection suggests a musical shrug of the shoulders. But this should occur only rarely and only on consonant tones. Its purpose is to momentarily break the line—therein lies its humor.

A triplet figure in the second of Schumann's *Fantasie-Stücke* for cello and piano provides an opportunity for this kind of good-natured lift.

Example 196

Sustaining the Line on "Up" and "Down" Beats

A simple way to keep the line going is to consciously play upbeat notes and arrival notes with a sustained quality. Often, upbeats are swallowed and downbeats are unnecessarily stressed, followed by an immediate diminuendo.

Using geometrical shapes to approximate the sound of unmusical phrasing (i.e., no line), the phrase illustrated in example 197 might look something like this:

Example 197

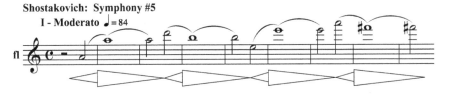

This manner of playing creates a deflated effect and should be avoided. No line is apparent. Example 198 is a visual representation of how this phrase should be performed in order to maintain the line.

Example 198

The upbeats should be slightly brought out, leading the listener forward to the longer notes. Those notes should then begin slightly softer than the end of the upbeats and be sustained at that lower level throughout their duration.

Upbeats have a natural forward-leaning intensity to them. They lead to their downbeat arrival notes. However, they should neither stick out nor be swallowed. This is a very fine distinction. Note that the rectangles below example 198, which illustrate this concept, are nearly the same width, both on the upbeats and the downbeats. The essential thing is to sustain both notes.

Bulging

A common habit that destroys musical line is bulging. Many musicians—sometimes even entire orchestral sections—play each note in a melodic phrase with its own individual hairpin (crescendo/diminuendo).

Example 199

This is caused by starting each note *piano* and then surging in order to give the music what some musicians perceive to be interesting musical impulses, when in fact such inflection results in a seasick effect. Other musicians do this unintentionally because they are insecure about the pitch of a note at its outset or because they wish to make a smooth connection between the notes by taking away the wind or bow speed momentarily as they change fingerings. Only after they are sufficiently satisfied with their pitch or connection to the next note do they then suddenly increase the dynamic. Marcel Tabuteau has been quoted as saying, "Play from the head of the note—not its *stomach*!"—meaning that the note should "sound" from its beginning.

Bulging out on arrival notes is also commonly heard. Give the lion's share of growth to the smaller upbeat notes. Let the long notes sail forward under their own power. Each arrival note functions like a landing in a long staircase: a few steps, then the landing—then a few more steps to the next landing. This feeling can also be likened to that of gliding in a canoe on a placid lake—first comes the row stroke (upbeat), then the forward glide (downbeat). The flute line from Shostakovich's Fifth Symphony can be used again to illustrate this point.

Example 200

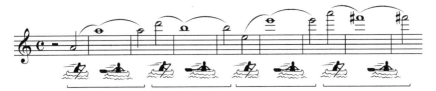

Diminuendo

Since music exists in time and since time never moves backward, we must guard against loss of forward motion. Even during a diminuendo, there must still be forward momentum so the line will not be broken. Think of a train that approaches from a distance at fifty miles per hour (crescendo), passes by (peak), and continues on its way down the track (diminuendo), never slowing as it recedes into the distance. Similarly, a diminuendo should also sustain its rate of forward motion as it recedes into silence.

How the last note of any phrase or composition is played has a profound effect on the listener. If the final pitch is supported with intensity until its extinction, the feeling of forward motion will continue in the listener's mind even after the note has faded to nothing. Sadly, it is true that the musical line can be destroyed even during the last note of a phrase or composition.

Broken Line

Destruction of the musical line is the destruction of the music's life. Like a deathbed illness that robs one of breath, rendering speech broken, unsupported, and incomprehensible, the loss of line in music also hinders one's communicative ability. Only when an infirm quality is desired should the line be broken intentionally. This happens in music, though rarely, most often in opera, where the words or situation help justify a broken line.

The Four Elements of Music

Violin I

I - Allegro

(*f*)

Vivaldi: The Four Seasons, *Spring*

Meter, rhythm, melody, and harmony each have an effect on musical performance. Along with note function, they are the immutable elements of music. Any musical phrase could be played in a different key, with various articulations or dynamics, but its meter, rhythm, melody, and harmony are endemic to its structure and dictate how each note within that phrase relates to every other note. These four elements form the basic grammar of music and follow an elementary principle of hierarchy. Meter is the bedrock, rhythm is the lay of the land, melody is the greenery, and harmony is the atmospheric condition—the weather—that colors the emotion of the phrase. Layer upon layer, they each influence how the music should be realized. Whichever element prevails depends upon the ever-changing *momentary* structure of the music.

Meter

Meter is the "gravity" of music. It defines the relative strength of the beats—strong and weak.

In 2/4 time, the basic rule is that beat one is stronger than beat two. This does not mean that the whole first beat is loud and the whole second beat is soft, but that the beginning of each beat is either louder or softer than the rest of that beat. The volume within the beat then progresses toward the volume of the next beat smoothly, as if breathing.

Example 201

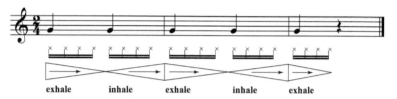

In 4/4, the pattern is most often like a subdivided 2/4 bar, with beat 3 as the softest:

Example 202

Or like two bars of 2/4 with beat 3 inflected not quite as loudly as beat 1:

Example 203

Or as in basic grouping:

Example 204

But this metrical shaping must be done subtly in order to pre-serve the integrity of the musical line—especially when longer note values are employed. The shorter the notes (e.g., sixteenths), the more emphatically this metric shaping can be applied.

In 6/8, which is often a variant of 2/4 time, it is easy to fall into the common habit of emphasizing each beat.

Example 205

Beethoven: Violin Concerto in D Major
III - Rondo (Allegro)

It is much better to feel whole bars as they pass by:

Example 206

However, slightly stressing only every other bar, or only one of every few bars, is preferable to leaning on all the downbeats. And, as with the internal beats of every measure, there are strong (S) and weak (W) bars within every phrase:

Example 207

In 3/4 time, there are a couple of basic patterns of beat strength:

Example 208

Example 209

The second of these patterns is found in the final movement of Sibelius's moving Fifth Symphony. The second beat should be played lightly while the lower line is brought out.

Example 210

There is a fairly common phrase structure in 3/4 time in which the third beat of each bar functions as a resolution. It is one of the rare exceptions where phrasing ends at the bar line. In the following example, the third beat is the resolution of the half note.

Example 211

There are two kinds of compositions that go against the basic beat strength inherent in 3/4 time: the sprightly *mazurka* and the somber *sarabande*. In these forms the formerly weak second beat is frequently emphasized, either explicitly, with an accent (example 212), or implicitly, with appoggiaturas (example 213), ornaments, or other melodic or harmonic devices.

Example 212

Example 213

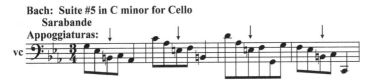

Bach: Suite #5 in C minor for Cello
Sarabande
Appoggiaturas:

Many advocate a strongly accented, early placement of the second beat in the accompaniment of a Viennese waltz.

Example 214

As written: As often performed:

This idea is often touted as an essential idiosyncrasy of "the Viennese Style," though it can be argued that this accenting changes the waltz, with its strong emphasis on beat one, into more of a mazurka in mood. However strongly or early the second beat is played, it should not challenge the downbeat's supremacy.

Rhythmic, melodic, or harmonic concerns can take center stage for a time, but meter remains the most basic element of music.

Rhythm

Rhythm can exist in either consonance or dissonance with the meter.

Example 215

Consonant rhythm:

Meter:

In example 215, the notes move at the same rate as the beats. There are no cross rhythms.

However, when a dissonant (or contrasting) rhythm occurs, then it affects phrasing. A rhythm of this nature exists in *friction* with the meter.

Example 216

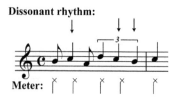

The notes highlighted with arrows in example 216 are those that do not move in consonance with the prevailing meter (strict subdivision of eighth or sixteenth notes creates no friction). The quarternote syncopation reaches a point of friction when the second, underlying beat of the bar arrives. The big triplet reaches a point of friction when its second note is sounded. The first triplet note exists in consonance with the third beat. It requires no special emphasis.

Rhythm can override meter in importance, if, for example, a syncopation occurs on an otherwise weak beat.

In example 217, the second beat—which is usually a weak beat—calls for some emphasis. This is not to say that an accent is needed but that the whole length of the note should be highlighted and carried forward to the next note on the fourth beat.

Example 217

Also, when a rhythmic pattern has been set and is then suddenly changed, one's playing should be sufficiently resolute at that moment in order for the change to clearly register in the ear of the listener.

Example 218

As ever, it is helpful to remember that the human ear cannot perceive a rhythmic change until the second note of that change has sounded.

Melody

The structure of a melody, like the structure of rhythm, can dictate phrasing contrary to the meter's natural points of emphasis even to the point of creating a new meter for a few moments. The famous cadential hemiola found mostly in baroque music is a common melodic variation of this sort. Of course, there is also a harmonic as well as a rhythmic component to the hemiola, but a hemiola is arguably felt as primarily a melodic event that affects meter.

Example 219

At the unaccompanied opening of Prokofiev's Second Violin Concerto, the violin states a melody that, to the ear, seems to be unmistakably in 5/4. However, the meter marked is 4/4. This theme has two eighth notes that could be considered upper and lower appoggiaturas (or upper and lower neighbors) that resolve on the following downbeat. They add an unusual melodic emphasis to the fourth beat of 4/4 time here. However, the fourth beat in 5/4 time could very naturally take a slight emphasis, outlining a 3 + 2 construction of the bar. This emphasis would show the dissonant functions of the eighth notes.

Example 220

Melody trumps meter here.
There are many other examples where questions remain.[1]

At a certain point in the last movement of Rimsky-Korsakov's *Scheherazade*, the repeated notes in the bassoon part are beamed together to suggest a grouping of two beats per bar while the upper voices play a melody in 3/8. Should the bassoonists place a light accent in the middle of the bar to give a feeling of "two," even though there is an accent already on beat one? This is, admittedly, a rhythmic concern, but it could create friction with the melody.

Example 221

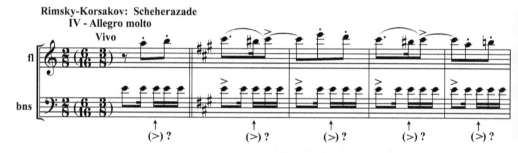

For a brief moment in the first movement of Brahms's Second Symphony, the oboe and bassoon have a transition over two bars where the opening lower neighbor tone idea has been stretched to twice its length. Should the first beat of the second bar be stressed slightly *within* the tied note in order to show friction with the meter?

Example 222

In Strauss's *Till Eulenspiegel* the famous horn solo is written across the bars without seeming reference to the 6/8 meter. Should the player play the figures as though they are free of any connection to the meter by simply emphasizing the appoggiatura at the center of the motif (example 223)? Or should the horn player give inner impulses in order to show these cross rhythms (example 224)?

Example 223

Phrasing emphasis according to the appoggiaturas:

Strauss: Till Eulenspiegels lustige Streiche
allmählich lebhafter

1 - 2 - 3 - **4** - 5 - 6 - 7,   1 - 2 - 3 - **4** - 5 - 6 - 7,   1 - 2 - 3 - **4** - 5 - 6 - 7,

Example 224

Phrasing emphasis according to the bar lines:

In his First Symphony, Shostakovich also plays with meter. In the second movement, there is a melody that outlines a feeling of 4/4 time while the meter reads 3/4 (example 225). Should the flutes inflect in 3/4 time, 4/4 time, or simply play it straight? During this dirgelike theme, the triangle sounds on each 3/4 downbeat. Should this influence the phrasing of the flutes?

Example 225

Shostakovich: Symphony #1
II - Allegro. Meno mosso

In Bach's Brandenburg Concerto No. 1, should the phrasing of the theme late in the movement be different from the beginning of the movement because it begins one half-bar later than its initial statement? Does the principle of strong and weak beats apply? What was the reason Bach wrote it this way?

Example 226

Example 227

And what about Mozart's Horn Quintet in E-flat major? Was Mozart pulling the leg of his favorite horn player (Joseph Leutgeb) when he began the theme of the last movement seemingly one beat too soon?

Example 228

Example 229

These are questions without definitive answers. Yet thinking about them is essential in order to arrive at an intellectually honest performance of the music.

Skeletal structure is also a melodic factor. Generally when that structure rises, the intensity and dynamic should increase unless the composer has specified otherwise. Likewise, when the skeletal line falls, so should the dynamic and intensity. Although skeletal structure relates strongly to harmonic structure, its ups and downs are melodic in nature.

Also, when there are dissonant tones in the melody (as in the earlier Prokofiev example), the performer should bring them out. Because of our increasing desensitization to dissonance, it often goes unnoticed by the performer. A great deal of the time, no effort at all is made to show the innate harmonic friction within these potent dissonant tones. In *Essay of a Method for Playing the Transverse Flute* (1752), Johann Quantz pointed out that one must bring out "above all the dissonances," that they "serve as the means to vary the expression of the different passions."[2] Still valid advice.

Harmony

The children's tune "Mary Had a Little Lamb" (example 230) can be used as an easily understood example of harmony's profound effect on musical phrasing. If this melody is harmonized in the traditional way, there are no surprises—no unusual points of emphasis.

Example 230

Harmony, being the strongest element of music, can usurp the strength of all the other basic elements. If, for example, the harmony suddenly changes to *minor* during this major key melody (example 231), more tension is created at the moment of that change—regardless of where it might occur.

Example 231

The normal emphasis would be on the two V7 chords in this phrase, but the unexpected change to minor in the fourth bar dictates greater harmonic weight at what would otherwise be a point of repose. Of course, it seems that no one could possibly slough over this harmonic surprise, but this is exactly what many musicians do quite regularly in well-known works. Beware of becoming dulled to harmonic meaning by over-familiarity with the music. It is not enough to play through all manner of interesting harmonies by offering little more than "beautiful tone."

When highlighting a harmonic change, one does not necessarily have to play louder. Sometimes a harmony can be effectively highlighted by lightening up the dynamic, intensifying the vibrato, or by slightly lengthening a note or two (although habitually lengthening certain notes can quickly become cloying). To highlight only means *to create contrast from* the surrounding musical texture.

As previously noted, when the skeletal structure of any melody dips downward, it is appropriate to lower the intensity of the sound. However, if an unexpected change of harmony occurs at that moment, then harmony's precedence over the other elements of music is once again proven. That harmonic surprise supersedes all else.

Harmony, like melody and rhythm, can also dictate a momentary change in the prevailing meter. Example 232, from Telemann's Sonata for Bassoon in F minor, shows how the underlying harmonies outline a pattern different from the 4/4 time signature of the movement.

Example 232

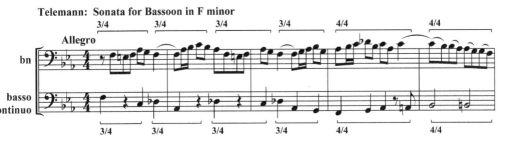

Telemann: Sonata for Bassoon in F minor

The bassoon line should reflect this unwritten meter manipulation. This kind of harmonic play allowed Telemann to slyly change meter at will without changing the time signature.

Additionally, if there are augmented or diminished chords, deceptive cadences, Neapolitan sixth chords, or any number of harmonic devices that may now sound fairly tame to our modern ears, bring them out. Though they may not immediately seem so to us in our present-day musical world of unresolved dissonance, they are still effective—*if noticed* and brought out by the performer.

The Mix

Layer upon layer, musical phrasing is built according to the blueprint of these four basic elements of music. Thinking of them in preparation for performance yields organic musical conclusions that carry a greater impact than sole reliance upon subjective inspiration.

However, one's musical instincts do have a role to play. Instinct can guide one as to how much to emphasize each element and can keep one from stepping beyond the boundaries of good taste. But instinct is only a hit-and-miss proposition if not supported by basic knowledge of the music's structure.

Be sensitive to, and aware of, minute changes of harmony, subtle variations in melodic contour, rhythmic surprises, and the ever-present magnetic, gravitational pull of meter. And keep the eyes open to the overall context. Opening the ears to the subtleties of the most seemingly banal music will allow you to enter a world of greatly enhanced musical understanding, enjoyment, and excitement. This newfound feeling of involvement will then be transmitted to the listener. By hearing you play the music in accordance with its natural structure, the listener may even feel that he or she is hearing an old standard for the first time—again.

Part 5

Wind Techniques

Wind machine
Schnell und heftig

p cresc.   **f dim.**

Strauss: Ein Alpensinfonie, *Gewitter und Sturm, Absteig*

Wind playing involves three fundamental aspects: control of the airstream, fingers, and tongue.

It is possible to relate much of this section of the book to string instruments. Quite a bit more can be applied to brass playing. Some adventurous singers will even find a few tidbits they can apply to vocal technique.

The following chapters address basic techniques that can help the performer achieve the control required to transcend the instrument so that the listener's reaction is not "What a great oboist," but rather "What a great musician" or—even better—"What great *music.*" The irony is that the principal goal of the instrumentalist is to help the public forget the instrument and immerse themselves in the music.

Breathing

Soprano
Lentamente   *pp*   ten.

Adriana: Ec- co: Re-spiro ap - pen - a.
"See: I am barely breathing."
Cilèa: Adriana Lecouvreur, Act I

Before breathing can be examined in relation to wind playing, it is necessary to define what takes place in normal non-musical breathing.

Normal Breathing

In the type of breathing we utilize almost every moment of the day, the diaphragm muscle pulls gently downward at the base of the lungs in order to inhale the air. Upon exhalation, the air is expelled without effort. The natural weight of the chest lightly presses on the lungs and causes most, but not all, of the air to come out. The air speed and volume rapidly decrease in this normal exhalation.

The Active Exhalation

In speech, singing, and musical performance on a wind instrument, where a line must be sustained, the muscles of the abdomen, which surround the base of the lungs, automatically keep the air pressure up.

Here is an experiment that demonstrates that the abdominal muscles are those that actively sustain the line: speak beyond the capacity of your lungs, continuing until you feel you absolutely must take a breath. As you reach your limit it becomes ever more obvious by their intense tightening that the abdominal muscles are responsible for pushing air out of the lungs. But they go into action without conscious effort.

Sometimes the advice is given to "support with the diaphragm" while playing. This is not physically possible because the diaphragm muscle is in a state of relaxation during exhalation. When a young wind player hears this dangerous advice, he or she then usually cramps the abdominal muscles in order to force the wind pressure up.

In truth, an active exhalation comes completely naturally to us. Yet for the obvious reason that they are wind players, young wind instrumentalists fixate upon expelling the wind. However, the air that wind players exhale can only be utilized correctly when a proper active *inhalation* precedes it. This—and not the exhalation—is what the wind player must focus upon.

The Active Inhalation

There are two types of inhalation. The first is the panting breath, which is how most of us breathe all day. It is enough to sustain life but inadequate to sustain the line of music. Avoid taking this type of shallow, upper-lung breath before playing.

The second type of inhalation occurs while yawning. This deep intake of air is what wind players must consciously utilize in order to reach their full capacity as phrase makers. Concentrate on expanding the waistline when inhaling, even for quick catch-breaths. This is where the diaphragm muscle works its magic. The diaphragm must be fully flexed so the lower parts of the lungs are fully filled with air. This lower air, most of which will never be used in performance, gives the abdominal muscles something to push against. A solid stream of concentrated, controllable air from the *upper* lungs can then be emitted during playing.

The lungs are like two giant tubes of toothpaste. A tube of toothpaste must be filled completely, or nothing will come out of its top when squeezed from the bottom. The abdominal muscles, which push against the air in the lower lungs, are, after all, located very near the bottom of the lungs.

The ability to play longer phrases, make smoother attacks, and produce a fuller tone are also welcome results of deep inhalation.

An attack made with only the air of the upper lungs will quiver. It is free-floating and, consequently, produces a tenuous sound. However, by filling the lower lungs, allowing the abdominal muscles to subtly control the airstream, even a diminuendo at the end of a very long musical phrase will be firm. Most important, all musical inflections are controlled by the abdominal muscles, which manipulate that crucial supporting air in the bottom of the lungs.

Reed players often blame the reed when they encounter problems attacking, sustaining, or releasing a note. Sometimes the reed is at fault, but deep inhalation alleviates these problems to a great degree—*without* resorting to the reed knife.

It is an interesting irony that the quality of all the sounds one makes as a wind instrumentalist depends precisely upon that moment immediately before the attack, when one makes no sound at all.

The Long Tone

Trumpet in A
Molto sostenuto e maestoso

Wagner: *Rienzi, Overture*

The long tone is the embryo of all music.

It comes from silence, reaches a climax, and returns to silence. Long tone practice develops the attack, control of the line, and the release. It is, by far, the most difficult musical exercise to perform well. When one can successfully negotiate its difficulties, the entire world of musical expression is laid open.

Developing Control

An ensemble musician virtually never has the luxury of choosing when to play. Concert dates and times are often scheduled more than a year in advance. Conductors may arrive on stage a little earlier or later for any given performance. Composers have also dictated exactly the bar and beat upon which one must enter, and have indicated the dynamic level and often the mood as well. Even the issue of tempo is not left to the individual musician. Playing orchestral music is the only profession that comes to mind, other than working on an assembly line, where one's pace is completely determined by outside factors.

Because of this, you should mentally create a framework that simulates the concert situation when practicing at home so that you can develop the ability to have the tone begin exactly at the moment required.

The framework for the long tone begins by setting a tempo. Before you play, think to yourself, "3–2–1" (quarter = c. 60).

During these preparatory beats, feel an imaginary diminuendo taking place as the embouchure evolves to a *pp* position. Then, when making the attack on 1, you will feel as though you have already been playing. These numbers (3, 2, 1) correspond to the dynamic—1 being the softest you can play. Begin the long tone at the lowest point of your mental diminuendo and grow from there.

In order to have the best chance for a successful attack, take your breath on 3, set the embouchure on 2, and contract the embouchure to the *pp* position up until the moment of the attack on 1. If you breathe immediately before the attack and set the embouchure at the last moment, your entrance will often be rough and predictably late. This is especially glaring in faster music and with entrances that take place on upbeats. Breathe well in advance of any entrance—at least two beats before—if possible. This applies to all the playing you do, not simply to long tone practice.

Once you have attacked the note, smoothly execute a dynamic progression up and down.

Example 233

As you reach each number during this progression, listen for a different color or thickness to the tone. When approaching the end of the long tone, think "up-up-up" as the note fades away. Do not let the intensity drop, even as the note fades to nothing.

A Note to the Unfortunate about Reeds

Often, when practicing long tones at home, young reed players simply try attacking the note again and again until the reluctant tone finally speaks satisfactorily. That will not do in concert. Train yourself and your reed to respond on cue on the first try. Having the reed respond when required is your first responsibility. What good is a reed with a "nice, big sound" if nothing comes out when *pianis-*

simo is needed? By insisting on delicate and immediate response from the reed every time, your reed-making abilities will grow to meet the challenge.

From the Bottom Up

The reason for working on long tones from 1 to 5, at the bottom of the dynamic range, is obvious: it is the range most neglected by students and professionals alike. In order to expand our limited dynamic palette and play *pp* with certainty in even the most difficult and exposed concert situation, it is necessary to develop the extreme soft register. When you master this ability, you will immediately stand out from the crowd. In an audition, exhibiting this fine degree of dynamic nuance can be the deciding factor that wins you the job. Musical freedom is attained only through dynamic control.

Remember that nothing in nature, if it is alive, starts out big and gets smaller. Develop your tone from the bottom up. If this means having a small tone for a year or two in school before you build greater volume, so be it. As you grow your tone over time, always strive to keep that soft control while increasing your dynamic range. Never surrender that.

The Long Crescendo and the Long Diminuendo

When students encounter a crescendo that lasts a long period of time, they sometimes ask themselves, "Does this mean every note is louder than the last?" With very rare exceptions, this is not the case. The high point of each subsequent note group within the long crescendo is simply played louder than the high point of each previous group. Unlike a long tone, where the dynamic progression is smooth, the up and down of musical phrasing still takes place during these long crescendo periods. Some notes are upbeats. Some are arrivals. Others are resolutions. The same situation arises in a long diminuendo. Remember, even a marching band that approaches from afar is still phrasing (hopefully!) as they march toward you. The same happens as they retreat.

By the way, when you see the word crescendo, think *piano*—then you have somewhere to go. Conversely, when you see diminuendo, think *forte*. The musical texture and prevailing dynamic will guide you in how strongly to apply this principle.

Conquering Fear

Beginning a long tone, or any exposed *pp* note, can be a fear-inducing event. However, there is a little trick that can eliminate all trace of trepidation. Think of that note (whatever its duration) as an upbeat to what follows—even if it is followed by a rest. The attack suddenly becomes much more reliable and gentle. You can even think of leading to a note two, three, or more bars *after* the troublesome entrance note. If you focus upon the moment of the attack itself, you can easily become tight and afraid. But by thinking of that note as an innocent upbeat to what follows, everything most often comes out just fine.

Example 234

Approach long tones in this manner as well.

Selfishness

In his woodwind class, John de Lancie often said, "Sound is a blotter; the louder you play, the muddier things become." He was directly addressing the selfish human tendency to play louder than your neighbor. Logically, if everyone attempts to do this in ensemble playing, then no one is heard well. He illustrated this by saying, "*Loud* is like a painting of a rainbow on a wall; its colors are opaque. *Soft* is like the real rainbow; it's transparent."

Mastery of this ethereal range of the instrument is only achieved through long tone practice.

The Singing Interval

Elgar: **The Dream of Gerontius, Part I**

Marcel Tabuteau taught his students a specific way to perform what he called the "singing interval." The singing interval is most often used on upbeats or "up" inflections to downbeats or "down" inflections. He said, "The point is to fill up the gap in between two notes. Like a horse jumping over a hurdle—*down, up-up-up, down*. The last *down* is the landing." He called the growth within the up inflection the "inner work."

This exercise is closely related to the long tone. Begin by choosing two notes—the first lower than the second. Then proceed with the preparatory 3–2–1 (quarter = c. 60). During 1–2–3–4 grow on the lower note. On 5 change the fingering to that of the upper note. No extra push of the wind will be needed to get this higher note to speak. All the work will have been done *within* the lower note. In this way, the upper note is contained in the line and does not stick out. Then, during 4–3–2–1 make the diminuendo in the same manner as a long tone but, as ever, thinking forward to the note's extinction.

Example 235

3 - 2 - 1 - 2 - 3 - 4 - 5 - 4 - 3 - 2 - 1 → → (forward)

Be aware that the diminuendo begins immediately at the moment the higher note begins (on 5). There is no growth or sustaining push required after that downbeat.

When a hairpin (crescendo/diminuendo) is written as in example 235, do not commit either of the two most common dynamic errors, illustrated in examples 236 and 237:

Example 236

The second beat of the second bar played loudest:

3 - 2 - 1 - 2 - 3 - 4 - 5 - <u>**6**</u> - 3 - 2 - 1 → → (forward)

Example 237

The highpoint stretched throughout the first two beats of the second bar:

3 - 2 - 1 - 2 - 3 - 4 - <u>**5**</u> - <u>**5**</u> - 3 - 2 - 1 → → (forward)

By practicing the singing interval with an exact highpoint in mind (the very moment when the note changes) one will become hyper-aware of the location of the loudest part of any hairpin played. Awareness is the goal.

A slight variation on the singing interval can yield striking results. Begin exactly as before, but at the moment of the change to the upper note, hold the dynamic back slightly, as illustrated in example 238.

Example 238

3 - 2 - 1 - 2 - 3 - 4 - <u>**3**</u> - <u>**&**</u> - <u>**2**</u> - <u>**&**</u> - 1 → → **(forward)**

The lightness and grace of this gentle inflection is more easily experienced than explained. However, take care not to overuse this special nuance, as it can easily become a distracting mannerism.

Of course, the singing interval technique can also be applied to downward intervals.

Satisfaction

Of the singing interval, Tabuteau said: "This fun was to explain how I duplicate the famous gliss*aaaaaaaa*ndo used by the string play- ers. . . . The understanding of this important lesson will help you to reach a high standard in your performance as an artist and bring you self-*satisfaction*!"[1]

The Fingers

Clarinet in B♭
Molto moderato
con licenza
17
gliss.
p
mf

Gershwin: Rhapsody in Blue

Attitude is the key to progressing beyond mere fingering of the notes.

"Fake" Fingerings

The question of fingering on a woodwind instrument is a sticky one. There are so many fingerings available. Quite often, the fingerings that are not the first ones learned are referred to as "alternate" or, more piously, as "fake." The problem with using these words is that they immediately give a negative connotation to many valid fingerings. A passage that might otherwise sound labored, sloppy, and indistinct when the "real" fingerings are used might very well sound clean, clear, and flashy when so-called "fake" ones are substituted. The bottom line is that those "fake" fingerings can make many passages sound more *real*. They should be referred to as *appropriate* fingerings.

Flailing Fingers and Tension

Moving the fingers excessively, as well as squeezing the instrument in a vicelike grip, can cause pain and tension in the hands and arms.

This can be very dangerous over the long term and can lead to tendinitis or other debilitating conditions. Relax the hands completely. Keep the fingers close to the instrument, hovering over the keys, ready for action, so they are required to move as little as possible. Tension in the shoulders can also cause problems. Not only is it distracting to see, but it also drains energy that could be used constructively in performance. Try to relax the body completely and channel all your energy through the instrument—through the music.

Legato Fingers

Slapping the fingers down on a woodwind instrument while playing makes one's progression from note to note sound "note-y." The art of smoothly changing from one note to another is crucial in diverting the listener's attention from the instrument to the music. Legato fingering must be cultivated in order to do this. Just slurring the notes together does not guarantee that one has played a true legato.

When practicing legato fingering, think of singing. In singing, every slurred note is approached or left with a quasi-glissando. In order to approximate this natural vocal quality it is necessary to move the fingers in a smooth—almost slow—way. First, practice chromatically, choosing two notes that require the movement of only one finger to go from one to the other. Sometimes, when an open hole is involved, one must roll the finger slightly to create this smoothness. Practice this technique as one would play a long tone.

Example 239

Try achieving the same legato effect on larger intervals that require many fingers to move. Experiment by first leading with one and then another finger (or fingers) in order to find the smoothest-sounding solution. Think "gluey" so there will be no unvocal "pop" between the notes.

Unfortunately, this popping sound is an extremely common occurrence in woodwind playing. It is so generally accepted as a normal part of the sound of moving from note to note that one must be taught to hear it. Once one learns how, this sound becomes very distracting. Eliminating it whenever possible brings one's playing one step closer to singing. Of course, in faster music the fingers will not move so deliberately, but if you remember this concept even in quick passages, greater fluidity will result. Do not be content simply to change fingerings with military precision at the expense of a true legato. The meaning of the word legato is "bound." Bind as many notes together as seamlessly as you can in your playing. It is difficult, but the result is well worth the effort.

One mental image helps. Imagine that your fingers are held in place by cables pulling from above as well as from below. When the fingers close the keys or holes on the instrument they must go against the resistance of the upper cable and, when they open the key or hole, they must then do so with resistance from the lower, imaginary cable. But the fingers must not be tense while thinking of this concept.

The End Result

Instrumentalists are naturally preoccupied with the fingers. But their importance must be kept in perspective. The famed pianist Josef Hofmann was once asked, "How can you play the piano so brilliantly with such tiny fingers?" "Madam," he replied, "I do not play the piano with my *fingers.*"

The payoff for all this seemingly thankless finger work is exactly what Josef Hofmann was alluding to when questioned about his short fingers. Without the extraneous finger problems so commonly heard, the perceptive listener will finally be able to understand that you are not playing the instrument with your fingers at all, but that you are making music—inspiring emotion—through the active use of your brain.

Scales

Violin I
IV - Adagio

Beethoven: Symphony #1

Speed

I once attended a master class conducted by cellist Zara Nelsova. She quoted an elderly cellist she knew as having said the way he kept his playing in such good shape over the years was by practicing slow scales every day. Nelsova said that instead of playing them quickly, as most musicians do, practicing scales somewhere between fast and slow is actually more difficult and accomplishes much more. Mastering the ability to play cleanly at this rather uncontrollable mid-range tempo will yield much more effective results in your fast playing because it will have the effect of fusing an engaged mind that is concerned with perfect evenness of execution with the muscle memory one attains through speedy practice.

Musical Scales?

Scales are music. They should always be played in a musical way. Music is very often made of scales, sometimes broken up into sections as small as two notes. The following is a method of playing scales that puts them into a musical framework and uses the entire range of the instrument.

Scales should be played with a pulse that anchors them to the beats. Then, they relate to the way one plays in concert. They are not simply free-floating.

Begin mentally by thinking "3–2–1" as when practicing long tones. Make the attack on the tonic (the lowest one on your instrument for that particular scale) on 1 and continue upward in deliberate sixteenths, making basic groupings while you crescendo all the way up to the highest note you can play in that scale. Make playing the extreme notes a routine, daily task. Do not hold the high note, but immediately continue with the descent and diminuendo. Continue down past the tonic to the lowest note in the scale within the range of your instrument and then go back up to the tonic, making sure to end *on* a beat. Place a fermata on the last note.

The oboe scale in example 240 illustrates that sometimes adding the supertonic is necessary in order to end on a beat. The oboe range is generally considered to extend from low B-flat below the treble clef up to its high G. The brackets show basic grouping.

Example 240

In example 241, even more notes are added at the end so that the last note falls on a beat.

Example 241

A variation on this long tone theme is to make small waves as one goes up and down the scale, as in example 242.

Example 242

1, 1- 2-3- 4,   4-3-2-1,   2-3-4-5,   5 - 4 - 3 - 2,   3 - 4 - 5 - 6,   6 - 5 - 4 - 3,   2-3-4-5,   5-4-3-2,   1 - 2-3-4,   4 - 3 - 2 - 1

When making the descent, maintain the wind support. If you allow the support to drop as you diminuendo, the pitch will droop. Think "up" while going down the scale.

Listen

Be able to play all scales—major, the three minors, whole tone, and chromatic—without relying on printed music. Too often, reading scales leads to trouble playing them away from the paper. They should be memorized and easily retrievable when they are spotted in the music one encounters.

There is a secret to memorizing scales: Do not think of their key signatures while playing them. Simply be aware of the sound of the intervals that make up that particular scale—half and whole steps (major and whole tone scales), and the augmented whole step contained within the harmonic minor scales.

Value

By practicing scales in this musically structured way you will also be practicing long tones and groupings—and you will be removing the scales from the page by not reading them. Although you may feel that you are practicing many things at once, the reality is that you will be making only one thing—music. You will be treating scales as the compositions they are. Mozart, Beethoven, and Brahms all wrote scales in their music. A scale in one of Mozart's greatest masterpieces and the scale you play in the practice room both have the same musical value.

Jane Orzel, my first bassoon teacher, wisely advised, "If you can spare only ten minutes to practice each day, make it scales."

Using the Wind

Tabuteau spoke of how his teacher, Georges Gillet, had him practice wind control by blowing on the flame of a lit candle. He was instructed to bring the flame close to extinction gradually and then slowly allow it to come back to full flame. This is precisely the kind of refined control involved in woodwind phrasing.

Conservation and Respiration

Since wind players have a finite supply of air, a good rule of thumb is to give a little more volume on shorter notes and conserve the air on longer notes, in order to play longer phrases. Fortunately, in addition to helping you play longer between breaths, applying this technique will simply make your playing sound more musical.

In example 243 this concept is illustrated geometrically beneath the notes. Think "give" on the half notes and "conserve" on the tied whole notes. You will be amazed at how much longer you can play on a single breath if you consciously give to upbeats or up inflections and conserve on downbeats or down inflections. The same principle applies to the bowing on string instruments.

Example 243

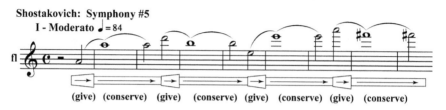

(give)   (conserve)   (give)   (conserve)   (give)   (conserve)   (give)   (conserve)

If this phrase were played in the opposite way, with more volume on the longer notes, as in example 244, the unmusicality is plain to the ear.

Example 244

Also, in example 244, you would run out of air much sooner.

Yet, even if the phrasing in example 243 is exaggerated, it still sounds somewhat musical, if a bit overdone.

This "give/conserve" technique goes hand in hand with making a plan for your breathing. Know exactly when you will inhale and also where you can exhale leftover air. Stick to your plan. It will provide you with a sense of security, as all plans in life do.

The Soft Attack

Wind players sometimes forget that when playing *pp*, concentrating on wind support is even more crucial than when playing *ff*. When playing loudly, support happens almost automatically, but when playing softly, musicians tend to associate the word "less" with their breath support. The result is a corresponding drop in air pressure. It is true that less wind is required for *pp*, but the softer the note or attack, the faster and more concentrated the airstream must be.

Think of a garden hose when applying this principle. When the nozzle of the hose is tightened, the water's stream is much more concentrated. Less water is coming out—but that water is under much greater pressure, and is propelled out of the hose at a greater rate of speed.

In playing a reed instrument, use the embouchure to focus the air by pulling in the corners of the mouth (as if saying "ooo"). This, and not biting, gives greater security when making a soft attack or sustaining a long diminuendo *al niente*. Do not fall into the trap of clamping the reed with the jaw while playing softly. This pinches the sound and causes the pitch to go sharp.

Marcel Tabuteau illustrated the concept of the relationship between the embouchure (the nozzle) and the wind (the water) with this simple diagram:

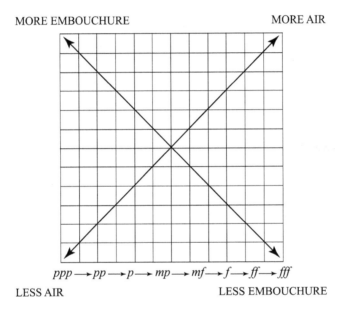

The line from lower left to upper right is the *Air*. The line from upper left to lower right is the *Embouchure*. When one is playing *ppp* the embouchure is at the maximum round support (the nozzle) and the air at its lowest volume (the water). When playing *fff* the situation is just the opposite; the embouchure is much more open and relaxed while the air flows at much greater volume.

The Loud Release

As wind players must develop the skill of beginning a note softly and tapering it gently to its extinction, they must also develop the ability to end a note loudly at full force. Sometimes wind instrumentalists stop a loud final note with the tongue. This is not related to singing. Even when an opera singer sings a word that ends in a harsh consonant, that word has a residual open quality, as in "stand(a)!" On a wind instrument, stopping a note with the tongue stifles this natural-sounding open end. Imagine the stilted sound produced by a string player who stops the final note of a heroic phrase with the bow still in contact with the string! This is the effect wind players should avoid.

Often, young players who do end a loud note in an open way sound like their air pressure is being cut off rather slowly—like a water faucet being turned off. Immediately after their conscious exhalation is finished, an unconscious trickle of leftover air follows, creating a flaccid impression as the tone rapidly deflates.

In reed playing, the embouchure should tighten from the corners of the mouth at the very end of the note while the abdominal muscles give a minute push with the air. This slight increase in air pressure at the final moment keeps up the intensity of the cutoff and prevents any residual feeling of deflation. Ending a triumphant note in this way, as a great opera singer might, can create a thrilling effect.

The "Life" of the Note

Just like the smallest and most short-lived of insects, every note—no matter how brief in duration—has its own life.

Yet, although each note is written as a separate, freestanding individual, music is really just one note that swims through different pitches. Visualizing the music in this way makes us more sensitive to what happens during the life of each note. Like blood coursing through the veins and arteries, music pulses through the notes, creating its line.

Marcel Tabuteau said that we must play the "life" of the note. Although it is a difficult concept to explain, the absence of life on any note, no matter how small, becomes conspicuous once one develops sensitivity for hearing it. Too often, wind instrumentalists focus on the attack, and tone quality, at the expense of paying attention to how that note lives after it has been born.

Louis Rosenblatt, former English hornist of the Philadelphia Orchestra, told a story that revealed Tabuteau's own idea of his mission in life. "I remember now that Mrs. Tabuteau invited . . . me to a party. . . . One lady said to Mr. Tabuteau, 'Oh, Mr. Tabuteau, you are the greatest oboe player in the world!' And so he said, 'Well, I don't know about that, but I want to play *zee life of zee note.*'"

Although this anecdote is amusing, Tabuteau was sincere in his reply. No one can rightfully say he or she is the "greatest in the world" in any area, but one can be sincere in stating one's goals.

Listen to the recordings of Tabuteau, Callas, or Kreisler for vivid examples of how to sustain the life of each note. Every note has music pulsing through it. It is not easy to revivify every note on the page, but they did it. Their example is encouragement to those who wish to put forth the necessary effort. It is exhausting work that demands constant vigilance, and it also requires that the performer know the purpose of every note. That is why so few performers do it.

The elusive "life" of each note rests in its progression from its beginning, *through* its duration, and in how it terminates or joins to the note that follows. The notes, when carefully spliced together like pieces of electrical wire, merely form a conduit through which the seamless electrical current of the music flows.

Articulation

Debussy: Golliwogg's Cakewalk

For many performers, articulation is simply the icing on the cake. However, all articulations hold the power to define the functions of the notes, and function determines emotion. Therefore, the articulations employed by the player should be able to withstand questioning from those who listen for logic as well as emotion in musical performance.

The Old "Stand-By"

Often, when wind players encounter a series of sixteenth notes without slurs, in a baroque or classical composition where the composer has not specified all the articulations, "slur two/tongue two" is arbitrarily pulled out of the hat. Unfortunately, many well-meaning music editors have also chosen this convenient route and, by doing so, have unwittingly contributed to over-popularizing this articulation.

Although "two-and-two" tonguing may give a certain simple pleasure to the player, it does not fit all sixteenth-note passages. Even if a historical precedent exists, tradition alone is no reason to apply this technique blindly. There are good and bad traditions. "Two-and-two" tonguing is, more often than not, merely an easily applied technical solution for getting through rapid articulated passages with a minimum of thought and effort.

As Tabuteau enjoyed pointing out, in truth, "slur two/tongue two" is really "slur *one*/tongue *three*" (example 245). Only the second of the four sixteenths is slurred into [S]. The other three are articulated with the tongue [T].

Example 245

T - S - T - T   T - S - T - T

This little illustration demonstrates that some of the labels we routinely take for granted are not as well thought out as they seem at first glance. It is worth questioning all widely held suppositions—and traditions—to test their logic. If they do not stand up to this testing, they should be discarded in favor of *reasoned* principles.

Example 246 illustrates how "two-and-two" articulation is sometimes used regardless of the functions of the notes.

Example 246

Mozart: Concerto for Bassoon in B flat Major
I - Allegro

This articulation obscures the underlying sequence of rising half-step intervals. When boiling this phrase down to its skeletal structure, it is easy to see that, aside from the first downbeat, each pitch occurring on a beat is preceded, in effect, by a leading tone (example 247).

Example 247

Each leading tone, in turn, has been given an upper neighbor tone (example 248).

Example 248

"Two-and-two" delineates groups that are completely foreign to this structure (example 249).

Example 249

The resolution of the trill at the beginning of this sequence (the D on the first downbeat) should not be connected to the following E-natural by a slur. This illogical slurring is analogous to connecting the last word of one spoken sentence to the first word of the next:

> *Incorrect: "To be or not to be that. Is the question . . ."*
> *Correct: "To be, or not to be. That is the question."*

The articulation that best defines the meaning of the notes is illustrated in example 250. Only the leading tone and the main pitch of the beat are articulated. They are, after all, the two main tones that define the structure of this rising line. The resolution of the trill is also joined to the trill by a slur.

Example 250

Choose articulations that work with the music's content, not against it.

There are instances where "slur two/tongue two" works. For example, if the first and second sixteenths of the beat are an appoggiatura and resolution, respectively, and if they are followed by scalewise figures or arpeggiations, as in example 251, this articulation is not only acceptable, it best defines the functions of the notes.

Example 251

Broken arpeggios with the contour outlined in example 252 also lend themselves to this articulation.

Example 252

There are, of course, rare moments when articulation is not crucial to the function of the notes at all, as when all the notes are scalewise or arpeggiated. This usually occurs in less profound music (virtuoso variations, e.g.) where a performer can indulge freely in his or her whims. No serious damage is done to lightweight show-pieces by highlighting articulation itself as the centerpiece of the moment from time to time.

Performers only need to reconcile themselves to the fundamental principle that in most instances the functions of the notes should be highlighted through the articulations chosen—unless the composer has specified articulations contrary to those functions.

This having been stated, the vast world of music often confronts us with frightful technical articulated passages. Sometimes, as a matter of sheer survival, "two-and-two" can get one safely home. It is not a musical solution, however. In these frenzied instances it serves only as a necessary life preserver in a storm at sea.

How to Avoid Choppiness

In his explanation of how to perform mixed articulations[1] (some notes tongued and others slurred), Marcel Tabuteau said that the last note of a slurred group that is followed immediately by an articulated note should not be clipped or stopped with the tongue. He used the word "long" when describing this note, saying that the following note is "expressed on the *length* of the *long*." He chose Ravel's *Le Tombeau de Couperin* as illustration, saying "tee-*long*-ta-tee" while singing the triplet notes (example 253).

Example 253

Ravel: Le Tombeau de Couperin
I - Prélude. Vif ♩. = 92

Tabuteau: tee- *long* - ta - tee-*long*-ta-tee-*long*-ta - tee-*long*-ta - tee

Tabuteau's message was that the end of the second triplet note doubles as the beginning of the third triplet note; one motion of the tongue, not two. The tongue does not remain on the reed between the notes stopping its vibration; it only lightly articulates the beginning of the third note.

Tabuteau contrasts this with a vivid example of how not to play (example 254), this time saying, "tee-*at*-ta-tee"—an articulation that does stop the reed's vibration.

Example 254

Tabuteau: tee- *at* - ta - tee - *at* - ta - tee - *at* - ta - tee - *at* - ta - tee

This style of articulation is undeniably jerky and creates an impression of amateurism. It can also distort the rhythm. By thoughtlessly clipping the second note in this way, and then leaving the tongue on the reed for too great a time before articulating the next note, triplets can be distorted into the rhythm shown in example 255.

Example 255

tee - *at* - ta - tee - *at* - ta - tee - *at* - ta - tee - *at* - ta

But thinking of the word "long" on the last note of a slurred group allows even the most complicated tongue and slur combinations to flow in a natural, speaking manner.

On with the Wind

Whether one plays a whole note, two halves, four quarters, or eight eighths, the wind should do exactly the same thing. It should make a line. The habit many wind players fall into is to pulse one's airstream on every note as if deliberately saying, "Ah—Ah—Ah." One should not play that way. Keep the wind moving, even when rearticulating the same pitch. Articulate on the line. Do not let the support drop at the end of each note.

The reason articulation on wind instruments can often sound grotesque is that some wind players try to articulate with their wind. But in normal speech, the articulation comes from the movement of the tongue, lips, and teeth. The linear use of the breath in wind playing should be exactly the same as in speaking.

Punctuating

Often, when a dotted rhythm appears, the dot carries the implication that a slight space, or punctuation, should occur before the following note (example 256).

Example 256

Handel: Concerto for Oboe in G minor
I - Grave

This type of punctuating is especially important when the dotted note and the following note of shorter duration are of the same pitch. Otherwise, in the concert hall, the repetition of pitch can be blurred.

Fast Tonguing

In order to increase the speed of one's tonguing, concentrate on moving the tongue the least amount possible, while coupling it with highly concentrated air pressure. Imagine that you are supporting the tongue on the airstream as a flapping flag is supported by a strong breeze. Mentally framing this concept in this way subconsciously relaxes the tongue and reduces the work it must do. Also, think of playing *long* notes when tonguing extremely fast passages— *even if the notes are marked staccato.* Begin each note cleanly with the tongue. Do not think of ending the notes at all (example 257).

Example 257

Beethoven: Symphony no. 4
IV - Allegro ma non troppo

Correct: ta - ta - ta - ta - ta-ta - ta-ta-ta-ta-ta-ta - ta - ta-ta-ta - ta - ta-ta-ta - ta - ta - ta - ta - ta
Incorrect: tat-tat-tat - tat-tat-tat - tat-tat-tat-tat-tat-tat - tat-tat-tat-tat-tat-tat-tat-tat-tat-tat - tat - tat - tat

Here again, the beginning of each note (except, of course, the first) in this example serves as the end of the previous note. In addition to its relation to speech, where the end of one word is often elided with the beginning of another, this is also related to the bowing on string instruments. Most often, when string players articulate rapid passages, the bow does not perceptibly stop between the notes. It simply changes direction.

Staccato

"... staccato refers to how a note is ended, not to how it is begun ..." —Philip Farkas (*The Art of Musicianship*, 36).

Staccato does not mean "short." It means "separated."

The wind staccato is analogous to the string pizzicato and both, in turn, are related to laughter. With a properly executed wind staccato, each note has an articulated beginning and an *open* end. Begin the notes with the tongue and finish them on the wind, as illustrated in example 258.

Example 258

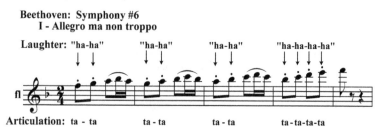

Beethoven: Symphony #6
I - Allegro ma non troppo

Laughter: "ha-ha"   "ha-ha"   "ha-ha"   "ha-ha-ha-ha"

Articulation: ta - ta   ta - ta   ta - ta   ta-ta-ta-ta

The ends of the notes are not stopped in any way—they are simply released.

There is a natural bounce to a refined bowed staccato in string playing that wind players should emulate. But one must first be aware that there is a fundamental physical difference between staccato string articulation and the chopped wind staccato often heard. With string instruments, the bow keeps moving between the notes and the string itself continues to vibrate after the bow ceases to make contact with it. No such reverberation happens with a wind staccato. In order to bring staccato off successfully in wind playing—to create and maintain a musical line—one must carefully judge how much a puff of air to give each note. The player must also build in a bit of resonance by controlling how much of a "tail" each note should have.

Marcel Tabuteau had his students practice the following kind of staccato separation (example 259). This exercise contains both growth during the crescendo notes and decay during the diminuendo notes while maintaining slight separations between them. Of course, while performing this exercise the student would bear in mind the true meaning of the word "staccato": *separated*. Sometimes, Tabuteau would draw a diagram to illustrate this point.

Example 259

Although the notes are disconnected, the overall line is still recognizable. Even with their longer duration, the notes are still open-ended—whether making a crescendo or diminuendo.

The Ugly Exception

There is a type of mechanical staccato where the wind player does stop the note with the tongue. This most often occurs in music written after 1900, but it is extremely rare. Unfortunately, many contemporary musicians have been unwittingly conditioned to approach all staccato notes as relatively harsh popping sounds because so many modern works do represent the uglier side of mechanized life. While modern composers often reflect this quite well in their compositions, performers today must choose what type of staccato best fits within the context of the music being played, by paying special attention to its character as well as to its vintage.

"Bad" Slurs

It may come across as musical heresy of a sort, but in some writing for wind instruments, certain slurs should be ignored. The following bassoon excerpts (examples 260 and 261) demonstrate this crucial lesson. They contain awkward downslurs that, if played on a piano, are completely without difficulty. Most composers compose at the piano and many are pianists. But on the bassoon, the resulting "downswoop" caused by slurring these difficult intervals can sound perilously close to the hee-haw of a donkey if the slurs are not broken by a subtle use of the tongue. Lightly tonguing the lower note of awkward downslurs also keeps the upper note from bending downward pitchwise in anticipation of the lower note's pitch. It can also guarantee that the lower note speaks without an accent.

Reed players must develop this delicate technique in order to avoid embarrassing mishaps. Be sure to keep the upper note moving forward *into* the bad slur and then "flip" the reed lightly with the tongue (T) at the moment of the change of note (example 260). The results will speak for themselves.

Example 260

Mahler: Symphony #1
III - Feierlich und gemessen, ohne zu schleppen

Each instrument has its own bad slurs. Sometimes eliminating them altogether is the only way to turn them into good "slurs."

Up or Down?

From time to time, it is beneficial to think of upward intervals when encountering a sequence of particularly awkward downslurs, as illustrated in example 261.

Example 261

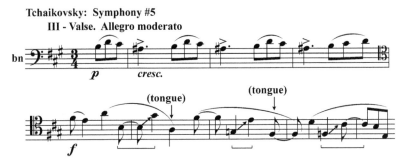

Tchaikovsky: Symphony #5
III - Valse. Allegro moderato

This technique avoids the aforementioned problem of the upper note bending downward as the embouchure prepares for the lower note. By mentally eliminating downslurs from time to time, many passages can be rendered with much greater security.

Integrity

It is important to realize that all the notations on the page (e.g., slurs, articulations) are merely a shorthand that attempts to show what the *end result* should sound like in performance. Those markings are not definitive instructions of literally what to do. Breaking printed articulations, from time to time, is not a punishable offense.

Part 6

Controversy

Horns in F

Stravinsky: Rite of Spring, *Sacrificial Dance*

In the profession of music, all is not in a state of perpetual harmony. There are many areas where colleagues disagree. The topics addressed here are looked upon as hot-button issues which have the potential to bring even the most outwardly placid of musicians to a boil. The silver lining is that dispute, properly reflected upon, can lead to artistic growth.

An art form such as music, which ostensibly involves displaying one's passion on stage for all to judge, could not possibly be divorced from passionate disagreement, due to the widely perceived emotional nature of the profession itself. But once the musician realizes that the goal in musical performance is not the transmission of one's own emotions, but rather communication of the composer's intent, then controversial issues can be discussed rationally.

Tone

Flute

Très modéré

Debussy: Prélude à l'après-midi d'un faune

The tone we are closest to all our lives is that of our own speaking voice. To an extent, a person's speaking voice is reflected in the tone produced on his or her instrument, both in quality and in volume. This is most noticeable on wind instruments, particularly the reeds. People who speak loudly tend to play loudly. Those who speak with varied inflection play that way. Those who have rich, dark voices tend to have a similar instrumental tone quality.

Unlike the voice in one's throat, however, one's instrumental voice must be consciously built from the ground up. An analysis of the components that make up a complete tone quality helps one to understand that the ideal instrumental tone should not be just one unchangeable sound.

Darkness and Light

As the monotony of perpetually overcast skies can become overwhelmingly depressing, and, conversely, the glare of relentless sunshine can make you wish fervently for the smallest cloud to provide a moment of relief, an unvaried instrumental tone quality can also create a disturbing impression. People use the words "bright" and "dark" to describe various tone qualities, but mastery of a subtle gradation between these two extremes is necessary in order to avoid monotony.

John Minsker, the longtime English hornist of the Philadelphia Orchestra (1936–59) and woodwind teacher at Curtis (1978–85), who was revered for his tone, described the variable tone one should strive for:

> You have to have the dark quality tone to which you can add color and intensity. If you start from this bright, white, shiny tone that they talk about the sopranos, for example, today; they say, "Well, she has that beautiful tone—it's like a diamond." Well, a diamond's great but a diamond all the time is *too much sparkle*. That sparkle has to have a background of a certain darkness and your basic tone has to be a dark one—which Tabuteau had and which Kreisler had.
>
> See, you start with *black*—which, according to the physicists, is a lack of all color—and *white*—which is the presence of all color—and you play with what's in between those two . . . then with *that* you can give color. You can give intensity and you have something to play with. If you start with that white, that brilliant sound . . . *so where do you go from there?* Then [you] have to play a *pp* and nothing sounds. It's a bright *pp*. It's not a dark *pp* from which you can expand and expand and add color to.[1]

Marcel Tabuteau said, "In my opinion, the quality that carries is the amplification of a *dolce* tone. The *dolce* tone is the nearest to zero."[2] In this way he described that the ideal tone at its loudest still has the dark and unforced quality as that produced when playing *pp*.

When visualizing the type of tone that has the ability to change color, think of the eight ball in the game of billiards. It is black, firm, smooth, and shiny, with the ability to reflect light. It is not like a black tennis ball—fuzzy and infirm—which never could reflect anything. If you shine a red light upon the surface of the eight ball, the ball glows red, and so it goes for all other colors. It is this ability to reflect light—to *become* light—that creates a vibrant, interesting sound.

Squillo

In the world of Italian opera, the word "squillo" describes the essential element that determines how much light one has in the tone. As the sound of the word itself reveals, "squillo" is closely related to the English word "squeal." In fact, the Italian meaning of this word is "shrill" or "ringing." Squillo is the light that reflects off the glossy black eight-ball tone. It is the sound of the higher overtones, which give the tone its life.

Squillo is heard in the greatest singers' voices. If it is not present in sufficient quantity, a singer's voice will lack focus and clarity, sounding as if the throat is coated with chocolate pudding.

Great speaking voices also have squillo. It is a necessary element for varied expression. In tender moments, the tone becomes more covered—warmer. In moments of anger or tension it become more wiry—drier.

Luckily for string players, squillo occurs naturally. It is the sound of the bow on the strings. George Bernard Shaw's characterization of the sound of the cello as "a bee buzzing in a stone jug" gives one a quaint sound picture that vividly illustrates the sound of the squillo overtones (the bee) and separates them from the deeper underlying fundamental (the jug).

Some wind instrumentalists forget the squillo and become obsessed with getting the darkest tone possible. Others try for the most brilliant and cutting sound. But constant gradation of the tone is necessary to reflect the many moods within music. A tone with too little squillo can be unbearably dull. By the same token, a tone with too much squillo can be strident. The ideal tone, at its darkest, is not completely devoid of squillo, and yet at its brightest it is also not totally bereft of its dark quality. Finding the proper balance is an unending pursuit.

Use of One's Tone

It is said that a person with a great voice can bring tears to the eyes simply by reading the telephone book aloud. However, beautiful tone quality alone cannot be relied upon to sell even the most interesting material—let alone the telephone book. Rather, it is the evolving and involved *use* of the tone—whatever its innate qualities—that creates an emotional listening experience.

As an illustration of the controversy surrounding the issue of tone quality, there is no better example than the voice of soprano Maria Callas. To her critics, her tone is lacking all that is truly operatic and plush. They call it thin or metallic. Yet, incredibly, she could also sound pure, serene, girlish; such was her control over the various tone *qualities* she produced.

In Franco Zeffirelli's documentary about Callas, conductor Nicola Rescigno observed, "Her voice was not of the most beautiful quality, and still she made this instrument the most expressive, the most telling, the most *true* to the music that she interpreted of all of the singers of her day." Conductor Carlo Maria Giulini made perhaps the most perceptive observation of all: "It is very difficult to speak about the voice—the *instrument* voice of Maria Callas. It was a very, very special instrument. You know, sometimes happens the same thing with string instruments—violin, viola, 'cello—where the first moment that you listen to the sound of these instruments the first feeling is a little bit strange sometimes. But after just [a] few minutes that you get used [to]—you become [a] *friend* for this kind of sound. Then the sound becomes a magic quality. *This* was Callas." Zeffirelli summed it up: "Her voice disturbed as many as it thrilled. . . . The controversy soon settled into an argument as old as opera: *sound*, versus the dramatic *use* of sound."

Value

Some listeners revel in the warmth of a velvety tone or thrill to a brilliant and penetrating one. This sensual element is an indispensable part of music, but tone, in and of itself, cannot lend profundity to musical communication.

In the equally sensuous culinary world, many people value the flavor of food far more than they do its nutritional value. The aspect of flavor gives fleeting pleasure. However, a food's nutritional value—*its content*—has the capacity to help us heal and grow. Furthermore, nutritious foods, as well as music making of value, simply make us feel good, sometimes for hours after eating or listening. Only with maturity can we more accurately assess the "nutritional value" of what we listen to.

Unfortunately, music is often viewed as a mere bonbon, something that provides fleeting pleasure. Many listeners expect ear candy when they listen to music. Luckily for them, this kind of music making is plentiful. Musical performance of substance is more difficult to find.

It is easy to be seduced by outward beauty, only to realize later that beauty is not always coupled with inner substance.

A "Beautiful" Tone

Tone is only a medium for conveying expression. One of the emptiest compliments is "What a lovely tone you have." Imagine if, after a tour-de-force live theater performance of *Mary of Scotland*, someone had said to the great actress Helen Hayes, "What a great tone your voice has," without any reference to the expressive use of her voice.

Although known for his tone, Marcel Tabuteau put the entire issue into perspective. He said, "By all means, if you have absolutely nothing to say, develop a beautiful tone. You will always be able to find *someone* who will enjoy listening to you for it."[3]

Your tone is your voice—but it is not what you say.

Intonation

Piccolo Trumpet in D
Trumpet in B♭

Stravinsky: Petrushka, *Death of Petrushka*

Despite its basis in mathematics, intonation is often a contentious topic among musicians. Some people practice a theory of tuning known as "expressive" intonation. Others believe in "equal-temperament." However, it is preferable to respect the nature of the overtone series and practice "just" intonation.

The subject of intonation is actually less subjective than it first seems. There are basic principles of physics that have a bearing on how to tune even before the notes have sounded. Just as knowing the tendencies of certain troublesome notes on your instrument makes a difference in where to place them, so too knowing the tendencies of notes, *related to their position in the chord,* affects how they should be tuned.

The Overtone Series

The fundamental is the lowest and loudest part of a musical tone. But there are higher elements accompanying this fundamental.

Objects of an inconsistent structure—a desk, a chair—will not demonstrate this overtone series if struck. The vibrations of their constituent parts conflict with one another and all they can emit is a muffled thud. But almost any object consistent in its structure, such as a vibrating string, a column of air, or any object capable of producing a recognizable pitch, will produce the universal phenomenon known as the overtone series.

A breakdown of the first few overtones is illustrated in example 262. Every pitch follows this principle. Only the first few of the overtones shown below are the ones that can be heard with the unaided ear.

Example 262

(fundamental)

*The 6th overtone of low C is pitched between A and B flat.

The first overtone is produced by one half of the vibrating body (e.g., string, column of air). The second is produced by one third of it. The third by one fourth, and so on. The overtone series continues ad infinitum into ever-smaller divisions of the vibrating body.

The following is an exercise that will help you recognize the first few overtones, using example 262 as a guide:

On an acoustical piano, silently depress the C in the middle of the bass clef. This note will represent the first overtone. Then forcefully strike the C fundamental (one octave below) *staccato*, without the sustaining pedal, while still depressing the C key one octave above. After you have released the low C, you will notice that the first overtone contained within it has caused the other C string to vibrate sympathetically. Try this with the twelfth above the fundamental, then two octaves above, and finally the third above that. You will be able to hear each tone faintly. The higher they are, however, the more difficult they are to hear. You will not actually be hearing the overtone while performing this exercise; rather, you will hear the string most closely tuned to the overtone vibrate in sympathy with it.

Now try the same experiment with a pitch *not* present in the overtone series of the fundamental—perhaps a sixth or a ninth above the tonic. No discernible sympathetic vibration will occur.

There are two reasons why the overtones in this exercise grow fainter as they go up. The first is that the portion of the string creating the higher overtones is smaller. The second is that the equal temperament of the modern piano is not in tune with the overtone series. Because of this, the sympathetic vibrations of the undamped notes are less strong than they would be if the piano were tuned perfectly with the overtones.

After this exercise, strike and *hold* the fundamental again without depressing any other key. Your sensitized ear will now be able to hear the first four overtones clearly as the note fades. Surprisingly, you will hear a full C major chord simply by playing a low C.

Forcefully play that low C once again and listen specifically for the major third (the E) overtone. After allowing it to decay for a few moments, softly play the E at the bottom of the treble clef, joining the natural diminuendo already taking place. You will hear beats between its pitch and the pitch of the pure overtone. The E overtone is markedly *lower* than the tuning of the E on the piano keyboard.

The fact remains that if a piano were perfectly tuned to the key of C throughout its compass it would be grossly out of tune when any modulation out of that home key occurs. Before J. S. Bach popularized equal temperament in the early 1700s, with his *Well-Tempered Clavier*, this was just how it was on keyboard instruments. Afterward, and to the present day, all keys became equally and, to most people, tolerably out of tune on the piano.

It is interesting to note that in order for a piano to be truly in tune it would require seventy-seven keys within each octave.[1] String, wind, and brass instrumentalists, as well as singers, are able to produce these seventy-seven pitches with effort and a little thought. They are able, therefore, to be much more in tune than today's well-tempered piano.

Why Is Minor Minor?

As shown, the overtone series is major. Only in the extreme upper overtones does the minor overtone appear, and then it is far too weak to hear. Because of the strong fourth overtone, major is the natural state of tonality. When we hear a major chord, the natural phenomenon of the overtone series itself is reinforced and we experience a sensation of satisfaction. So what makes a minor chord sound minor?

A minor chord has, as its distinguishing element, a lowered third. This minor third clashes directly with the strong major third overtone contained within the root of the chord; hence the feeling of unease created when a minor chord is played. Minor chords exist in dissonance with nature.

Know Your Place

Before the proper tuning adjustments can be made, musicians must first cultivate the ability to discern the position of their individual note in any given chord: root, third, fifth, or seventh (or one of many possible appoggiaturas or dissonant tones). Be sensitive to whoever is playing the root of the chord—if you are not already playing the root—and you will have greater success ascertaining your position. The key to playing in tune lies not in simply hearing yourself but in hearing those around you.

Octaves

In tempered tuning on the piano, octaves are the only acoustically correct interval (if the piano tuner has not unnecessarily spread the octaves). On wind, brass, and string instruments, they are the easiest to tune. If one has difficulty tuning octaves, perhaps an alternative career should be considered.

Fifths and Fourths

When fifths and fourths are out of tune, the result is excruciating. The beats caused by the clash of their lower overtones is quite apparent. Because of the strength of these overtones, fourths and fifths are relatively easy to tune.

Example 263

fifth   fourth

The overtone series provides an unerring guide to tuning these intervals.

The second overtone of the harmonic series is 2 cents higher than equal temperament.[2] Since the low C is the root of the first interval in example 263, and since the root is the strongest note in any chord, the other note in this interval of a fifth (the G) must be raised from equal temperament by 2 cents in order for its fundamental and first overtone to mesh with the second overtone of the low C.

The interval of a fourth, illustrated in example 263, reveals the correlation between the third overtone of the lower note (C) with the second overtone of the upper note (F). That second overtone of the F is 2 cents higher than equal temperament so, in order to be in tune, the C must be raised slightly because the F is the root here.

Adjusting only a small amount makes a great difference in tuning fifths and fourths. The rule is that fifths should be slightly wider than equal temperament. Fourths should be slightly narrower.

Thirds and Sixths

The tendency when playing the major third of a chord is to place it high. Players think "major" and they go up. This is exactly the opposite of what should occur. A major third should be kept down in order to be in tune with the fourth overtone of the root. The major third overtone is actually 14 cents lower than the same note in equal temperament. Conversely, the minor third of a minor chord must be raised 16 cents in order to be in tune. Careful practice with another musician will convince one of this.

Sixths are simply inversions of thirds. A major sixth must be narrowed and a minor sixth must be widened (when the root and the third are the chord tones involved). Once one of the notes is determined to be the third of the chord, that note can then be adjusted accordingly. But, of course, the tonic must also be in tune. All ensemble tuning must be a group effort.

Example 264

The rule is: wide minor thirds and sixths and narrow major thirds and sixths. But these intervals (as all "just" intervals) should be tuned only until they are in tune, not until they sound "narrow" or "wide." If that happens, one has gone too far.

The Devil Incarnate

During medieval times the tritone was referred to as the *diabolus in musica*. Vatican authorities of that era expressly forbade its use in compositions for the church. It was regarded as the most dangerous interval, inherently unstable and unsettling in its sound. Its clash with the second overtone (the twelfth above the lower "root" tone) causes extreme dissonance. The tritone should be slightly lowered in order to be farther away from this strong second overtone.

Example 265

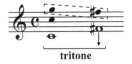

tritone

Sevenths

Even though the remaining intervals—seconds and sevenths—are dissonant, the fact remains that they, too, must be played in tune.

The minor seventh in a dominant seventh chord should be lowered a full 29 cents from equal temperament (practically a third of a tone!). Then, it produces resultant tones that reinforce the V7 chord. Detailed explanations about resultant tones can be readily found in other texts.

Example 266

A major seventh should also be lowered. Just as in tuning tritones, a major seventh is simply more effective if widely separated from the octave overtone contained in the tonic. This also relates to the wide tuning of half-step appoggiaturas mentioned later.

Example 267

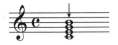

If this interval occurs as the last note of a composition (as in much impressionistic music), the seventh should not be felt to be leaning "northward" as the piece comes to a close.

Seconds

Seconds are usually encountered as appoggiaturas. A major second upper appoggiatura should be lowered. Conversely, a half-step upper appoggiatura should be raised slightly.

Example 268

Major second   minor second

Try these appoggiaturas with colleagues or play a major chord on the piano while depressing the sustaining pedal. Play your intruding appoggiatura and adjust it. You will be surprised at the simplicity of tuning even the most dissonant intervals. Your ear will be, as it must, the ultimate judge of how far to go in either direction, even when tuning with a piano.

Appoggiaturas occurring below the main tone need to be lowered. But those occurring above the main note must be raised. As ever, the opened ear (and not the eye looking at printed sharps and flats) must be your guide.

The Leading Tone

There is vehement disagreement about how to tune a leading tone. However, a leading tone leads far more with intensity than it does with pitch. In harmonic music it is almost always the major third of the V chord and, as such, must be definitively lowered from its equal-tempered position to be in tune.

Electronic Tuners

Mechanical tuners are adequate for letting one know if one is playing the tuning A at the preferred pitch level of the ensemble (A = 440). They can also be relied upon to tune the root of a chord

Example 269

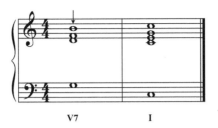

V7   I

and can be helpful in reed making. But tuning every note in a given phrase or chord to a tuning device leads one down a dangerous path. The very act of tuning by eye is fatally flawed. If everyone in an orchestra played while staring at a tuner, the intonation of the entire ensemble would be atrocious.

Until electronic tuners can be programmed to discern a given note's position in the chord, to register the minute voice-leading tendencies of the bass line according to the harmonic movement of the composition, *and* to hear the other voices playing with the note to be tuned, the only true tuner remains the human ear firmly linked to an engaged mind.

Instrumental Proclivities

Each instrument has its tendencies regarding intonation. The clarinet and oboe tend toward the flat side in their low register. The bassoon is sharp in its low register. The dynamic can also affect the intonation. The flute has a tendency to be flat when played softly and the reeds and brass go sharp. Temperature also has its effect. Colder temperatures lower the pitch of the winds and brass and raise the pitch of the strings. Warmer temperatures create the opposite result.

Being aware of these factors helps tremendously in ensemble playing. Group music making then becomes a much more pleasant experience for everyone—especially the audience.

Also, when playing in an orchestra, although the oboe gives the tuning A, it is the strings that set the pitch during performance. Adjust to them.

When playing or singing with piano, many pitches must be tempered in order to be in tune with it. And, by the way, never forget that no matter how loudly you play, intonation remains an important consideration. Never sacrifice intonation for vulgar effect.

My pragmatic first teacher, Jane Orzel, told me early in my studies with her: "Intonation *never* gets any easier. Get used to it! It's a lifetime struggle."

She was right.

Vibrato

Leonora: Io tre - mo!
"I tremble!"

Verdi: La Forza del Destino, Act II

The subject of vibrato can ignite fiery passions, in part because it is one of the most elusive of techniques to define and refine.

A Brief History

Early written evidence that vibrato has been a part of musical performance far longer than generally thought comes from Martin Agricola's 1528 treatise *Musica Instrumentalis deutch*, one of the very earliest treatises on musical performance in existence—if not *the* earliest. In it, Agricola (1486–1556), a German author of several treatises on music and musical performance, states that the flute should be played with "quaking breath" (*zitternde Wind*), an obvious reference to vibrato. That vibrato is alluded to at all in this treatise bolsters the supposition that it has, without a doubt, always existed. Supporting evidence for this can be found in the songs of the most primitive tribes even today. To assume that vibrato is a recent human invention implies that the human voice never trembled with emotion before recent times.

More than two centuries after Agricola, Leopold Mozart wrote of using vibrato ("tremolo") of varying speeds "charmingly" on "a closing note or any other sustained note" on the violin, poetically remarking that vibrato "is an ornamentation that arises from Nature herself."[1] He cited examples "which can very well be played with the tremolo; yea, which in truth demand this movement" and advises its use on double stops. He suggests that the violinist "take pains to imitate this natural quivering." But he criticizes its overuse by remarking caustically, "Players there are who tremble on *each* note as if they had the palsy." This is hardly a glowing endorsement of constant vibrato, but an admission, nonetheless, that there were string players of his time who used an ever-present one.

In 1751, five years before Mozart's treatise, eminent Italian violinist Francesco Geminiani wrote in *The Art of Playing on the Violin* that in addition to using vibrato on long notes, "when it is made on short notes, it only contributes to make the sound more agreeable and for this reason it should be made use of as often as possible."[2]

Geminiani, student of Corelli, advocates, in all practicality, a constant vibrato. And so, variance of opinion and usage were, as ever, rampant.

Flutists Johann Quantz and Johann George Tromlitz wrote of a "key" vibrato on wind instruments called the *"flattement."*[3] Tromlitz, in his 1791 book, *The Virtuoso Flute Player*, goes so far as to include a fingering chart of the best fingerings to create this vibrato effect on every note possible, throughout the entire range of the flute. These tentative attempts were obviously reaching toward imitation of what the human voice did naturally when filled with intense emotion.

Tellingly, C. P. E. Bach felt the clavichord to be a superior instrument in expression to the newer pianoforte, partly because it was able to produce a vibrato.[4]

There is an amusing anecdote involving J. S. Bach and a bassoonist that suggests the kind of animosity the touchy subject of vibrato can engender.

> The young J.S. Bach . . . held a low opinion of bassoonists. Indeed, his first recorded difficulty with a musician involved a bassoonist whom he publicly insulted. According to the protocols of the Arnstadt consistory from 1705, Bach nearly came to blows with a student named Geyersbach. . . . Whether Bach actually offended Geyersbach himself (calling him a Zippelfagottist, a "nanny-goat bassoonist" according to the document) or merely reviled his instrument remains unclear. Geyersbach failed, in any event, to appreciate the difference between the two. As he put it: "Anyone who insults my bassoon insults me."[5]

Another account stated that Bach had

[a] quarrel with Johann Heinrich Geyersbach on the night of August 4, 1704. Because of his allegedly having insulted the pupil—Bach is supposed to have called him a Zippel Fagottist (greenhorn bassoonist), perhaps in connection with a performance—they came to blows. Geyersbach hit Bach in the face, and Bach defended himself with his sword. One of the students who had accompanied Geyersbach had to intervene and separate them.[6]

Bach's use of the insult "Zippelfagottist" in this sordid affair seems to imply that Geyersbach's playing was reminiscent of a bleating sound. Thus, Geyersbach himself may have had a noticeable quaver in his sound—possibly his vibrato.

Doubtless, players through the ages looked for ways to emulate the voice in song. There were those who used vibrato and others who swore that it was to be avoided at all costs. This situation exists today. However, by the twentieth century, through the widespread use of vibrato, most instrumental playing was brought closer to its vocal roots.

The Modern Vibrato

THE STRINGS

The emergence of Fritz Kreisler (1875–1962) on the musical scene was to change the face of modern string playing, especially concerning vibrato usage. Kreisler was one of the first notable proponents of using a constant vibrato, even in faster passages. His friend and fellow violin virtuoso Carl Flesch once described his playing as "the personification of sin" partly because of his ever-present vibrato.

The preeminent violinist of two generations before Kreisler, Joseph Joachim (1831–1907), Brahms's longtime friend and collaborator, lived long enough to make recordings. Those few documents, made in 1903, show how different his approach to vibrato was from Kreisler's. He judiciously chose where to apply it. His recording of the Bourée from Bach's Partita in B minor for solo violin has only a handful of noticeably vibrated tones, and his rendition of the Adagio from Bach's unaccompanied Violin Sonata in G minor provides a stunning contrast to Kreisler's vibrato-filled 1926 recording.

Kreisler's vibrato lent his playing a vocal quality that seemed to remove it from the realm of instrumentalism. String players who did not vibrate as Kreisler did simply sounded dull, so a great many of those who heard him adopted his method. The recordings of the fine string players of the mid-twentieth century who followed in Kreisler's wake are worth studying. The influence of his playing, by virtue of its dissemination through the medium of the gramophone, is still felt today.

THE WINDS

The prevailing style of woodwind vibrato in America from 1900 up to about 1940 featured a very rapid and more or less unvarying pulsation, if it was used at all. This is now referred to as a "nanny-goat" vibrato because of its generally faster speed than what is heard today. Some brass instrumentalists followed suit.

Admittedly, American wind instrumentalists, more than Europeans (with the possible exception of the French), were more inclined to use vibrato because there was no long-standing tradition against vibrato in wind playing. There were no long-standing American traditions at all. Varying speeds of vibrato were developed later, which led to the current variety of playing now found worldwide.

In the application of vibrato to wind playing, do not pulsate the air with the abdominal muscles, momentarily increasing the pressure of the wind. This will give one's playing a pop music sound, where the vibrato raises the pitch. The wind vibrato should emanate from the throat, just as in fine singing. A well-modulated string or wind vibrato starts on the main pitch and then *drops* slightly, so rather than thinking of vibrato as a pulsation of the pitch, it should be thought of as a relaxation of pitch—a momentary lessening of pressure.

To give a more concrete image of this integrated, internalized vibrato, picture a great lone tree as a light breeze fans its leaves—not enough to disturb its branches—just enough for the leaves to flutter gently. That soft rustling is equivalent to a refined musical vibrato. Some vibratos literally shake the tree trunk and whip up the dust around the roots! Avoid this common overindulgence. And never compromise the pitch of a note to a wild vibrato.

Some wind players prefer an operatic quality to the vibrato that involves a noticeable fluctuation of pitch.[7] This is particularly discernible in the playing of certain flutists. There is also a distinctive vibrato heard in the playing of many European oboists that is wider and slower and involves greater pitch fluctuation than that heard in the playing of North American oboists. This is often produced by the pulsation of the abdominal muscles and results in a vibrato that rises above the main pitch of the note.

Other wind players have developed a jaw vibrato. This is an acceptable sound in jazz music, particularly on the saxophone, but in the classical world its value is suspect.

By the way, there is no such thing as a "diaphragm vibrato." The diaphragm flexes upon inhalation (and I have yet to hear someone produce a vibrato while inhaling). In reality, it is the contractions of the abdominal muscles that produce what is erroneously referred to as a diaphragm vibrato.

Non-Vibrato

Although string players sometimes opt for a vibrato-free tone, while otherwise playing with a constant vibrato, many wind players feel that vibrato should be used sparingly. Other wind instrumentalists feel that it is an integral part of the tone that should nearly always be present on the oboe, flute, and bassoon. If used on the clarinet and horn, it must be done subtly; there is an inherent purity to their tones that can be easily sullied by the ornamental nature of vibrato. However, in a jazz context, even a wide vibrato on the clarinet and horn works well.

The question of why the tone of one instrument lends itself more readily to the use of vibrato than another has been clinically studied. Tentative conclusions about this issue seem to rest upon the relative strength or weakness of certain upper partials produced by the various instruments. Those instruments favoring the lower overtones (e.g., horn and clarinet) seem to sound well without vibrato. Those favoring the upper partials (flute, oboe, bassoon) seem almost to require its use as a general rule, so as to keep the sound from boring itself into the ear.

In classical performance, the special effect is the *absence* of vibrato. For example, when playing placid accompanimental chords with the brass (a sound reminiscent of Gregorian chant, a boy's choir, or an organ chorale) a wind vibrato can be decidedly out of place.[8] There are also certain moments in both string and wind playing where a glazed or innocent sound is desired. Other moods, such as religious piety, utter disbelief, hopelessness, exhaustion, or the frigid quality of an icy atmosphere, call for a straight tone. These moments are operatic, to say the least, but with imagination they can be portrayed in purely instrumental music as well. But, once again, this absence of vibrato is the exception to the rule. Leaving the vibrato out of a particular musical moment should be a musically justifiable act.

Almost There

Just as Kreisler set a new standard for the strings, soprano Maria Callas did so in the vocal world. When listening to her recordings, be especially aware of how she continues her vibrato on the note just before an arrival, in the way illustrated in example 270.

Example 270

Some musicians have acquired the chronic habit of leaving the vibrato off the penultimate note of a phrase or note group. Playing that way can make that note stick out, breaking the natural flow of the line (example 271).

Example 271

The extreme example of thoughtless vibrato usage is also often heard—using it on every other note (example 272). Avoid this like the plague![9]

Example 272

Another disturbing mannerism is that of habitually starting the vibrato late (example 273) or ending it early before changing to another note (example 274):

Example 273

Late start:

Example 274

Early ending:

There are many recordings of famous singers and instrumental-ists, past and present, that provide vivid examples of what *not* to do. Always listen to recordings and concerts critically. This will help you incorporate the good and eliminate the bad in your own play-ing.

Getting It Going

Beware of the tendency of starting a long note without vibrato and then letting it "kick in" halfway through the note. Although there are instances when a long note can take this device (such as when a suspension reaches its dissonance), if this is routinely done, it quickly becomes too much of a good thing.

Keeping It Going

Vibrato should continue to the end of the last note of a phrase or composition unless the mood of the moment is a reflection of one of the aforementioned states where vibrato is not called for. When the last note is kept alive by vibrato all the way to its extinction, the listener feels a sense of continuation even after the note ceases to sound—especially on a note that diminuendos to a *pp*. The vibrato should become progressively narrower as the dynamic fades. As the note recedes, think of the rapid heartbeat of a baby bird: so much life in such a small package.

Awareness

Do not hide behind a vibrato at the expense of developing a tone that should comfortably stand on its own without it. One should be able to produce variance within the vibrato and to control that variance. It should be just as possible to play a loud, intense vibrato as it is to play a soft and intense one. Similarly, a *pp* and *ff* relaxed vibrato should be cultivated. Gradually speeding up or slowing down the vibrato as the music demands is also something to be developed. And, of course, there are those times when any vibrato at all is grossly inappropriate.

At the very least, the use or non-use of vibrato should be *conscious choices*—not unconscious accidents.

Ornaments

Clarinet in A
etwas bewegter
p dolce   *p*

Wagner: Tristan und Isolde, Act III, *Liebestod*

If you were to see a group of Christmas trees for sale and one of them was adorned with decorations, it is only natural that the ornamented one would stand out from the others. In the same way, musical ornaments highlight a note. When ornamented, almost any note, no matter what its position in the bar, usually calls for greater emphasis.

Grace Notes

Because grace notes are normally of such short duration, they can be swallowed in performance, so one must consciously emphasize them. A slight puff of air or a little more speed of the bow accomplishes this.

Many composers wrote a slash mark through the tail of certain grace notes to indicate that they should be played before the beat. However, because many other composers did not make such a specification, the absence of a slash does not always imply that a given grace note is supposed to be played *on* the beat. As a result, one must judge how to play each grace note according to its context, by taking melodic, rhythmic, and harmonic consequences into account.

In a fast tempo, where a figure such as that in example 275

might occur, there is not much time to subtract the grace note's value from the preceding sixteenth.

Example 275

The dotted rhythm runs the risk of distortion if the grace is played before the beat, and might sound something like that illustrated in example 276.

Example 276

The length of the grace note could be taken from the following note without risking this kind of rhythmic distortion (see example 277). However, this placement usually works best in minor music and in slower tempos where the mood is somewhat melancholy.

Example 277

But if the character of the music is martial, boisterous, or even impish, a whiplash grace before the beat might be more appropriate. If you choose this option, and the tempo is fast, you must snap the grace note extremely quickly.

There is no definitively correct way of playing such a grace note; therefore, performers should consider the mood of the passage before arriving at a conclusion.

The opening theme of the second movement of Beethoven's Octet for Winds (Op. 103) presents a harmonic difficulty worth studying.

Example 278

Harmonic implications if grace notes played on beat:

If both grace notes are played before the beat, a skipping rhythm is created. However, the character of this theme is not a skipping one; it is romantic and singing. Playing the first grace note on the beat creates a 4–3 dissonance that fits the yearning mood of this phrase.

The second grace note presents a thornier problem. If played on the beat, it converts the seventh of the V7 chord (the E-flat) into a passing tone between the preceding F grace note and the following D. If the E-flat were solely present in the oboe line, this placement of the F grace note would greatly reduce the expressive dissonance in this chord. However, the seventh is fortunately also stated in the accompaniment, so the dissonance between the tonic and seventh is preserved *even if* this grace note is played on the beat. Therefore, playing both graces on the beat highlights the melancholy mood of this phrase.

The score guides the decision-making process. Studying only the oboe part would not have been enough to reach an educated conclusion in example 278.

The composers of the classical era often wrote appoggiaturas as grace notes (example 279).

Example 279

Haydn: Sinfonia Concertante for Violin, Cello, Oboe and Bassoon
III - Allegro con spirito

The reason composers wrote these appoggiaturas in this way per-
plexes many modern-day musicians. I am convinced they often did
this so the performer would recognize them and stress them accordingly instead of playing through them plainly, unaware of their dissonant function. The performers of the classical era were, after all, just
as capable of sloughing over dissonance as are present-day performers. If the appoggiaturas had simply been written out just as all the
other sixteenth notes, they might not be readily identifiable as dissonances and, hence, possibly ignored. There are, of course, many consonant grace notes of this sort, but the very fact that composers wrote
them as small grace notes convinces me that they too should be
played with emphasis, if not expressly *on* the beat on every occasion.

Like the melody in Beethoven's Octet, the placement of the
first three grace notes in the second movement of Mozart's Concerto for Bassoon in B-flat major (K.191) presents some interesting
difficulties.

Playing them consistently, either all *on* the beat or all *before* the

Example 280

Mozart: Concerto for Bassoon in B flat Major
II - Andante ma adagio

beat, creates problems. Each grace note should be considered individually.

If the first one is played on the beat, parallel octaves occur between the bass line and melody and, obviously, the G grace note
would then also be in consonance with the bass, eliminating the
harmonic friction created by the 4–3 appoggiatura figure that follows; the F appoggiatura becomes a passing tone. But if the grace is
played before the beat, the parallel octaves are eliminated and the
dissonant appoggiatura is preserved.

If the second grace note is played on the beat it creates a color-
less 5–4–3 progression. The ear latches onto the first note (the 5)

and perceives the next (the 4) to be a passing tone that leads to the third of the chord. If this grace note is played before the beat, again a beautiful 4–3 appoggiatura figure becomes clear to the listener.

However, if the third grace note is played before the beat, like the previous two graces, it becomes a lame repetition of the preceding pitch with no harmonic reason to exist. It would serve only a rhythmic function, creating a skipping rhythm. The resulting 6–5 appoggiatura is also quite pale when compared to the expressive 7–6–5 that would result if this grace note were played on the beat.

Therefore, in this instance, the bassoonists' tradition of playing the first two grace notes *before* and the third one *on* the beat is best. The search for expressive dissonance leads inexorably to this conclusion.

Sometimes, tradition is a good thing.

AGOGIC GRACES

Because grace notes have a natural tendency to highlight, they can create agogic accents. Agogic accents cause unexpected rhythmic inflections that can, in effect, change the beat pattern the listener perceives. In the introductory bassoon solo of Igor Stravinsky's monumental *Rite of Spring,* the grace notes achieve the effect of changing the pulse by creating just such agogic accents.

The opening motif is stated in four differing metrical ways, either stretched out or compressed from its original statement (example 281).

Example 281

The grace notes are placed on the B each time the falling figure (the skeletal C-B-A) occurs, but they occur at varying points in the beat: first on the beat; then on the third triplet note of the beat; on the beat again; and finally on the second quintuplet note of the beat. Because of these grace notes, the emphasis should fall on the B every time it occurs, regardless of its position in the beat or bar. It should sound as though the B always occurs on a downbeat.

When the graces are lightly stressed, the resulting pulse felt by the listener is that shown in example 282.

Example 282

This is complicated to write, even more so to perform if written this way. Stravinsky ingeniously achieves this complicated metrical effect simply by placing the grace notes in various positions within the beats in order to create agogic accents.

Example 283 presents the same phrase with phrasing numbers under each note. The presence of the grace notes has determined which notes are emphasized. The brackets underneath show the subgroups as well as the larger note groups. The first note has a 2 in parentheses during its value, signifying slight growth during the fermata. The 5 within parentheses in the second measure indicates an emphasis on the G grace note. These phrasing numbers signify intensity; they do not literally indicate volume.

Example 283

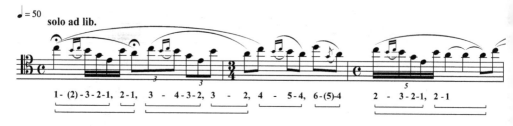

Trills

There is a widely accepted rule about trills: "All trills in classical and baroque music must begin on the *upper* note."

Blindly following this rule limits one's expressive options because it functions as the dictate of an unquestioned supreme and unknown authority. The convenient way of passive submission to this rule pays no heed to the functions of the trill and removes any responsibility for thinking about those functions. Because the baroque and classical masters of composition placed trills in all contexts, each should be viewed with an eye toward its environment.

Treatise writers of the baroque and classical periods wrote about trills. Some, like C. P. E. Bach, advocated starting on the upper note. But others, such as the noted flutist Johann George Tromlitz (1725–1805), wrote a dissenting opinion:

> Some people think the trill should begin from above, and consider the upper notes at this fast speed as simple appoggiaturas, consequently putting the weight on them, and treat the second note, which is supposed to be the main note, as the passing-note, on which for my feeling the weight ought to come. Anyone who wants to do it like this may do so; for me it is impossible, and unnatural to my feeling; the note over which the trill is written is the main note, and this must be clearly heard for the sake of good and expressive melody just as if the trill were not there; but by this reversed method the main note is supplanted and exterminated, the sequence of the melody interrupted, and the real melody made unrecognizable.[1]

Which of these performers and teachers is correct?

Rather than passive submission to either of these writers, or to the general "rule" cited above, each trill should be judged on a case-by-case basis in order to extract maximum expression.

MEANING

A trill is the excitement of a pitch. Like an ebullient child, a trilled note simply cannot remain still. That excitement is derived from one or the other of two basic emotions: happiness and sadness. Each of these heightened states can cause trembling.

There are three things to keep in mind when choosing how to start a trill: dissonance, direction, and, above all, character.

EXPRESSIVE DISSONANCE VS. MILITARY PRECISION

Generally, starting a trill on the upper note and on the beat creates a dissonance with another note in the chord. Starting a trill on the upper dissonant pitch can greatly enhance the element of sadness or tension in a phrase.

But if innocent simplicity or military precision is desired, as in example 284, then starting on the main note is best.

Example 284

Although an expressive 6–5 dissonance would be created by starting the trill on the upper note here, starting this trill on the main pitch preserves the toy soldier feeling in this figure. The contrast Mozart has crafted between the two opposing ideas that make up this phrase will then be much clearer.

There are also innocent-sounding trills, such as those illustrated in examples 285 and 286, that do not call for the pathos generated by starting on an upper, dissonant pitch.

Example 285

Example 286

The character of the music is paramount when choosing how to trill.

LINE AND DIRECTION

If trills are present in an upward-moving scalewise line, it is usually best to start them on the main notes regardless of the dissonances that would be created by starting them on the upper notes.

There are two reasons for starting trills on the main pitch in a rising line:

1. To preserve and show the upward progression of the scale.
2. To avoid anticipating, and therefore spoiling, the trill's resolution on the next note.

Example 287 contains a rising scale ornamented with trills on the second half of each bar.

Example 287

Haydn: **Trumpet Concerto in E flat Major**
I - Allegro

If these trills are started on the upper note, the ear perceives a down-trill. The other note of each trill—the written note itself—then becomes subservient to that upper note. Whichever note begins a trill registers in the listener's mind as the main pitch. Be sure that the starting note is the one you wish to emphasize.[2]

Example 288 outlines the aural structure delineated by beginning these trills on the upper note.

Example 288

A chord, rather than a rising scale, is spelled out in the listener's mind. The scale is camouflaged.

However, when the trills are played starting on the note, the rising scale is clearly communicated (example 289) and a greater sense of increasing tension is created.

Example 289

The search for dissonant expression is important, but the line often takes precedence.

An intriguing example that proves the supremacy of the first note of any trill is found in the first movement of Ravel's Piano Concerto in G. Only a few bars from this passage are quoted in example 290.

Example 290

Ravel: Concerto for Piano in G Major
    I - Allegramente
    Cadenza: Andante a piacere

Each trill in this unorthodox phrase is a *down*-trill. The upper note is stated at the beginning of each beat and, as such, is held in the listener's mind as the main note, even though listeners are far more accustomed to hearing trills that involve the main note and its upper auxiliary. If the pianist were to begin each trill in this phrase on the lower note, this would yield an entirely different, *bitonal* result because the lower tone would then be taken by the ear as the main pitch.

THE APPOGGIATURA TRILL

Appoggiaturas are dissonant tones. Their very reason to exist can be negated if one begins an appoggiatura trill on the upper (possibly consonant) note.

If a trill on a 4–3 appoggiatura is started on the upper note, it will sound like a 5–4–3 consonant progression (example 291) with the dissonant fourth degree rendered as a weak passing tone.

Example 291

Likewise, a 2–1 dissonant appoggiatura will sound like a 3–2–1 consonant progression, as shown in example 292.

Example 292

If appoggiaturas are transformed into passing tones by trilling in this way, then it is impossible to "lean upon" them (the very meaning of the word appoggiatura). Their dissonant function has been eliminated.

However, some appoggiatura trills can effectively begin on the upper note if the upper note is still a dissonance. A 6–5 appoggiatura is a case in point. If you begin a trill on the upper note here, an expressive 7–6–5 dissonant progression is created. Beginning the trill in this way is a matter of preference because both the 6–5 and 7–6–5 progressions are dissonant. Often the 7–6–5 is preferred because the seventh formed with the root is usually a major seventh—highly dissonant and expressive (example 293).

Example 293

Even if there is a preexisting pattern of appoggiatura trills that begin *on* the note, this 7–6–5 upper-note trill can create the welcome feeling of breaking the mold.

Mozart writes upper grace notes on a 6–5/4–3 double appoggiatura in the second movement of his Flute Concerto in G major (example 294). The fact that Mozart writes upper graces here implies that it was not always the fashion to begin a trill on the upper note in his era. By notating specifically to do so, he ensures that the principal flute player in the orchestra highlights the major seventh dissonance created with the bass line by starting this 6–5 appoggiatura trill on the upper note.

Example 294

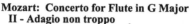

Mozart: Concerto for Flute in G Major
II - Adagio non troppo

TRILLING ON THE DOMINANT SEVENTH

Beginning a dominant seventh-degree trill on the upper note eliminates its dissonance. The trill then begins on a consonance—the tonic—rendering the seventh as a passing tone between the tonic and the resolution that follows. However, in a V7 chord, one can effectively start the seventh-degree trill on the tonic as long as the seventh is present in the underlying harmony (as in the grace note example, 278). Then there will still be friction created regardless of which note is sounded first. But if no seventh is present in the other voices, then starting the trill on the seventh is preferable.

THE "SKIPPING" TRILL

Sometimes trills are started with a skipping rhythm, as illustrated in examples 295 and 296.

Example 295

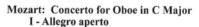

Mozart: Concerto for Oboe in C Major
I - Allegro aperto

As printed:

Example 296

With added skipping pre-beat grace note:

The addition of what amounts to a pre-beat grace note is actually an ornamentation of an ornament. It is more than a trill.

If an appoggiatura trill is started with a skipping grace, before the beat and on the upper note, as illustrated in examples 297 and 298, how could one then "lean upon" the appoggiatura if it has not had a resolute beginning?

Example 297

Example 298

One can rationalize this skipping method of trilling by saying, "The *second* note of the trill—the note which occurs on the down-beat—can be emphasized. *There* is the appoggiatura" (example 299).

Example 299

But the logical question follows: Why start this trill on the *upper* note if you wish to emphasize the *lower* one? Could this "skipping trill" simply be an attempt to follow the widely accepted rule of starting every trill in classical and baroque music on the upper note, while still trying to emphasize the dissonant appoggiatura by play-ing it on a beat?

Although I am not an adherent of much of the dogma put forward by C. P. E. Bach in his famous treatise, it is interesting to note that he stated quite emphatically that all the "voices including the bass must be struck with the *initial* tone of an embellishment."[3] According to him, this, in effect, means no pre-beat grace notes. In fact, Bach goes so far as to mention his abhorrence of what he referred to as the "repulsive unaccented [pre-beat] appoggiatura, [which is] so extraordinarily popular."[4] This is difficult to square with the "skipping" trill so often heard in performances of baroque and classical compositions by musicians who profess their historical "correctness," unless they are emulating those whom Bach reviled. Perhaps they would not mind that he would have labeled their pre-beat graces as "repulsive."

THE CADENTIAL TRILL

A leading tone cadential trill leads to its resolution much more effectively if begun on the main note. The feeling of anticipation is dissipated if the resolution pitch is given away at the start of a leading tone trill, even though starting on the upper note creates an expressive 4–3 dissonance, as in example 300.

Example 300

Mozart: Concerto for Clarinet in A Major
III - Rondo. Allegro

Effect created by starting trill on upper note:

(trill anticipates the final pitch)

Beginning the trill on the note, as illustrated in example 301, results in a much greater feeling of anticipation.

Example 301

Effect created by starting trill on main note:

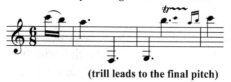

(trill leads to the final pitch)

If a cadential trill occurs on the fifth degree of a V chord, one may begin it on the upper note without disturbing the line. This creates a beautiful 6–5 dissonance that in no way takes away from the resolution because the line descends into the cadence (example 302).

Example 302

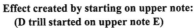

6-(5)

Examine mood, harmony, and line to reach an educated conclusion that reflects the musical character of every trilled moment.

SPEED

The speed of a trill and its *nachschlag* (defined below) should also relate to the mood of the phrase. Often, instrumentalists cultivate only an extremely quick trill, but one speed of trilling is not enough. A trill that sounds like a buzzing doorbell in an otherwise sleepy moment of the music is extremely disturbing. Sometimes planning the number of pitch alterations helps preserve a placid mood.

INNOCENT EARS

All these ideas about trills should be considered as though one is an uneducated audience member whose feelings are completely without prejudice. The aforementioned affects created by playing a trill one way or another can be felt by even jaded, educated musicians if the ears are cleared of preconceptions, and wiped clean of the misinformation preached so vociferously about historical "correctness."

Nachschlags

A *nachschlag* consists of the two terminating notes usually played at the end of a trill. This word translates literally as "after stroke." Notwithstanding this translation, a *nachschlag* brings attention to the note that follows it. All *nachschlags* belong to the following note—not to the preceding trill. They carry the trill to its resolution. In most circumstances, they should be emphasized. However, after an appoggiatura trill, the situation regarding *nachschlags* is very different.

When a composer has written a *nachschlag* after an appoggiatura trill, that is one of the rare times when an ornament should be played in an understated way so as to keep it from creating a bump before or on the resolution note. Then the resolution should be played much more softly than the dissonant trill that precedes it.

Example 303

Cadential trills should practically always have a *nachschlag* because of the much-desired leading impulse toward resolution (example 304)—but, as ever, exceptions will be found.

Example 304

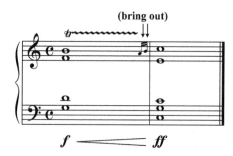

The Turn

Composers often use turns to add emphasis to a leap (see example 305).

Example 305

A portato inflection, as illustrated in example 306, often works well on the first note of a turn, if time permits, and the mood of the moment is sufficiently sentimental.

Example 306

Often, turns occurring on a weak beat should be played more softly than the surrounding tones. In the main theme from the first movement of Beethoven's Seventh Symphony (example 307) the turn after the strong appoggiatura on the downbeat of the fourth bar should be played lightly. This guarantees that the turn will not sound like it is part of the pick-up to the next bar.

Example 307

Turns on inner figures, such as in example 308, should also be played more softly, by virtue of their placement in the subservient voice of an individual dialogue. These turns create a feeling much like a shrug of the shoulders.

Example 308

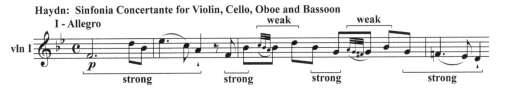

It's Just Wrong!

One cannot rightfully say it is wrong to play grace notes, trills, *nachschlags*, or turns in one way or another. One can only observe that opportunities for expressive dissonance may have been passed over or that the direction of the line or the character of the passage has not been preserved.

There is controversy about how to play practically every ornament in baroque and classical compositions. These questions are best answered by a thorough examination of the musical text, rather than by adhering to a specific dogma that may have been less than universally accepted even in its own time. After study of these questions, I have concluded that there was no consensus that can guide today's musician absolutely. Your own musical judgment, based upon the harmonic functions of the notes, the motivic structure, the shape of the line, and the character of the music itself, must be the final arbiter. Otherwise, you risk negating your own interpretive intellect.

Was There a Baroque Style of Playing?

Violin I
  I - Allegro

Bach: Brandenburg Concerto #3

A great many musicians believe there was a specific baroque style of playing. A baroque performance practice movement began to take hold in the 1970s. Yet the climate of curious, open-minded trust that first welcomed that movement has steadily given way to an ever-greater skepticism among professional orchestral musicians.

Communication

It is interesting that in the modern world of mass transportation, mass media, and master classes, there is still no consensus regarding how to play today. Contemporary recordings of orchestras from all over the globe are testament to the diversity of playing styles encountered and are available at our fingertips. Because of these persuasive forms of communication, one might reasonably conclude that we would all have been swayed by now into a mass worldwide style of performance. But this has not occurred. Exposure to different ways of playing has not created a present-day uniformity.

Unlike our own time, the baroque era was an age when people generally lived out their lives near the city of their birth and musical clinicians rarely traveled. In light of this, how has it come to be generally accepted by today's well-connected and yet *diverse* musicians that during the time frame of roughly 1600 to 1750 there was a European way of playing we can imitate today that we call "baroque"?

Although certain musicians were able to travel internationally, most were restricted to their local ways for obvious reasons, i.e., hampered international communication, difficulties of long distance travel, lack of financial resources.

C. P. E. Bach wrote:

> My Prussian duties [at the court of Frederick the Great] never left me enough time to travel in foreign countries. . . . This lack . . . would have been harmful to anyone in my profession had I not had the good fortune from my youth on to hear at close range the finest of all kinds of music and to meet masters of the first rank, many of whom became my friends.[1]

Thus, the most famous son of the great Johann Sebastian states that in adulthood his work kept him from traveling. He was indeed lucky to have been surrounded by many of Europe's leading musicians early on, but how many others were not so lucky to have had the luxury of the world literally at one's doorstep? If he, with his advantages, was too busy with work to travel, it is not hard to imagine how free his struggling contemporaries were.

Logic dictates that a patchwork of styles existed across the European continent. From city to city and country to country there could not have been a truly homogeneous style. People heard and emulated local tradition. There were surely regional and national differences but they were not shared by every player in a given area. In any group of musicians today differences in playing from person to person will be found.

The *Treatise on the Fundamental Principles of Violin Playing* (1755) by Leopold Mozart (1719–87, father of Wolfgang), the *Essay on the True Art of Playing Keyboard Instruments* (1753) by C. P. E. Bach (1714–88), and the *Essay of a Method for Playing the Transverse Flute* (1752) by famed flutist Johann Quantz (1697–1773) are the three books generally regarded as the cornerstones of baroque performance practice. All three of these musical giants were educated at the height of the baroque era (1710s–30s). Their books give us glimpses into the minds of the three musicians who wrote them. They wrote in order to fix the musical problems they heard every day. The critical nature of much of their writing makes for entertaining and enlightening reading.

Leopold Mozart writes about the players of his day:

So long as they play an allegro, all goes well: but when it comes to an adagio, there they betray their great ignorance and bad judgment in every bar of the whole piece. They play without method and without expression; the *piano* and *forte* are not differentiated; the embellishments are in the wrong place, too overloaded, and mostly played in a confused manner; and often the notes are far too bare and one observes that the player knows not what he does. For such people there is rarely any more hope of improvement, for they, more than anyone, are taken up with self-esteem and he would be in their great disfavour who would candidly attempt to convince them of their errors.[2]

Johann Quantz points out the defective results he heard in performance:

Yet if we consider the condition of the majority of musical establishments at courts as well as in republics and cities, we immediately note considerable defects ... stemming largely from the great disparity in the manner of playing found among the musicians of the same chapel or orchestra. No one can imagine the extent of these defects unless he has personally experienced it, and has heard many different orchestras ... therefore ... it is necessary to remedy these mistakes made in performance.[3]

C. P. E. Bach puts them both to shame with his comments about music treatise writers:

Vain and selfish addlepates are no longer satisfied with playing their own fabrications creditably and forcing them on their students. No! They must seek immortality through authorship. As a result so many school and textbooks have appeared since my Essay that no end of them can be seen. ... I can assert without anger, and in truth, that every instruction book that I have seen since the publication of my Essay (and I believe I have seen them all) is filled with errors. What I say can be proved if necessary.[4] ... What miserable nonsense can be found in some![5]

Teachers also do not escape Bach's irate sarcasm:

Our pedants can often play nothing but their own fabrications; their abused, awkward fingers deliver these stiffly. They can compose only what their hands can subdue. Many are held in high esteem who hardly know how to perform tied notes. Consequently there arise great quantities of miserable works and abominable students.[6] ... Teachers try to make amends for a stiff left hand by teaching their students to favor the right and garnish adagio or expressive passages with a wealth of pretty little trills to the revulsion of good taste. These are often interchanged with senile, pedantic embellishments and fumbling, inept runs in the playing of which the fingers seem to grow choleric.[7]

The unavoidable implication in these strong statements is that there was no uniformity—no overriding baroque style,[8] but rather a plethora of varying levels of musicianship and diversity of opinion. These three authors criticize many of the wide-ranging musical habits of their time—*habits equally baroque as their own*. They wrote about how to be different from the majority of other baroque musicians and hence, to a certain degree, *anti*-baroque.

To propose that an orchestra in Edinburgh in 1731 played a work by Bach in substantially the same way an orchestra in Leipzig or Rome might have played it seems a bit presumptuous. Yet this is the implication when musicians today speak of playing a baroque composition in the "baroque style." Despite the existence of treatises by well-established musicians of the time, which disagree on many points, it is simply impossible to prove there was a baroque way of playing.

Variables

One needs to look no further than the basic element of pitch to point out the extent of the variables that acted upon musical performances of the baroque. Contrary to current popular belief, there was no so-called "baroque pitch." There was no pitch standard at all.

The exhaustive volume *On the Sensations of Tone* by Hermann Helmholtz contains a chart: "*Historical Pitches in order from Lowest to Highest.*"[9] In it, no fewer than 242 measurements of a' taken from various tuning forks, organs, harpsichords, spinets, and pianos made between 1511 and 1885 are methodically listed. Surprisingly, the a' varied from a low of 373.1 cps (cycles per second) to a high of 567.3, a measurement from 1619—a full century before J. S. Bach's prime. This is a variance from today's F-sharp up to C-sharp. Interestingly, there is no strict trend regarding the dates and pitches. The older measurements are not necessarily the lowest ones. Only in the mid-1800s does one begin to see the pitch uniformly rising, settling between $a' = 440$ and 450.

Where the musicians played also had a profound effect on their performance. Many professional musicians at that time relied upon the church for their livelihood. If the Kapellmeister (literally, chapel master) of the local church preferred short articulations because of boomy acoustics, the musicians he prepared then played in a clipped way for clarity's sake. In a large sanctuary, musical articulation must be exaggerated to have any definition at all. Many European cathedrals have reverberation times of well over five seconds. Fortunately, the clearer sound environment of most contemporary concert halls permits a much wider palette of articulation options open to today's performer.

Additionally, during that time, there was no such thing as a conductor. There was generally a leader who played the harpsichord, organ, or violin, but the personal stamp he put on the group's performance was surely not as rigid as the interpretations of today's autocratic maestros. In performance, he would generally start and stop the group and keep the tempo while playing nearly all the time. Although the Kapellmeister, acting as the leader, undoubtedly coached the instrumentalists in rehearsal, the musicians were more or less left on their own regarding their individual performance. Solo improvisation and ornamentation were highly regarded as modes of self-expression, and few, if any, dynamic and expression markings were written into the music by the composer. Those things were expected to be supplied by artistic performers.

Consensus

In his introduction to the 1966 edition of Johann Quantz's book, the editor, Edward R. Reilly, bluntly states:

> Yet, important as the treatise is, modern performers must remember that the work is the synthesis of the experience of one man active at a particular period in time and in a certain milieu. Solutions to the various problems of performance were as diverse during that time as they are today.[10] . . . Criticisms of certain parts of the *Essay* must also be noted, as they emphasize the variety of opinion and practice of the time, a variety that must be constantly stressed for the benefit of those who seek to dogmatize about the performance of music in the past, or expect to find "definitive" solutions to artistic problems.[11]

The editor of the 1949 edition of C. P. E. Bach's book, William J. Mitchell, notes, "Most easy to discover are those points on which he and his contemporaries disagreed. Although he rarely mentions anyone by name, it is clear that he and Quantz [who worked together at the court of Frederick the Great] were divided on several matters."[12]

In order to dissuade readers from concluding that Leopold Mozart spoke for his illustrious son, Wolfgang, Alec Hyatt King, in his "Note to the 1985 Reprint" of Leopold Mozart's treatise, writes: "[The *Violinschule*] is not a guide to the music of Wolfgang Mozart and other composers of his generation."[13]

Frederick Neumann's *Ornamentation in Baroque and Post-Baroque Music* (1978) is one of the most exhaustive books about baroque performance practice. In it, Neumann quotes the opinions and writings of many of the baroque period's most illustrious musicians. The countless contradictions of one source with another contained within this book lend credence to the reality that it is, and always has been, human nature to disagree.

For example, at the end of a thirty-nine-page chapter solely concerning J. S. Bach's one-note graces, Neumann states, "After all this is said, the performer's taste and judgment, tempered by the framework staked out by our historic investigation and enlightened by stylistic insight, must have the final word here as everywhere else in the field of performance."[14] He is, like Messrs. Reilly and Mitchell, reminding the reader that the various viewpoints quoted in his book are *opinions*.

Earlier, after a discussion of whether grace notes written by composers other than Bach should be played on or before the beat, Neumann writes: "Not only in matters of the Vorschlag, but also with regard to all the other small graces, the age-old Italian freedom and flexibility remained fully alive well beyond the mid-18th century."[15] Thus, he admits in a roundabout way, Italians retained both types of grace notes—on and before the beat.

Neumann also writes: "However, prebeat and onbeat styles continued to coexist in the second half of the century in France as well as in [Italy and Germany]."[16] Now, France and Germany enter the fray. In the same paragraph, he quotes Jean-Jacques Rousseau, an eminent French musician of the baroque, as dryly stating that a grace note's "very short value is taken from the preceding *or* from the following note." Drawing the obvious conclusion, Neumann observes: "That means, of course, they are either prebeat or onbeat graces." Then he concludes: "The last word, of course, belongs always to the *goût* [taste]."[17]

And so it goes for approximately 500 pages. It seems that then, as ever, there was no consensus.

C. P. E. Bach writes without equivocation about grace notes:

All embellishments notated in small notes pertain to the following tone. Therefore, while the preceding tone is never shortened, the following tone loses as much of its length as the small notes take from it. . . . The other voices including the bass must be struck with the initial tone of an embellishment. Yet as often as this rule is cited, so often is it violated.[18]

There it is in black and white. All grace notes in baroque music should be played on the beat. No further thought is required.

But aren't there baroque stylists who play some graces before the beat? Are they un-baroque because they disagree with C. P. E. Bach? Do they have other sources that back up their way of playing? Is it important that they have sources?

And what about all those baroque musicians who "violated" C. P. E. Bach's rule? Were they bad musicians, or were they simply uninformed about the "baroque style"?

The more one reads on the subject of historical performance, the clearer it becomes that there was no single style or method of playing. Even concerning the performance of simple one-note grace notes of one composer's music, there is no agreement—except with regard to the indispensability of an educated taste.

Familiarizing one's self with the various writings on baroque musical performance can be enlightening. But one should remember that simply because a few prominent musicians wrote down their *opinions*, that does not make those opinions, by default, the prevailing mode of their day.

As Mr. Neumann notes, good taste is essential, but taste must be guided by knowledge of the music's structure. Instead of depending upon the written opinion of a single individual or even those of a handful of writers to guide your phrasing decisions, filtering the music through your own store of knowledge will yield results that sound logical, natural, and expressive. And if anyone feels you have played something in a way that is contrary to the "baroque style," it is virtually assured that you can, if you wish to put in the time and effort, find at least one baroque writer who will back you up.

How to Become a Baroque Expert in Less than Five Minutes

Many busy orchestral musicians believe that the techniques heard in the recordings of modern baroque groups are the result of rigorous studies that they themselves have not had the time to pursue. They have assimilated what they have heard into their own playing so as to appear as though they too are in the know. Highly trained orchestra members politely eliminate their romantic habits when they play baroque compositions in order to be more "baroque."

The most pervasive example of how this "baroque" mode affects a modern orchestra's playing is in how the last note of most baroque compositions are played. Usually we hear a massive space occurring immediately prior to the last note (example 309), as if one would sing:

Example 309

If this effect were written out by the composer, it would appear as in example 310:

Example 310

This practice flies in the face of the sacred, vocal origins of baroque concert music. The roots of instrumental concert music are found in the church. In church music, a great many compositions end with the word "Amen." The church-employed musicians of the baroque would have been very aware that their own music sprang from the church and that the final cadence very often related to that word. In addition, manufacturing a space here needlessly separates the dominant or subdominant chord from its resolution into the tonic.

Another "baroque" phrasing device that has become popular often manifests itself in the phrase shown in example 311.

Example 311

Handel: Messiah, Second Part, XX - Air: *"He was despised"*

In many performances, the violins answer the singer with a space after their first eighth note (example 312).

Example 312

In this fashion, there is no relation between what the singer "says" and how the violins answer. In a well-intentioned attempt to be "baroque," modern musicians play this motif in a disjointed way throughout the movement, without regard to its relation to speaking or singing. It seems to be generally agreed that, in baroque music, one must "lift and separate" all unslurred eighth notes—especially if they are pick-ups.

However, this chopped quality of the bow stroke in string playing was a source of controversy even in the baroque era. Johann Quantz's book was generally praised by a contemporary expert, Johann Friedrich Reichardt, who nonetheless wrote this reservation: "I must, however, warn everyone against the frequent detaching of the bow [advocated by the flutist Quantz]."[19] This "frequent detaching" is generally taken today as an essential element of the "baroque style."

Another generally accepted "baroque" practice is the flagrant use of open strings. Not surprisingly, Leopold Mozart himself repeatedly warns against using them in no uncertain language: "The tone of the open strings contrasts too sharply with that of the stopped notes, and the inequality arising therefrom offends the ears of the listener";[20] they "pierce the ear too sharply."[21]

In addition to the habits already mentioned, there seem to be other unspoken rules applied. Perhaps they are left unspoken because those who use them do not wish to be seen as having a simple formula that they apply to all baroque music. It is telling that singers do not generally observe these precepts because of their obviously unvocal nature. Three of the following rules have already been mentioned.

1. A space should occur before the last note of each movement.
2. All unslurred eighth and quarter notes should be well separated (refer to Reichardt's remark earlier).
3. All trills should start on the upper note (see Tromlitz's comments in "Ornaments," Part 6).
4. The last note of a slur should be clipped, *especially if there are sequences of slurred groups of two* (even if the second note under the slur is a dissonant passing tone and not the resolution of an appoggiatura; the functions of the notes are *subservient* to the slurs) (see C. P. E. Bach's comment in "Sound Connection," Part 4).
5. A hairpin [crescendo/diminuendo] should occur on long notes.[22]
6. No vibrato should be used (with some exception) (see Geminiani's comment, "Vibrato," Part 6).
7. Use the open strings frequently (see L. Mozart's comments above).

There you have it—the Baroque Style in a nutshell. Life would certainly be simpler if every subject were so quickly mastered.

Invariably, when a modern-day performer plays a baroque composition without utilizing these practices, he or she is recognized by the "*cognoscenti*" as being "un-baroque" and dismissed as being un-informed. Even if the performance is lauded for its expressivity, the smug caveat remains: "But it wasn't played in the baroque style."

Their Instruments

The baroque performance practice movement of the late twentieth century resurrected many of the original instruments used centuries ago. It is interesting to hear what those extinct instruments sound like with modern players. To hear the music of Bach or Vivaldi played on instruments that existed in their day gives us a glimpse into what one may have heard in terms of tone quality, intonation, and balance of the ensemble. It can also show us quite clearly why those instruments were subsequently improved.

Composers and performers alike, through the ages, have expressed joy over the technical improvement of musical instruments. Whenever a problem with an instrument was lessened or eliminated, both felt freed of one more impediment to expression. Never mind the primitive wind and brass instruments of that era—violinist Leopold Mozart entreated "mathematical friends" to "further the cause of music by means of useful research" in order to develop better *string* instruments. They would, in Mozart's words, "be of invaluable assistance."[23]

Their Ornamentation

C. P. E. Bach wrote about ornamentation at length. One comment he made should be better known.

> Above all things, a prodigal[24] use of embellishments must be avoided. Regard them as spices which may ruin the best dish or gewgaws which may deface the most perfect building. Notes of no great moment and those sufficiently brilliant by themselves should remain free of them, for embellishments serve only to increase the weight and import of notes and to differentiate them from others. Otherwise, I would commit the same error as orators who try to place an impressive accent on every word; everything would be alike and consequently unclear.[25]

Whether or not all baroque musicians agreed with him is immaterial. This is simply intelligent advice given by a very intelligent musician.

On the same subject, in a footnote, Mozart wrote:

> Many imagine themselves to have brought something wonderfully beautiful into the world if they befrill the notes of an *Adagio Cantabile* thoroughly, and make out of one note at least a dozen. Such note-murderers expose thereby their bad judgement to the light, and tremble when they have to sustain a long note or play only a few notes singingly, without inserting their usual preposterous and laughable frippery.[26]

Who Were "They"?

The musicians active during the baroque era would probably not appreciate their playing being reduced to a handful of clichés.

Never before in the history of musical performance have musicians tried to imitate what their predecessors from a distant era *might have done* at the expense of their own artistic sincerity. Musicians trusted themselves more completely in the past. They played in *their* way for the people of *their* time. Even Wolfgang Mozart, who held C. P. E. Bach in high esteem, said, "We can no longer do as he did."[27]

The "they" we refer to when we ask ourselves, "How did *they* play it?" are no different from us. They were individuals. Their emotions were no less passionately felt. They tried to express joy and sadness through their instruments as we do. They did not possess any less imagination or intellect than we and they did not play in a way that reined in their intelligence or their natural musical impulses by following the "baroque rules" of performance that have only recently become *de rigueur.*

Correctness

Studying various musical treatises of the baroque leads one to the inescapable conclusion that their ideas were just as diverse as our own on the subject of "how to play." Some industrious individuals did take the step of writing down their ideas but they did not mean to imply that all or even most other musicians thought in the same way as the writer. If there had been artistic unanimity, there would not have been the need for a book to straighten out other musicians in the first place!

We should read what the treatise writers had to say, but to stop there is to progress only halfway toward understanding. As in musical notation, everything is not printed on the paper in those treatises. Using the good sense we have is the least the composers of the baroque would expect of us. Common sense is one element they used which still remains with us. Hopefully, it has not faded with the passage of time. It is not the instruments or a self-imposed set of rules applied to the music's surface that are important; it is the performer's understanding and communication of the music's structure and emotion that matter.

Without the mental convenience afforded by blind adherence to the "rules" of baroque performance practice, the baroque music one plays must be studied with renewed diligence. And this can be quite disconcerting to those who have nothing more to hold on to than those "rules." That which communicates greater expression should be the answer sought by thoughtful musicians, regardless of how those conclusions square with the "rules." However, it is undeniably easier to whitewash all baroque music with the aforementioned affectations so that one can rest securely in the misguided belief that one is playing "their" music the way "they" did. Stock answers are comforting, but absolutes in music as well as in morality are suspect.

So the questions remain. Is today's musical language of inflection unmusical when applied to the music of the baroque? Have the baroque performance practitioners successfully traversed the gulf of silence that separates us from that distant time and found the elusive truth of how music was then performed? Nobody knows. Nobody can know. But the inescapable reality that remains is that we today listen to all music with modern ears. We simply cannot perform or appreciate any musical work of the distant past as did those alive at the time of its creation. Playing old music on old instruments is one thing. Stating that one's style of playing is *the* way or even one of the supposed ways that music was performed in a long-dead era is another thing altogether. The value of any composition from any era lies in what it says to us now. Like Shakespeare's plays, the great works of musical art stand the test of time through thousands of renditions.

The kind of conviction in music making that communicates sincerity is reflected in an anecdote about conductor Fritz Reiner (1888–1963):

> In Chicago he once engaged for a Bach keyboard concerto a pianist who made much of playing Bach in an authentic style, "as Bach intended." After their rehearsal, an exasperated Reiner exploded privately, "If that is how Bach intended his music to be played, *Bach* was wrong!"[28]

C. P. E. Bach deserves to be heard once more:

> My principal aim, especially of late, has been directed toward playing and composing as vocally as possible for the keyboard, despite its defective sustaining powers. This is no easy matter if the sound is not to be too thin or the noble simplicity of melody ruined by excessive noise [read: ornamentation]. . . . I believe that music must, first and foremost, stir the heart. This cannot be achieved through mere rattling, drumming, or arpeggiation, at least not by me.[29]

Leopold Mozart summed it up simply:

Who is not aware that singing is at all times the aim of every instrumentalist[?][30]

We must endeavor to produce a singing style . . . so that the instrument, as far as possible, imitates the art of singing. And this is
the greatest beauty in music.[31]

Understanding the profound relationships of music to language, language to singing, and singing to instrumental technique is
the ultimate key to being musical no matter what music one plays.

With regard to performance, "style" should refer to the mood
of the moment in music, not to an entire era. Playing all music in a
singing way, with attention to both its surface elements and deeper
structure, is a road to musical expression at least equally valid as that
taken by the baroque performance practitioners—not less expressive and most certainly not incorrect.

Music Speaks

Bass
IV - Allegro Assai

Voice: Al - le Mensch-en wer-den Brü - der, Wo dein sanf-ter Flü-gel weilt.
"All men become brothers where your gentle wing rests."
Beethoven: Symphony #9

There is nothing that rivals the deep-seated nature of language in the mind except perhaps music. We hear both our language and our music from the first moments of life. The first musical sounds we hear are usually songs sung to us by a loving parent. As we grow up, we speak and hear our language every day. We also sing and hear our language sung. Its cadences, inflections, and structure influence and determine to a large extent what we will feel is musical for the rest of our lives.

Language itself is arguably the basis of all national styles of music.

Mandarin

The relationship of the Chinese language of Mandarin to that country's music provides a particularly vivid example of how the characteristics of a given language can influence a specific country's compositional style and instrumental playing.

Mandarin is a tone language, filled with sudden upturns and downturns of inflection that completely change the meaning of a word depending on the tone employed. For example, the basic sylla-ble "ma" can have at least five meanings, given different inflections:

SYMBOL	INFLECTION	MEANING	PART OF SPEECH
嗎 *ma*	→ [straight]	*question mark*	*punctuation mark*
媽 *mā*	→ • [straight/staccato]	*mama*	*noun*
麻 *má*	↗ [up]	*linen*	*noun*
馬 *mǎ*	↘↗ [down up]	*horse*	*noun*
罵 *mà*	↘ [down]	*to scold*	*verb*

It is quite clear that in Mandarin, proper inflection is critical to communicating one's desired meaning. If the intonation is off, one could easily call one's mother a horse or scold the linen! Although slight variance of spoken inflection is possible, there is far more freedom of inflection permitted in the Western languages. The advantage in this linguistic freedom is that it can be present in every word, changing the meaning by degree. That freedom is reflected in Western music and musical performance.

The singsong nature of the Mandarin language is easy to detect. This characteristic is also present in the great Chinese culture's distinctive music, with its many sliding tones. Listen to Chinese music and the Mandarin language back to back to appreciate their deep connection.

Finnish

The strongest characteristics of the Western languages tend to manifest themselves most profoundly in the beginnings and endings of musical phrases. In Finnish, the first syllable of each multisyllabic word is almost always stressed. The remaining syllables resolve softly. Though Finnish composer Jean Sibelius was born into a Swedish-speaking home, he later learned the Finnish language with a vengeance and asserted his Finnish pride, personality, and language in his music. The opening of his Second Symphony is a clear example of this, with its trailing-off figure of remaining syllables found at the end of each phrase group (example 313).

Example 313

There are many examples of this throughout Sibelius's musical output. It is simply a Finnish linguistic trait that has quite naturally found its way into his music.

Hungarian

Hungarian language and music are also inextricably linked to one another. Here, as in Finnish, the first syllable is nearly always stressed. But there is a clipped nature to this accenting. This is often reflected musically with a sixteenth note on the beat followed by a dotted eighth (example 314). This yields a pseudo-Scottish inflection somewhat reminiscent of the word "laddie."

Example 314

French

The French language is similarly reflected in French concert music. Veiled phrases with fade-ins and fade-outs attest to that language's impact on the French compositional style. The soft entrance and exit made by the strings and oboe at the very opening of the first movement of Camille Saint-Saëns's "Organ" Symphony is illustration of this kind of French smoothness (example 315).

Example 315

Italian

The Italian language is also strongly reflected in that country's music. Italians have long maintained that it is a particularly Italianate trait to sing full-throated. Their language backs up this claim because most words in the Italian language end in a vowel. This allows for smooth connections between words when spoken and sung.

The long lines of the melody in example 316 clearly illustrate this characteristic.

Example 316

Verdi: **I Vespri Siciliani**, *Overture*

German

German is somewhat baffling. Here we are confronted with a situation where music has softened a language instead of that language being directly reflected in that country's music. Although widely regarded as a rather harsh language because of the frequent percussive endings to words, its guttural and spitting sounds, as well as its many diphthongs and triphthongs, the greatest German composers have compensated for this to such a degree by creating so much superior vocal music as to make the listener all but forget those rough elements and actually revel in its sound. German composers have so often elongated the vowels over such achingly beautiful melodies that the frequently hard consonants become a proportionately smaller part of the overall picture than when the language is merely spoken. Perhaps this is the secret to the success of German vocal composition. This linear characteristic has bled over into purely instrumental German music as well.

Schubert was the absolute master of setting the German language to music (example 317).

Example 317

Schubert: "Nacht und Traume"

Of course, German composers also use the coarser elements of the language to great effect (example 318).

Example 318

Wagner: Das Reingold, Act I, scene i

English

The English language is much like German—intrinsically not the most beautiful. The frequently harsh consonant endings of most words do not place it near the top of the list of the most singable of languages.

Historically, since there was not a strong tradition of outstanding English composers until relatively recently, it is hard to generalize about the English language's effect on English music. Most music scholars agree that between Henry Purcell (1659–95) and Edward Elgar (1857–1934) there were no English composers of true greatness. Furthermore, many of the more prominent English and American composers of the 1800s and 1900s emulated the Germanic School, which did nothing to further the development of a truly English style. Recognizable English and American styles did not crystallize until the appearance of Elgar in England and Copland in America. Now, schools of composition do exist, but as for their relation to the English language, I cannot say. The manner of composition currently in fashion does not, to my ear, relate strongly to any spoken language.

The "International" Language

By and large, through the ages, and until very recently, music has been a reflection of natural human speech. "I love you" is spoken as it has been for centuries. The German citizens of 1731 said, "Ich liebe dich," just as they do today, i.e., with no spaces between words and on the line of the breath. The Italians say, "Io t'amo"; the French, "Je t'aime"; Hungarians say, "Szeretlek"; the Finnish, "Minä rakastan sinua"; the Chinese—it doesn't really matter. The point is that vocal delivery is most certainly linear. It is simply unnatural to break the spoken line. The vocabulary of language changes—but the physical way of speaking does not. Our lungs, larynx, and abdominal muscles still work in the same way as they have for millennia.

The vocabulary of music also changes—the combinations of notes, the chord progressions, and so forth—but if one appreciates the relationship of speaking to singing, then accepting the relationship of singing to instrumental music is as logical as it can be. Music speaks. However, if one believes that instrumental music exists independently of singing, then anything goes. One must first accept the hypothesis that singing is the root of all music for one's music making to achieve its deepest attachment to the human heart.

Portato: Herald of a New Romanticism

Trumpets in D
IV - Allegro, ma non troppo

Dvorak: Symphony #8

Portato is often confused with *portamento*, a word we sometimes use today for a glissando. Yet a century ago, portamento was sometimes used to signify what we now call portato. Confusing?

In his Third Symphony (1895), Gustav Mahler writes *molto portamento* under the horn parts at one point (example 319).

Example 319

Mahler: Symphony #3
I - Sehr weich und ausdrucksvoll hervortretend

molto portamento

Here are two definitions of portamento from older music dictionaries:

Portamento. Sliding or "carrying" the voice from one sound to another; also on bow instruments, sliding the finger along the string from one place to another. —Clarke, *Pronouncing Dictionary of Musical Terms*, 1896

Portamento. A smooth gliding from one tone to another, differing from the legato in its more deliberate execution, and in the actual (though very rapid and slurring) sounding of the intermediate tones. —Baker, *Pronouncing Pocket-Manual of Musical Terms*, 1933

The word "portato," on the other hand, is not to be found in either of those old dictionaries.

Obviously, Mahler did not mean to direct the horn players to perform a glissando between all the notes in example 319. By virtue of the hairpins and dashes he wrote into this passage, he clearly meant for the notes in the horn line to receive what we now refer to as a portato inflection.

Here are some more recent dictionary definitions of "portato" that help to shed light.

> Portato. Also called a "Louré"—a lifted, on the string stroke; a slurred staccato. —Grove, *Grove Dictionary of Music and Musicians*, ed. Sadie, 1980

> Portato (Portando). A style of performance between legato and staccato—separate bow pressure for each note. —*New Oxford Companion to Music*, ed. Arnold, 1983

Portato is most often performed by placing minute bursts of wind or bow speed on each note of a given figure while maintaining a slight connection between the notes, thereby obtaining a pulsating quality.

The words "portato" and "portamento" are both derived from the Italian word *portare*, which means "to carry." This root definition suggests that these notes cannot carry their own weight and must be lifted effortfully by the performer. The paradox here is that a portato inflection itself is usually very light, but nevertheless it can suggest a giving in to weariness. Portato is often a musical representation of regret, resignation, or sadness.

Written Portato

Normally, portato is represented by a slur with either dashes, dots, or carats over each note under the slur (example 320).

Example 320

Brahms: Symphony #2
    II - Allegretto grazioso (Quasi Andantino)

Portato usually occurs on a falling figure or at the end of a phrase or note group, but some composers indicate portato in both rising and falling figures at varying points in the same phrase, as in example 321.

Example 321

Schumann: **Piano Concerto in A minor**

However, this inflection, like most others, is usually not written at all. Most often, it is left to the performer's discretion as to where a portato inflection is appropriate.

Musical Meaning

A mental image that helps one understand the emotion behind a portato inflection follows:

A rejected suitor descending the stairs after being spurned by a love interest would hesitate a moment at the *top* of the stairs, then an acceptance of fate would propel the would-be lover down the last few steps more precipitously. Accordingly, a portato inflection is usually played with a slight lingering on the first note, while those remaining are played more quickly.

Another representation of the simple physics of portato is a bouncing rubber ball. The first bounce is larger and each subsequent bounce is smaller and faster than the previous.

Example 322

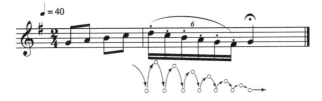

Although the first note is slightly lengthened, the last few notes catch up to where the next beat would normally fall. With a prop-

erly rendered portato, no distortion of the beat occurs—only a freedom *within* it is accomplished.

In a melody, portato can create the impression of sobbing. It
most naturally occurs at the end of a phrase but, as illustrated in example 321, can be used on occasion at the beginning.

Wind players, in particular, are often unwilling or unable to utilize
portato because it is so difficult to bring off with a sense of dignity. It
cannot be done half-heartedly and still be expected to evoke the desired pathos. An extremely subtle control of the wind, allied to a real
belief in the deeper meaning of this special inflection, is required.

Although more players on every instrument are beginning to
use this inflection again, it is still so infrequently heard that many
young musicians are not aware of its great musical value or even of
its existence as a musical inflection with a name.

The Contrast of the Ritardando

The opposite of descending the stairs—climbing those same stairs
wearily—requires much more effort. This is where the *ritardando*
comes in. Sometimes a slight ritard is warranted as one ascends
pitchwise, especially if leading to an important cadence or dissonance. This is completely different from portato and is included
here for contrast.

While making a ritard, keep inner subdivisions in mind. If you
make a ritard within eighth notes, feel sixteenth subdivisions. If you
make a ritard within sixteenths, feel thirty-seconds. This prevents
the last note before the arrival from being disproportionately long.
Also, group those inner subdivisions in your mind as you execute
the ritard (example 323).

Example 323

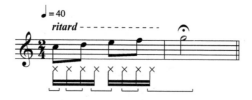

Portato usually involves stretching the first note and catching
up toward the end of the beat. A ritardando is just the opposite. The
first note can sometimes even be shortened by playing the second

note slightly early, while the remaining notes are further stretched; each a bit more than the last. And unlike a portato, the ritardando definitely does change the tempo by stretching the beats.

Rubato

Some musicians seem to feel they must stretch and push practically every note and phrase around with constant accelerandi and ritardandi. A seasick quality can result when rubato is the main element of one's "phrasing." But real phrasing is, rather, a matter of bringing the notes into relief, not one of toying with the pulse. Tempo, like the beating heart, must have a context of regularity in order for changes in pulse to be meaningful. A constantly fluctuating heartbeat would be rightly considered to be a serious affliction.

Rubato is a device applied on top of musical phrasing that simply heightens a given musical inflection or harmonic event. Locations for it must be judiciously chosen. Overuse will brand one's musicianship as undisciplined and self-indulgent.

The Romantics and Recorded Portato

Violinist Fritz Kreisler was perhaps *the* master of portato in the early part of the twentieth century. There are countless examples of this inflection in his many recordings made between 1903 and 1950.

Portato can also be found in the oboe playing of Marcel Tabuteau. Both he and John Minsker, student of Tabuteau's and English hornist of the Philadelphia Orchestra from 1936 to 1959, can be heard using it effectively in the Walt Disney film *Fantasia* (1940) in the "Arabian Dance" from *The Nutcracker.* In the phrase illustrated in example 324, which the oboe first states, followed by the English horn shortly afterward an octave lower, both Tabuteau and Minsker linger on the first thirty-second note and catch up to the next beat during the next three thirty-seconds.

Example 324

There are also many examples of portato in the recordings of Tabuteau's successor, John de Lancie. In example 325, de Lancie highlights a chromatic passing tone by using a pronounced portato inflection in the Philadelphia Orchestra's 1962 recording of Strauss's "Dance of the Seven Veils" from *Salome*.

Example 325

Strauss: Salome, *Dance of the Seven Veils*
Ziemlich langsam

ob

p grazioso

Maria Callas, too, used this device to great effect in her 1959 recording of *La Gioconda*. In the following example, she clearly realizes Ponchielli's indication to begin the phrase with portato. Ponchielli has marked a carat over each note under the slur. Afterward, Callas reclaims a resolute quality on the smooth repetition of the phrase.

Example 326

Ponchielli: La Gioconda, Act IV
tranquillo   *dolciss.*

sop

Gioconda: ciel, domando al cie - lo di dormir que-ta, di dormir que - ta dentro l'a vel,
                              portato   smooth

Sentimentality

Certain performers have, for some time, looked upon portato with derision, yet not so long ago it was considered an essential color within the palette of a musical artist's expression. Those musicians who reject this inflection are generally willing to accept portato when it occurs in an accompaniment of repeated eighths or quarters of the same pitch but summarily dismiss it when it occurs within a melodic line. These musicians have cleverly drawn a barrier between "sentiment" and "sentimentality" by equating sentimentality with cheap emotion while contradicting themselves by admitting it is all right to show sentiment in music. Where is the line drawn? Philip Farkas wrote, "The musician who tries to hide any show of emotion, either as a composer or as a performer, is negating the very reason his art exists."[1]

The word "sentimental" has been used as an insult when describing performers. Yet who has not shared sentimental moments with dear friends or had deeply moving experiences while rummaging through mementos that remind us of lost times? The nostalgia we all feel from time to time should be reflected in music making from time to time. In a gentler and not-so-distant era, sentimentality was highly prized as a mark of one's humanity. Far from being garish, the depiction of sentiment in music through the judicious use of portato is a wistful event most often realized with quiet resignation. Being a sentimental musician is part of being a complete musician.

It is, of course, possible to overburden a performance with sentimentality. But demonstrating no sentiment at all is equally undesirable. The key to remember is that sentiment should always be accompanied by mental restraint—an approach that will have the greatest impact on the listener because it illustrates the performer's capacity for both feeling *and* intelligent thought.

The Pendulum

In contrast to the many musicians trained between the 1950s and the 1970s who wince at the suggestion of heart-on-the-sleeve emotionalism, their teachers—trained between the 1920s and the 1940s—were taught to revere direct emotional musical communication. But that romanticism became too much for many of their students so a reactionary, antiseptic school arose. Literalism regarding the printed page and emotional detachment became the new fads. Since the 1950s, this unsentimental school of thought has prevailed musically. Thankfully, during the last half-century, there were many notable musicians who proved to be exceptions to this rule.

With the new century the pendulum is swinging back toward direct emotionalism. I believe the humble portato is the herald of things to come. Like the return of an endangered species to a formerly polluted environment, the burgeoning use of portato is a signal that the winds of change are again beginning to blow. I believe we are likely to see, during the next forty years or so, a new flowering of romanticism in performance and in composition.

"Technique" vs. "Musicality"

Violin I

Vivace

pp

Rimsky-Korsakov: Flight of the Bumblebee

Many musicians have the impression that the world of musical study is cut from two different cloths: "technique" and "musicality." The truth is that if either of these elements is missing, there can simply be no music. Music cannot exist without notes and cannot live without expression. If one believes that a separation between technique and musicianship exists, one's performance risks becoming a patchwork of "technical" passages interspersed with "musical" ones.

Proof

Musical thinking solves technical problems. Conquering technical hurdles is not simply a matter of good old-fashioned elbow grease but often it is a question of mind over matter. Note grouping—musical thinking—makes one's technique much more fluid. The mind is not cluttered with the thought of the individual notes as they fly by. Larger gestures are felt and communicated. The simple act of physical repetition in the practice session is not enough. When the mind becomes actively involved in musical preparation, technical difficulties melt away one by one.

For example, proper musical note grouping can mentally eliminate awkward intervals. Often, the two notes involved in the interval do not belong in the same group.

In Mozart's overture to *The Marriage of Figaro* (example 327) there is just such an interval in the bassoon part that often causes a fingering slip-up (C-sharp down to A).

Example 327

But by grouping the A with the D on the following beat, the troublesome downward interval (C-sharp to A) mentally disappears and is supplanted by the upward interval that follows. The seventh note of the second bar (C-sharp) is the *end* of a note group with a lower neighbor at its center. The following A is the root of the V chord that then resolves to the tonic on the next downbeat, forming a harmonic grouping (example 328).

Example 328

Example 329 contains a possibly hazardous upward leap; do not grow on the resolution note (R) of the appoggiatura (A) in anticipation of that leap.

Example 329

Mentally eliminate this large interval by tapering on the resolution of the appoggiatura and then growing within the high note *after* it has begun. That upward leap will, in all practicality, cease to exist, yet it will still be smoothly contained within the slur.

Technical ease is the natural dividend of musical thought.

One Note That Swims

Music is not a bunch of separated notes strung together, but rather *one* note that swims from pitch to pitch on a line.

Example 330

Written notes are simply momentary containers for the music through which passes the living current of musical emotion. The music flows through one pitch into the next.

Even a musical phrase made up of staccato notes is still one note that swims. Although the notes are disjointed, they still create forward motion in the mind of the listener if the notes are played on a line.

Oneness

In all areas of life where discipline is involved, whether diet, exercise, or music, one's thoughts must first change, then behaviors easily follow. How one thinks about any subject colors one's perception absolutely. Redirecting habitual patterns of thought is not so hard to accomplish if the arguments that seek to change those patterns are logical. Logical thinking about musical phrasing mentally unites the elements of technique and musicality into the truly indivisible entity that music is.

To stress the relationship of language to music yet again: the words or notes are the "technique"—their underlying meaning is their "musicality." In purely verbal communication, one cannot have detailed meaning without words but there can be words without meaning if they are not phrased coherently. Likewise, in music, one cannot have meaning without notes. Unfortunately, in far too many performances, there can be, and often are, many notes played without coherent meaning.

The specific words used in a sentence are not indispensable. Almost any word could be substituted with several synonyms without severely affecting the underlying message. It is the cumulative meaning of the words that is important.

In the same way, individual notes are not as important as they first seem. A different note here or there would probably not severely affect the deeper message of any well-constructed and well-played musical phrase. In fact, when repeating a theme or motif, composers often vary the notes. It may seem heretical to suggest, but one could even miss a note or two and still manage to convey the composer's emotional message.

Discarding the false mental barrier between technique and musicianship will enable your music making to always speak with coherent, unified meaning.

Part 7

The Profession

Tenor
Andante sostenuto

Rodolfo: Chi   son?   Son un po - e - ta.
"Who am I? I'm a poet."
Puccini: La Boheme, Act I

Now to the economic point of all this musical analysis—getting and keeping a good job. And, most important, passing the tradition to the next generation.

Practicing

Violin
Allegro moderato

Kreutzer: 42 Studies for Violin, #2

Through practice, we learn to hear ourselves. The process of opening the ears to the sounds we make is a constant struggle. Our idea of what we wish to produce often obscures the reality of the sound coming from the instrument. However, do not despair when you can finally hear your problems. The identification of a musical problem is 90 percent of its solution.

The Virtuoso

We are tantalized at an early age by the colorful word "virtuoso." We are told that if we want to become one, we must "practice, practice, practice." But what is a virtuoso? The image commonly held by the public is that of a long-haired Paganini-esque figure reeling about with sparks flying from the instrument, as cascades of notes spill out in a whirlwind of breathtaking showmanship. But the Italian meaning of the word is simply "virtuous one." Therefore, in order to be considered a true virtuoso, the young musician should strive to possess many virtues. This means not only having fast fingers but also having control. The ability to play slowly and softly with expression is at least as important as the garish acrobatics romantically associated with that deceptive word. Of course, we practice in order to obtain technical facility, but without developing delicate control as well, complete artistry—complete virtuosity—is not possible.

What Makes Success?

Given good health, there are two basic elements necessary for success: *talent* and *drive*. Of these two, the more important one, by far, is drive. There are many people who have very little native ability who nonetheless manage to achieve a high level of success. What they do have is the drive to achieve. On the other side of the coin, there are those who have been blessed with prodigious aptitudes and formidable intelligence (the most important talent) who do not possess the burning desire necessary to achieve. They cannot succeed. But when talents and intelligence are allied with an unquenchable drive, success is practically assured. One practices only if one has the required drive.

Notes and Music

Students often feel they must practice "the notes" first and then add "the music" later. This disjointed concept only prolongs the practice session. It divides the mind between "technique" and "music," leaving one to accomplish half as much in twice as much time.

Always practice musically.

Warming Up

Warm up musically from the first note, as if in performance—no mindless finger flapping. Do not make sounds in your warm-up that you would not want to be heard in concert. Make musical progressions from note to note. Compose your warm-up. Each figure you play should have important notes that are led to and resolved from. And test your ability to play softly by sustaining long tones during the warm-up. Avoid warming up in a mechanical or thoughtless way only to suddenly switch gears to become "musical" once the practice session, rehearsal, or concert proper begins.

Building Speed

When attempting to master fast technical passages, try this method of building speed: After identifying the groupings, practice them individually. Start slowly. Then gradually speed up each note group to the desired tempo. Finally, piece them together one by one. Theoretically, if you can play each little group up to tempo, you should be able to play the whole passage in tempo once they are joined together.

Example 331

Strauss: **Till Eulenspiegels lustige Streiche**
   Volles Zeitmass (sehr lebhaft)

The groupings in example 332 help in building speed.

Example 332

Rhythmical exercises such as those in examples 333 and 334 can also iron out technical difficulties.

Example 333

Example 334

Although this rhythmic routine is helpful, it does not reinforce musical thinking. The proper musical groupings illustrated in example 332 must be reinstated once the phrase is played in its proper rhythm and at its proper speed.

In all physical endeavors it has been demonstrated that the earlier one acquires dexterity, the greater its proficiency later in life. There are countless examples of musical virtuosos throughout history who began their training in earnest at the tender age of five, four, or even three years. Adults will definitely improve their instrumental abilities through practice, but without that crucial foundation of early training, they will still come up short. I believe that at least 95 percent of one's technical development is achieved by the age of twenty.

Consider this: The former Eastern Bloc countries long had Olympic training facilities for very young children who showed natural talents for certain sports. Those children developed into adults with astounding physical control. Without early training to reinforce specific chemical pathways in the brain, those amazing results would never have been possible. Diligently sharpening one's skills later in one's development can and does yield subtle and important improvements, as with adult athletes training for the Olympics, but the work that has made these athletes of Olympic caliber in the first place was done years in advance of these crucial but relatively minuscule improvements.

The same is true in language. Young children who relocate to a new country with a different language most often learn to speak the adopted tongue fluently without an accent. Their parents usually struggle with it forever. Adults may develop dexterity with the new language, but in the vast majority of cases their accents remain strong for the remainder of their lives. (Marcel Tabuteau, with his heavy French accent, springs to mind—and he landed in the United States when he was only eighteen.)

Memorization

Memorization most often happens by accident when practicing with intensity. The music becomes ingrained in the brain without conscious effort. Only when there are slight note variations that could cause confusion from one passage to the next does memorization become the main concern.

Play whatever you are working on from memory from time to time. Let the sound of the music imprint itself upon your mind. Do not become mesmerized by what you see, to the exclusion of fully hearing the music. It is possible to become immersed in the musically irrelevant world of sight. Close the music and "see" how far you can get.

Even if we need our eyes on the printed notes to keep us on track, we must remove the mind from the page. There is nothing worse than hearing an actor who sounds like he is reading the words. The same goes for musical performance. It should seem as though the sounds we make are improvised in the moment. Memorization, whether by design or by accident, makes it seem so.

In addition, there will be terrifying moments when you lose your place on the page in performance. It is at these exceptional times that you will be grateful that memorization kept you from straying from the right notes.

Programming

The brain is like a computer. When practicing, we program in the information that will be retrieved later. If we put the information in with errors, by practicing too quickly, errors are what we will get back in performance. Resist the temptation to practice technically demanding passages at speed before mastering them slowly. Slow practice makes quick progress.

Once the glitches have been worked out, always practice the music in its correct rhythm—as written. Do not touch each note in a randomly arrhythmic way in order to save time. Practicing as though you are in performance helps you judge your breathing or bowing distributions, not to mention your scaling of inflections, crescendos, and diminuendos. If you long for consistency in performance, practice in a consistent way. John de Lancie quoted Tabuteau about preparation: "You lose 50 percent when you perform; therefore, when you go on stage you have to be 150 percent prepared."

Violin virtuoso Fritz Kreisler detested practicing and did as little of it as possible throughout his long career. What allowed him to reach such great heights was what he termed "mental control." He believed that "technique is truly a matter of the brain."[1] Of course, his early manual training served him well all his life.

Hornist Philip Farkas referred to the brain as a computer when addressing the most frequent practice mistake:

> When, finally, that perfect run-through is accomplished, then, and only then, is the performer ready to start *practice* of that passage. The previous run-throughs only demonstrated the many ways of how *not* to play the passage. Now, after finally achieving

one perfect performance, the repetition process actually starts. . . .
Definitely, there is no more potent cure for stage fright than the
knowledge that you *can* do it. And the only way you can *know* that
you can *do* it is to *know* that you have *done* it—perhaps hundreds of
times. The more often the better. That computer cannot be ignored.[2]

Farkas and Kreisler approached the issue of practicing from
different angles. Yet both recognized that the brain is the key. Mere
repetition without mental understanding cannot yield worthwhile,
or even dependable, musical results.

Auditioning

Oboe

Allegro

Rossini: La Scala di Seta, *Overture*

What is the secret to winning an audition? *Have a plan for every note you play.* Relying on inspiration to strike is a sure recipe for failure, but knowing what you will do at every moment of the music will keep you focused on your playing instead of on the audition situation. Make your playing the priority. The human mind can be aware of more than one thing at a time, but it cannot actively *think* of more than one thing at a time. Making music is an all-consuming activity if you focus on your plan.

Do not provide the audition committee with ammunition to use against you. Quirks like leaking air from the embouchure and excessive movement or grimaces can put people off. All your energies, which are finite, should be channeled through the instrument and not wasted on extraneous and distracting body motions.

All of us have made mistakes in concert that we feel to have been massive disasters, but when we hear a recording of the performance, we are usually amazed at how quickly the harrowing moment passed. In this same way, in an audition, time seems compressed and we tend to feel that our tempos are not fast enough, so we rush. But those listening are not worked up as you may be. They hear everything at its real speed. To be safe, and to avoid being your own worst enemy, take each quick excerpt one or two metronome markings slower than you feel it should be played. Clarity adds a sense of speed. Fast and sloppy versus a little less fast and clean—you be the judge.

Perhaps most important, in an audition or even a concert, do not try to be better than you are. This attitude will distract you and can detrimentally affect each note you play. Do not try to do anything in an audition that you have not done in your practice. An audition should simply be a representation of your everyday playing. Show what you play like, not what you wish you played like. Sincerity is the key to musical communication. Only with sincerity can you hope to convince the committee and the conductor that you really do know what you are doing.

Teach the audition committee how the music should be played by scrupulously observing all that is on the page. Do not attempt to spice up your playing with spur-of-the-moment inspiration.

Each audition experience builds on the last and prepares you for the next. Each is an investment in your future. Do not pass up audition opportunities unless you have absolutely no desire for the job available.

Finally, if you have a high standard in your everyday playing, you need not fear a substandard performance in an audition. Make every day an audition—then audition day will be nothing special.

Orchestral Protocol

Violin I
(Largamente)
p legato e cantabile
Elgar: Pomp and Circumstance March #1

After winning the audition and beginning your tenure in a symphony orchestra, your musical life takes on a different hue. From the life of a student who has played in school ensembles, or perhaps here and there in freelance situations with constantly differing personnel, you are thrust into a new, fixed situation where most of the musicians have worked together for years. They have evolved into an entity with a certain professional code of behavior. You will have to adapt to this way of musical life once you have made it.

Dealing with Colleagues

What makes one a good colleague? Although the complete picture is hard to define, common courtesy, cooperation, and, above all, respect for one's co-workers are involved. Being aware that our behaviors in concert and rehearsal have the potential to disturb others keeps us in check. This understanding is vital to healthy relations among colleagues. Here are guidelines to help one avoid difficult situations:

1. During the warm-up on stage, do not practice the same phrase a colleague is playing nearby. This breaks the other player's concentration. Wait until it seems that person has finished and

then, after a decent interval, go on to that passage if you must work out your own difficulties.

2. If you hear a colleague practicing a phrase where intonation discrepancies have existed between the two of you, do not just chime in during his or her practice in order to check the pitch. Ask the other player if you might check the note or phrase.

3. When tuning, tune only when the A is given for your section of the orchestra. Play only that note and a few other intervals—no concertos. Tune quickly and quietly.

4. Never write anything in another person's part. It is not hard to imagine how disconcerting it is to notice that something has been written into your music while you were away.

5. If you need to write something in your music and you do not have a pencil (which you should have at all times), ask a colleague if you may borrow one rather than grab one that may be handy from your neighbor's stand.

6. Because our musical partners are trying to maintain their concentration, one should not fidget, especially during solos of nearby players. By not fidgeting you will also be ready to make your entrance. After you have finished playing, remain as motionless as possible while counting your rests.

7. Never turn around to look at another orchestra member who is playing a solo phrase—especially during a concert. If you are curious about who is playing, ask someone later.

8. If a dispute arises between you and a colleague, have the courage to address the issue directly (albeit as tactfully as possible) before speaking with the personnel manager. Keep the number of people involved in any sensitive issue to a minimum. Only when it becomes apparent that an agreement cannot be reached without arbitration should management then be brought into the picture.

Dealing with Conductors

Treating the conductor with an extra measure of respect goes a long way toward keeping you on the maestro's good side.

1. Keep eye contact with the conductor as much as possible—without losing your place on the page. Conductors notice and appreciate this. This also helps you react immediately to the conductor's sometimes vague gyrations and makes you a more flexible musician.

2. In rehearsal, when the conductor has stopped the orchestra to

speak, stop playing immediately. Do not continue until that particular composition evolves into your personal cadenza.

3. When the conductor asks you to play a passage a certain way, simply nod your head in agreement without speaking, even if you feel you just did it that way, or if the suggestion is something you do not agree with. This will placate even the most persistent conductor. The art of being agreeable is much appreciated. Having an argument with the conductor in front of the orchestra, no matter how well justified, only serves to make one appear difficult. If a serious problem arises, wait until the break to speak privately to the conductor to resolve the issue.

4. Do not try to explain yourself to the conductor with the orchestra present. Comments such as "I dropped my pencil and missed the entrance" are not needed. If at all possible, avoid speaking altogether. Even brief responses are superfluous, unless they are in answer to a direct question. The sooner the conductor can go on to the next concern, the sooner any incident involving you will be forgotten.

5. If you have a question, raise your hand and say, "Question" or "Maestro" after the conductor has stopped the orchestra, and you will be recognized. Then, *accept the answer you receive.* If you have discovered something within the music that may contradict the conductor's often-hasty conclusion, discuss your revelation later with the conductor privately. Never question a conductor's conclusions in front of the orchestra. You may feel you are scoring points with your colleagues by setting the conductor straight, but you will be losing footing with the one person who has the power to make your life miserable.

6. Play with conviction. Resolute phrasing can persuade even a conductor who has strong opinions about how to phrase your part. However, when a musical vacuum is perceived within your playing, then the maestro may feel the urge to lend a helping hand. Also, never ask a conductor for advice or an opinion of your playing ("Was that OK?") because this signals weakness. Conductors latch on to insecurity and can destroy sensitive musicians by exploiting their well-meaning uncertainty. Conductors know they hold this power. Some rarely hesitate to use it.

7. Predict where the conductor's next beat will fall, instead of reacting to the previous beat. That beat is dead and gone. Nothing can bring it back. It is only that beat's relation to the upcoming beat that matters. Everything one plays relates to the following beat. If you concern yourself with the next beat, the conductor will be amazed at your clairvoyance!

THE MAGIC HANDS

There are conductors who seem to think that the musicians of the orchestra are their musical children or, at the very least, their students. Let them believe this. It is a small price to pay. It is possible to learn something from even the least palatable conductor, and a great deal from a fine one.

There are magnificent conductors who shape concerts into life-changing events. They remember that they are on stage, like the instrumentalists they lead, to serve the music and not the ego.

Marcel Tabuteau had his own ideas about conductors. At the end of *Marcel Tabuteau's Lessons*, he says, "My dear little friends, between us, don't give my secrets away to anyone—especially to conductors. Let them believe it was [their] *magic hands* which did the trick! Ha! Ha! Ha! Ha!"

Performing

Piano

I - Allegro molto moderato

Grieg: Piano Concerto in A minor

All of one's musical study is not simply learning for learning's sake; if a musician wishes to be a great performer, he or she must apply that schooling in performance.

"Monkey See, Monkey Do"

"As a good advice to my young friends—wind players—I want to warn them against the general tendency to try to imitate without having had the basic technique necessary to perform." Marcel Tabuteau says this at the outset of *Marcel Tabuteau's Lessons.* He warns against a "monkey see, monkey do" method of trying to be great. Trying to imitate artists whom one admires without first knowing what they are saying through the music renders one's playing as no more than an empty exercise filled with meaningless gestures. It is meaningless because the monkey doesn't know why he is doing any of the things he is mimicking and has no idea what any of it means. However, once one understands what a great musician is saying, then one is able to *emulate*. Imitation is the hollow act of aping what another person does. Emulation is a living process of understanding that leads one closer to sincerity.

Whims

Many musicians feel that when struck by a feeling of inspiration, that whim must be acted upon in order to be sincere to themselves. However, when you have a whim, there must immediately follow a period of self-examination: "Does my momentary feeling have any relation to what the composer has left for us on the page?" The score is, after all, the composer's only clue we have as to what he or she wanted. It is not everything, but it is a guide that can act as a filter to guard against whims that do not relate to that particular moment in the music. A truly musical whim finds support in the score. An unmusical one has no such support and should be quickly discarded.

The following anecdote, possibly apocryphal, illustrates that in performance one's non-intellectualized feelings can easily cross the line into gross excess. In one of his master classes, the great piano virtuoso and teacher Artur Schnabel (1882–1951) listened to a student play a movement from one of Beethoven's piano concertos. The student proceeded to over-inflect each phrase, alternately rushing and stretching them with orgiastic abandon. After the student had finished, Schnabel waited a few moments and then asked, "Why have you played this piece in this style?" The student thought awhile and answered, "I just felt it like that." Schnabel quietly retorted, "I would like you to go outside and take a walk around the block—*until that feeling goes away.*"

Sharing

A parlor musician who plays for no one but him- or herself may be enjoying music—but is that person really *making* music? The riddle "If a tree falls in the forest—and no one is there to hear it fall—does it make a sound?" illustrates this concept. Music making must be shared by one person with another in order to be complete, just like a conversation, where an idea is put forth and then absorbed by another person.

Performing is shared communication. It is the time when we show our hard-won understanding of the composer's message to the listener. We help the paying customer understand and feel the music's structure and, therefore, its emotion.

Projection

For actors on stage, stage makeup is necessary. Without it, the expressions on the face of the actor fail to make much impact upon the audience. Actors must wear enough makeup so those sitting in the last row of the theater can see their facial features. From close up that makeup can appear to be quite exaggerated—almost grotesque. Much is needed, but over-applying it can make the actor look like a clown, even from a great distance. Only enough is needed to highlight and project the natural features of the face unless, of course, the actor *is* playing a clown.

When performing, musicians should remember that, like theater actors, we too are on stage. We must use a form of *aural* cosmetics to project the natural features of the music out into the auditorium. It is often the case that when music students have the opportunity to sit next to their teachers on stage, they are taken aback by the grandiosity of the musical gestures their teachers utilize in performance. Great performers sell their phrasing with a three-dimensional quality the audience can almost reach out and touch. Like actors, we musicians must animate our delivery to a certain extent so that what we say is remembered not only for its content but also for its presentation.

The musical makeup performers use is "projection." This word is not used here in its tonal meaning—as in producing a penetrating or loud tone so as to be heard—but as in *getting one's ideas across to the audience.* It is not enough that we know what we are saying or even that our colleagues receive our musical message. Our educated colleagues are attuned to hearing subtle nuances of phrasing. They are also near us on stage. Our intent must project beyond them to the ears of even the most indifferent and distant listener in order to have any value as a performance that communicates.

Show your ideas clearly by inflecting your phrases with conviction. Your phrasing should be so clear that your intent cannot be misunderstood. Of course, it is possible to overdo it. Crossing the line that divides character from caricature can be disturbing to one's colleagues and to the audience. But if a choice must be made, opt for over-inflecting rather than under-inflecting. Blandness leaves an emotionless impression. Without the performer communicating a sense of involvement, music quickly becomes no more than ordered noise. If you really overdo your phrasing, rest assured that someone will let you know.

John de Lancie said of musical performance, "Make every statement a positive one. Say *something*."[1]

He explained his philosophy of critical listening:

> I have held three positions on judging how people play:
>
> 1) If I heard someone play and I agreed with what they were doing, that was great.
>
> 2) If I heard someone play and make a *positive statement* of something I didn't agree with, I still had respect for them.
> —BUT—
>
> 3) If I heard someone play and I couldn't figure out what they were doing—*no point of view*—I could not have respect for their musicianship.[2]

Enjoyment

Oboist Alfred Genovese, principal of the Metropolitan Opera (1960–77) and Boston Symphony (1990–99),[3] remembered an incident in the wind class at Curtis where Tabuteau picked on another oboe student for quite a while. The student finally blurted to Tabuteau, "I'm very sorry that I can't please you!" Tabuteau, momentarily stunned by the reply, started the ensemble up again. After a few seconds, and without warning, he suddenly stopped conducting and exploded, "Please *ME?!* Don't please me! PLEASE *YOU!*"

No musician can please everybody. Of course, we do play for the audience and for our colleagues, but if we are completely honest, we must admit that we play, most of all, for ourselves. Please yourself and at least you can be sure that someone has enjoyed your performance.

Pressure

In an orchestra, all of us are subject to a host of pressures. Coping with them is part of professional life. A mutual understanding of the shared stresses we face as performers forms a fraternity among ensemble musicians. Reeds, technically demanding music, conductors, the presence of colleagues on one's own instrument, the rest of the orchestra, former teachers, the general public, students, friends, guest artists, and the radio or television audience, as well as knowing that there is no second chance can all conspire to upset one's confidence and ability to perform up to one's own critical standards. It is all too easy to become distracted by these things. But if we stay focused on our musical plans derived from within the music, the welcome reward will be a marked reduction in nervousness.

Choreography

Resist the impulse to swing and sway in concert. Musicians need not act out the part of a virtuoso for all to see. Although the music may move you profoundly, do not let it move your body excessively. We have all attended concerts where the face-making and bodily contortions of some performers have made us forget what we should be hearing. At those times, the ears of the listener close and the listener becomes a viewer. The performance changes from an aural to a visual spectacle. This is certainly not a performer's musical objective.

John de Lancie said, "The closest you will ever come to really hearing your own playing objectively is if you practice without moving at all. You can then concentrate on the motion of the music and not of your body."[4]

In his book Leopold Mozart wrote:

> There are a great many bad habits. The most common of these are the moving of the violin; the turning to and fro of the body or head; the twisting of the mouth or wrinkling of the nose, especially when something a little difficult is to be played; the hissing, whistling, or any too audible blowing with the breath from the mouth, throat, or nose when playing a difficult note; the forced and unnatural distortion of the right and left hand, especially of the elbow; and finally the violent movement of the whole body whereby the floor or the whole room in which he plays is shaken and the spectators are moved either to laughter or pity at the sight of so laborious a wood-chopper.[5]

Of course, we are not divorced from our bodies as we play. Music often does make us feel like moving. Some motion is inevitable—even desirable—but gratuitous choreography detracts from the listening experience, especially if it does not seem to stem from the music itself. Sometimes, a strategically placed mirror in the practice room is a good and honest friend that can tell us when we cross the line that separates expressivity from eccentricity.

Switching Gears

A warm-up is a performance. A practice session is a performance. An audition is a performance. A rehearsal is a performance. All the playing one does is a performance. Therefore, there are no gears to switch just because an audience is present.

Fame

Music making should not be an act of shameless self-promotion. Yet some musicians are smitten with the thought of fame and seem to stop at nothing in their quest for celebrity. They sacrifice artistic integrity by creating effect in order to be noticed. Fame is often achieved in this way. Sadly, artistic integrity is a far rarer commodity than fame itself.

Accompanying

Viola
I - Molto Allegro

p

Mozart: Symphony #40

As professional orchestral musicians, we will spend the greater part of our musical lives accompanying our colleagues. Unless we are opera stars or soloists who travel the globe playing concertos, we will be subservient to a much greater degree than we will be dominant. Often, when we do have a solo to play, it is fleeting. An orchestral player must try to say as much as possible in the shortest possible time. The bassoon plays the melody maybe two percent of the time. My guess is that even the oboe, arguably the prima donna of the orchestra, has the melody perhaps only fifteen percent of the time. During the course of their careers, even the mighty first violins will surely accompany others at least fifty-one percent of the time. These are arbitrary figures, but they attempt to show that our main function as orchestral instrumentalists, in terms of the time spent on stage, is to accompany.

Accompaniments provide the cushion upon which the melody rests. They also create mood. A melody, repeated in the same key and tempo as its first statement, can have a completely different effect upon repetition if the accompaniment is sufficiently altered by the composer the second time around.

When one accompanies, one enters a realm different from that of the soloist. It is interesting that many solo artists have felt the need, usually later in their careers, to focus more intently on cham-

ber music. Chamber music provides the welcome opportunity to accompany one's musical companions while providing the sensation
that one is still a soloist. Playing in an orchestra is simply chamber
music on a grand scale. The main difference, aside from the size of
the ensemble, is that many musicians often play the same part.
Whether in chamber ensembles or in a full symphony orchestra, one
gains a special sense of accomplishment through accompanying.

We are frequently required to accompany our co-workers extremely softly. These moments, which require the utmost skill and
sensitivity, can provide great satisfaction. Although seemingly covered, by playing these tender accompaniments with involvement—
filling out the inner harmonies in a meaningful way and leading
from one harmony into another—the music benefits. The difference is felt more than heard. By thinking of note grouping in even
the most seemingly uninteresting accompaniment, one's musical
life will never be boring.

As an example of the kind of impact a sensitively realized accompaniment can have, consider the main theme of the first movement of Schubert's "Unfinished" Symphony. Schubert has given no
indication of how he would like its syncopated accompaniment to
be phrased. It is conventionally played with an accent on the first
note followed by a diminuendo, as illustrated in example 335:

Example 335

The entire bar fades away. There is no forward motion. However, if it is played with a slight inner impulse on the *middle* note, it
dovetails beautifully with the phrasing of the melody (example 336).

Example 336

The impulse in the accompaniment occurs during the long note in the melody, adding a subtle inner pulsation to the phrase. However, this inflection must be played very gently and should not call attention to itself.

This phrasing also works well in the commonplace accompaniment shown in example 337.

Example 337

Here, the first eighth functions as an upbeat, the second as an arrival, and the third as a resolution. This is preferable to the tired tradition of accenting the first note and having the remaining notes die away (example 338).

Example 338

This principle works beautifully in the piano theme of the first movement of Mozart's Quintet in E-flat major for Piano, Oboe, Clarinet, Horn, and Bassoon (K.452). Incidentally, Mozart proudly referred to this work in a letter he wrote April 10, 1784: "I myself consider it the best I have written in my life till now."

Example 339

As in the Schubert example, the accompaniment here works beautifully if lightly inflected at precisely the point at which the theme has longer notes. However, the third time this accompanimental figure occurs, it is followed immediately by a longer note;

not by a rest. Therefore the inflection should go forward to that note on the third beat of that bar. The accompanimental figure of an eighth rest followed by three eighth notes here is simply a series of upbeats in *search* of a downbeat. Here, the third figure finally finds its wayward downbeat. The absence of a note on the strong beats of the first bar (beats 1 and 3) gives greater importance to the otherwise weaker beats (2 and 4). This is the reason a light inflection works so well on these weaker beats.

Figures like the one illustrated in example 340 also follow this principle.

Example 340

Beethoven: Violin Sonata #3 in E flat Major
II - Adagio con molt' espressione

In his 1935 recording of this work, Fritz Kreisler phrases this figure in this way.

The Bass Line

It may not seem so at first glance, but it is a privilege to be a bass-line instrumentalist. Certain compensations are to be found within this nether region of the musical world.

Humans, being melodic creatures by nature, are nearly always aware of a melody line. A bass-line instrumentalist does not need to be taught to hear it. Thus, bass-line players learn from an early age to listen to music in a two-tiered way. They hear the melody *in relation* to their bass line. However, melody instrumentalists must be taught to be aware of the bass line and of its effect upon the phrasing of their melody.

The binary mode of listening to music that comes naturally to the bass-line player should be every professional's goal. Once the upper-voice player is sensitized to the bass, he or she becomes attuned in a new and profound way to music's meaning, beyond "I have the melody—I am the *important* one."

Play as though you are playing all the parts. Reflect the harmonic movement in your single line—whether you are playing the melody, the bass line, or an inner voice. In music, all the voices have their function and each has the potential to affect the way every other line is inflected. To be able to play different roles is the greatest gift of ensemble music.

How boring it would be if one were always the "important" voice.

Teaching

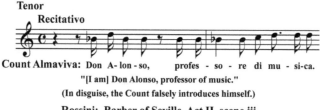

Tenor

Recitativo

Count Almaviva: Don A- lon - so, profes - so - re di mu - si-ca.

"[I am] Don Alonso, professor of music."

(In disguise, the Count falsely introduces himself.)

Rossini: Barber of Seville, Act II, scene iii

Teaching is the noblest aspect of a musician's life. Passing to the next generation of performers what one has learned assures the ever-upward progression of the art. John de Lancie was fond of saying, "Teaching is 5 percent explaining what to do and 95 percent repeating those same explanations." This is true, and like the repetitive process of practicing, the tautology of teaching also helps the teacher's abilities evolve to a higher level. Often, the teacher rightfully discards ideas previously taken as absolute truth once a student asks the simple question, "Why?" This questioning keeps the teacher honest and also keeps him or her searching for meaningful and logical reasons to support phrasing choices. Teaching defines one's musical beliefs.

The Purpose

Many musicians feel it is possible to teach technique but not musicianship. However, it is the student who must develop his or her technical abilities (fast tongue, fast fingers) on his or her own. There are pieces of advice to give and etudes a teacher can assign that help these things become more efficient, but the student must develop these physical skills at an early age through endless repetition—

alone in the practice room. *The musical development of the student* is what a music teacher should focus on. Musicianship is a thought process that can evolve and develop through careful direction.

The goal of teaching is to teach the student how to be his or her own teacher after the student's formal education has ended. In order to accomplish this objective, the teacher must strive to open the young musician's ears. A dedicated teacher can help the student achieve musical awareness by providing the student with a solid foundation of knowledge that can be applied to all music that will be encountered later in professional life. The young musician will then be able to develop musical arguments with certainty after the teacher is out of the picture. This gift of self-sufficiency is the greatest a teacher can give.

The Example

In addition to teaching lessons, we teach through our performances. By putting into practice those techniques we espouse, we provide a concrete example for our students. By listening to the teacher in concert, the student is able to analyze the value of those concepts. Far from the "monkey see, monkey do" approach utilized by teachers who are unable to verbalize their ideas, listening specifically for what has been *discussed* and *analyzed* in one's lessons reinforces a mental, rather than a visceral, approach to making music. Of course, there are instances in private lessons where demonstration on the instrument is paramount, but a student must be able to respond to verbal cues. After all, survival in a symphony orchestra depends on responsiveness to a conductor's spoken instructions.

Music students are not the only ones who learn through listening to performances. Maria Callas said, "You see, the *public* has to be taught. . . . We [performers] are a bit like teachers. We are professors and we have to teach this art. . . . How can the public know beforehand what we have taken years of devotion and study and scientific work [to grasp]? We perform an opera and they have to understand in one evening?! It's not possible! We teach [the public] what they should appreciate *later on*."[1]

Listening Sessions

Having students study commercial recordings is also a great help in the learning process. Sharing with them how to listen, by showing them what to listen for and by repeating portions of the recording a few times, can change a young musician's life. What one is *prepared* to hear affects absolutely what one *will* hear. From that point of understanding, students will begin to decipher which performances they hear are of real value. Paradoxically, it is also important to listen to recordings that provide contrary examples to those principles put forward in the lessons. Those recordings can actually reinforce one's musical convictions just as strongly as recordings that demonstrate proper musical thought by the performers.

Point of View

Teacher and student should both be engaged in a struggle to free their perception from subjectivity. They should strive to gain objectivity in order to see clearly what the composer is saying, without fogged-in personal preconceptions. Only after objectivity is achieved can they then step back inside the music to become intelligently subjective, *to assume the composer's viewpoint.* After intense study, this new awareness shows one that to remain blissfully confident of one's first impressions of the music can be a big mistake. First impressions are often wrong.

Like any communication, all art forms must come from a point of view. An informed point of view is always the most persuasive. The informed subjectivity striven for, through objective musical analysis, is that which conforms most closely to the natural structure of the music. Musical compositions *are* subjective forms of communication. But, for the most part, strictly speaking, musical performance is not.

Trust

The motto of the Curtis Institute of Music came from Josef Hofmann, its director from 1927 to 1938: "To hand down, through contemporary masters, the great traditions of the past; to teach students to build on this heritage for the future." The duty of a teacher is not to hand down all traditions but to hand down only those that are deemed worthy of being perpetuated—the *great* traditions.

Teachers are placed in the lofty position of judges of what is and what is not worthy in musical performance. Because of this, they should forever strive to educate themselves thoroughly—never remaining complacent or self-satisfied—in order to assure that their idolized position in the lives of their students is not a misplaced trust.

Part 8

The Search

Violin I
Andante
legato e sostenuto
ten.
p   molto espress.
Elgar: Enigma Variations, *Theme*

This book is not a replication of Marcel Tabuteau's teachings. It is my concept of his teachings as handed down to me by my teachers. They have added their perspective; I too have added mine. I cannot know what Marcel Tabuteau would have done in any specific musical instance but I have tried to apply his methods to discover what is inside the notes. Each performer who applies these methods will find his or her own way.

My book is an attempt to explain how to discover the music's natural structure and then how to bring it out through the development of concrete playing abilities. Along the way, I have thrown in liberal amounts of my own musical philosophy. However, as written notes are a poor substitute for music itself, written words can only hint at the real meaning in musical performance. Hundreds of details above and beyond those principles enumerated here will, of course, be required from each individual in live performance.

Beyond this, it is proper to remember that each of us brings to our music our accumulated life experience from which we draw expression. My woodwind instructor at the Curtis Institute of Music, John Minsker, imparted to his students his philosophy of life and music's place in it. He said, "Read great books. Experience life. Go places. Educate yourself beyond the study of music and all of that will be reflected in the music you play." Tabuteau himself said, "The more you take from the world, the more you can give to the world."[1] Music can only reflect life. Express your humanity through your music. Do not live only music. Giuseppe di Stefano, the renowned tenor who frequently sang with Maria Callas, said in reference to her exploitation as an artist, "[She was] a woman with a voice—[she] was not a *voice* with a *woman!*"[2] Likewise, we instrumentalists are whole people who just happen to play instruments.

Music is not a magical gift of the gods. It is a human creation that can and must be understood by professional musicians. Music's effects are magical but it is not magic to create those effects. The magic happens in the mind of each listener. All these words are simply an attempt to explain how the magic created by the composer can shine forth from every note, unobstructed by misguided or traditional thinking by the performer. To free one's self from ingrained tradition is difficult. There is truth in the old saying, "Tradition means only being as good as the last bad performance." Arturo Toscanini said, "The tradition is to be found only in one place—in the music!"—meaning, within the score itself.[3]

Often, as young professionals, we reach a point where we feel at our wits' end. The traditional ways of playing excerpts and solo pieces have a way of freezing up what we call our inspiration. We suffer from burnout and feel we must do something—anything—to wake up our playing. But more often than not, the end result is simply an imitation of what has been heard a thousand times on recordings and in live performances. The way to break free of this depression, to refresh and reinvigorate one's music making, is to look anew at the composition without preconceptions. Forget all that has been heard before and study the music's structure. Then the cycle of pressure that forces us to look within ourselves for answers, instead of within the music, is ended. We can then assume a thousand personalities and points of view instead of remaining bottled up within our limited selves. Like actors portraying many characters, we portray the different states of mind within the music—the music does not portray us. When the structure of music is understood and communicated, instead of "me, me, me" in performance, the audience will be truly exposed to Bach, Beethoven, and Brahms.

Approaching music making by first unearthing the grammar leads to the building of meaningful phrasing. This creates true expression of the musical ideas of the composer in performance, which then can elicit the proper emotions in the listener.

GRAMMAR → PHRASING → EXPRESSION →
EMOTION → FANTASY

Approaching music from the opposite direction, with the performer starting with either an unformed fantasy or raw emotion, can almost never lead one to communicate the composer's true message.

The search for musical truth—the meaning behind the notes—is our perpetual pursuit. But what is truth in music? I believe the truth we search for—whether in art or in life—is *sincerity*.

Maria Callas said, "Music is the straight way to go to the heart and to the minds of people. . . . You must serve music. . . . Music is so enormous and can envelope you into such a state of perpetual anxiety and torture, but [to serve] it is our first and main duty."[4] When questioned why she continued this sometimes agonizing struggle for musical sincerity, she replied unhesitatingly, "Devotion and love. *To serve what you adore.*"[5]

This ongoing struggle for perfection in musical performance, fueled by love, keeps us working diligently to improve our abilities. This is the human paradox: being human yet striving for perfection. Why don't we just give up? Perfection is not attainable, is it? Yet perhaps the very quest for perfection is a sort of perfection in itself.

Keep searching within the music for answers that reflect its underlying structure. Those answers must be logical in order to appeal to the intelligence as well as to the aesthetic sensibilities. Musical phrasing shaped by logic has greater impact on the listener than musical phrasing shaped only by feeling because its grip upon the emotions is supported by a simultaneous grip upon the intellect. The arts are, after all, rationalized representations of life that attempt to communicate. Works of art do not simply appear in their completed forms. Thoughtful artists rationalize, that is, they think out and search for ways to communicate what they are trying to say in their art, whether in stone or in tone.

It may sound surprising, but the word "art" itself is derived from the word "artificial." This is because a painting of a horse is not a real horse; a sculpture of a man is not a real man; the actors on stage are not really the people they portray. A musical composition that kindles feelings of sadness or glee is also not these things. Art is artifice. The irony is that through artificial means the artist can evoke very real emotions. Fabled artist Pablo Picasso said, "Art is a lie that helps us to realize the truth." Once the musical performer accepts this, the doors of expression are flung open and the artist is freed to create the tantalizing illusion of musical "magic."

Abraham Lincoln felt the written word to be humankind's greatest achievement, "enabling us to converse with the dead, the absent, and the yet unborn." Written music too has this almost supernatural ability to bridge the yawning gap between the living and the dead, the present with the future. When music is performed with a heightened sensitivity for motion, the emotions the composer wished to communicate through the composition live again. An entire sequence of emotions felt by the long dead can then be experienced by us, the living. This is as close to time travel as we can achieve. For the fleeting moments when this occurs, the boundaries of time, and place, and self cease to exist.

Sound in motion is *emotion* in sound.

Postscript

Soon after Marcel Tabuteau's death on January 4, 1966, his remains were interred in the *Cimetière de l'Est* in Nice, France. The crypt, as is the custom at this particular cemetery, is only rented. If the rent is not paid, it is cleared and then re-rented.

The lease for Marcel Tabuteau's site was to expire in 1995, and it was made known that his remains and those of his wife, Louise, would be removed to "a common grave" if the lease was not renewed. Having no heirs, it looked as though Tabuteau's final resting place would be, like Mozart's, unknown and unmarked.

Through the diligent efforts of John de Lancie and Laila Storch, this was happily not to be the case. The lease was renewed with donations given by friends, colleagues, students, and admirers of Marcel Tabuteau. The two who coordinated this endeavor are to be commended for their loving efforts on behalf of their mentor more than a quarter century after his death.

The lease was paid until the year 2005, at which time Anne and Alain de Gourdon of the Lorée oboe factory in Paris assumed responsibility for the perpetual care of the mortal remains of Marcel Tabuteau.

His musical legacy, however, remains in our hands.

Appendix 1. Recommended Recordings

As intelligence should not be suspended while playing music, it should not be suspended while listening to music. Unfortunately, some seem to feel that when they listen to music it should simply wash over them, bathing them into a stupor. But when we listen, we must involve ourselves both emotionally and intellectually; otherwise we cheat ourselves. Hearing music and listening to music are very different things.

"Who Do You Listen To?"

When I tell people about the recordings of the musical artists whom I most admire, I am often met with the question: "Yes, but who do you like who's alive?" It is disconcerting to hear this question because I believe that, through their recordings, the great performers of the past are as alive today as they ever were. The public who never saw Callas or Stokowski on stage only knows them from recordings, television, and film. Most of those documents still exist. Simply because an artist's heart no longer beats does not diminish the intensity of his or her recorded artistry.

Mozart and Beethoven; Chaplin and Keaton; Jefferson and Lincoln; how much the poorer our experience of life would be without an appreciation of the greats who came and went before us. Their greatness is not related to fad or fashion. It is timeless and, therefore, just as much of our time as it is of their own. When questioned about the longevity of her seventy-plus-year career, the incomparable actress Lillian Gish is reported to have said, "I've never been *in* style, so I can never go *out* of style."

Vocal Recordings

"In my opinion, the oboe technique is similar to the human voice technique." —Marcel Tabuteau (*Marcel Tabuteau's Lessons*, CD).

As instrumentalists we must constantly reinforce our vocal connection—for it is our main goal to sing, whatever instrument we play. The voice is the first and greatest instrument. However, the sad truth is that many instrumentalists say they do not like to listen to singers. They only listen to other instrumentalists on recordings or in live concerts. Amazingly, many listen only to recordings of those who play their own instrument. However, without a connection to the human voice in song, something vital is lost.

"La Divina"

Soprano Maria Callas (1923–77) has changed my life. She has had a similar effect on millions the world over who, had they never heard her, might have gone on describing themselves as opera haters their entire lives. Because of her towering musicianship in the often less-than-musical world of opera, it is quite consistent for one to say, "I don't like opera, but I love Maria Callas."

It is safe to say that there has been no more controversial figure in operatic history. When the name Callas comes up in conversation, inevitably someone will say, "She was a great actress, but I didn't like her voice." Her detractors did call her a "singing actress." But the truth is that she was first and foremost a singing *musician*.

First, her acting, or rather her *actions*, were dictated by the music itself. She said that her mentor, conductor Tullio Serafin, told her, "When one wants to find a gesture—when you want to find how to act on stage—all you have to do is listen to the music. The composer has already seen to that."[1] Metropolitan Opera general manager Rudolf Bing said of her, "Once one heard and saw Maria Callas—one can't really distinguish it—in a part, it was very hard to enjoy any other artist, however great, afterward because she imbued every part she sang and acted with such incredible personality and life. . . . *One move of her hand was more than another artist could do in a whole act.*"[2] Thankfully, there are a handful of films of her in concert. Though she stands next to the conductor in front of the orchestra, without aid of costumes, scenery, or props, Callas creates the illusion of fully staged operatic performances through her vivid characterizations.

As for her voice, because of the astounding variety of colors she employed, it simply cannot be compared to any other. A *forte* sound for one character in a given opera was different from a *forte* for another. Whether she was singing the wispy Amina in Bellini's *La Sonnambula* or Verdi's murderous Lady Macbeth, the totality with which she molded her voice to fit the musical and dramatic needs of the personality being portrayed was and is without peer. Opera was

---

1. *Maria Callas: The Callas Conversations.*
2. *Callas: A Documentary,* dir. Franco Zeffirelli.

a chance for her to portray many characters, rather than—as is often the case—a chance for the character to portray the diva on stage!

Callas's ability to assume the vocal garb of widely divergent characters was only one aspect of what made her performances so compelling. She also possessed a shockingly accurate coloratura ability that rendered each note in a scale or ornamental passage as clean as one might hear it realized in fine instrumental playing. She had the ability to produce a true trill, with both pitches clearly discernible. The caressing warmth with which she shaded gentler phrases is similarly remarkable when contrasted with the scalding power she sometimes used. She demonstrated clear and accurate diction, no matter how high the note or how uncomfortable the vowel. Her voice had an extremely wide compass, ranging from low F-sharp below the treble clef to F above high C. Her marvelous breath control and rare command of portato and portamento also point to her sublime musical sensibilities. Additionally, her sustaining of the musical line was, without a doubt, superior to practically all other recorded artists—vocal or instrumental.

But beyond all these marvelous qualities, the crown jewel of her artistry was the profundity of her musical phrasing. Her searching intelligence allowed the music to speak as never before, or since. She built her phrases architecturally, which proves that her artistry was founded upon thoughtful musical analysis and not simply upon musical instinct. She was a trained pianist and learned her roles while accompanying herself. She knew the functions of the notes she sang.

Although the basic tone of her voice put off many opera aficionados, most of her detractors recognized her astounding attributes. The tone she produced was never one that sounded artificial or affected, as though her throat were coated with *crème brûlée.* What Callas possessed was a human quality, a voice which was not manufactured in order to fall conveniently into a vocal category such as spinto or dramatic coloratura. It actually encompassed these types and more. It was a big voice that was essentially dark in color, and she had the ability to heat up that dark sound to a white-hot intensity. When she did this, a quality that has been termed a "Greek resin" came into the sound. Like a fine dry wine, her voice could have bite to it. Yet, conversely, she was able to sweeten her voice to portray the most delicate of operatic heroines.

Besides her basic tone, the flaw that so many of her detractors revel in pointing out is the wobble she acquired over time in her highest notes. This was not a vibrato, as some claimed, and it was also not present in all her high notes. I can think of no other soprano (except for perhaps Birgit Nilsson) who has hit such dizzyingly high pitches so accurately and forcefully as did Maria Callas. This wobble was a physical problem that caused some of her high notes to undulate, sometimes—as in her later performances—almost out of control. Some have hypothesized that this problem was the result of her having developed an unnatural upper extension to her naturally mezzo-soprano voice. However, careful examination of the register breaks in her voice reveal that she was a true soprano. Others attribute this ever-worsening problem to her sudden loss of over eighty pounds in 1954. She also experienced years of serious sinus problems that caused her great pain when reaching for the highest notes. Perhaps this, along with her chronically low blood pressure, was a factor. There is also the theory that the wobble was caused by over-singing. Whatever the reason, this problem was restricted only to the very top notes, unlike many other sopranos whose vibrato wobbles on every note, regardless of range, rendering the pitch almost unrecognizable. Callas's vibrato was actually quite focused.

Through Callas's superhuman domination of her unusual and unruly voice, she communicated an unsurpassed range of expression. The seeming irony is that through her academic study of the music's structure, she left such direct *emotional* documents in her many live and studio recordings. Her scholarship enhanced her expression. The more one analyzes what she is doing with each note, the more one is taken by the realization that a rare intellect of genius is at work. Through her informed performances, she teaches us.

In the same way that Marcel Tabuteau revolutionized American woodwind playing through his teaching and playing, Maria Callas, through her consummately instructive singing, transformed the world of opera. Callas, like Tabuteau, had the ability to define the natural in music. Years after their deaths, both continue to cast ever-lengthening shadows over the musical landscape.

RECOMMENDED RECORDINGS

With Maria Callas, it is important to which of her recordings one is initially exposed. Her later ones can unfairly prejudice one against her. However, if one first becomes familiar with those made during her peak (1949–59), the riches to be found are never-ending. Only after familiarity with these earlier recordings can one then begin to appreciate what she achieved in the difficult last years of her career (1960–65). Her sad comeback tour (1973–74) is only to be listened to for the sake of completeness. By then, her voice was only a shadow of what it had been. Fortunately, during her greatest period she recorded many discs that have since become "desert island" recordings. More than thirty years after her death, they are still top-sellers. They will propel her legacy into the foreseeable future.

BELLINI: *Norma*. La Scala Orchestra; Tullio Serafin, conductor (1960). EMI.

Although Callas recorded this opera commercially in 1954 when her voice was at its freshest, this, her second recording, is the one I find myself returning to. In it, there are a handful of high notes which threaten to career out of control, but the rest of her singing is on a higher expressive level than she had ever before achieved in this role.

There are literally hundreds of striking details that could be pointed out. However, the melody that begins the second act duet, "Mira, o Norma," provides clearly demonstrable evidence of her scholarship, her detailed scaling of notes, and her ability to show their functions. Christa Ludwig first sings the melody, which Callas takes up immediately afterward.

First, an analysis of young Ludwig's singing (example 341): In the first part of the melody, Ludwig gives a curious push on the second syllable of the word "Nor*ma*," almost losing control as her vibrato needlessly intensifies. She actually loses the pitch of the note (1). She does this again in the next bar on the last syllable of the word "gino*cchi*" (2). Later, in the sixth bar of the melody, she accents the resolution of the appoggiatura on the word "to*cchi*" (3). She uses the very next note, a syncopated high A-flat on the second beat of the bar, as an opportunity to show that she can start a high note softly (4). Yet, laudable though this may be, this note is a syncopation and, as such, it demands intensity from its beginning. Ludwig then makes no discernible attempt at defining the rhythmic change to triplets that follows (5). At the end of her descent there is another appoggiatura. Inexplicably, as before, she stresses its resolution (6).

Now Callas takes up the phrase and plumbs a whole new world

Example 341

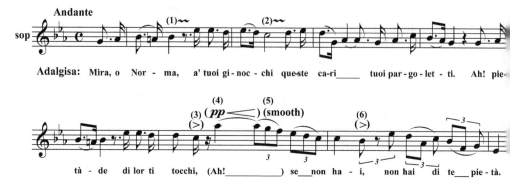

Adalgisa: Mira, o Nor - ma, a' tuoi gi - noc - chi que-ste ca-ri____ tuoi par - go - let - ti. Ah! pie-

tà - de   di lor ti   tocchi, (Ah!_____) se__non ha - i,   non hai   di te__ pie - tà.

of expression (example 342). The first and third notes at the beginning of this melody are chord tones. The second and fourth notes
are, respectively, a passing tone (1) and a lower neighbor (2). It is
these dissonant pitches that Callas subtly brings to the fore. She
then resolves on the second syllable of the second "perchè" so gently that it is hardly heard (3). Callas saves her volume until the crucial appoggiatura in the sixth bar of the melody (4), resolves delicately to the C and then gives a strong attack on the high A-flat
Ludwig had inappropriately sung so softly (5). Callas then sustains
this syncopation until the following triplets, investing them with
pathos by performing a portato inflection on each note (6), all the
while with her eye trained on the upcoming appoggiatura. These
are triplets that exist for a reason. Callas creates a palpable rhythmic
friction between them and the accompanying eighths. She then appropriately leans on the appoggiatura at the beginning of the next
bar and resolves gently on its resolution (7). Compare the way she
sings both of the appoggiaturas in this melody. The first one is an
eighth note (4) and the second one a quarter (*mor*-te). The quarter-
note appoggiatura, although lower in pitch, receives much more intensity due to its longer duration and the strong sentiment implicit
in the word "morte." There is no guesswork here as to Callas's intent; this note is the high point of the phrase. She then takes the line
to a remarkable close with an ethereal lingering on the penultimate
note, which is an escape tone (8).

The clarity of Callas's thought throughout this phrase demonstrates that her intellect was not disengaged from her expression in

Example 342

Norma: Ah! per- chè,   perchè   la mia co-stan - za vuoi sce-mar_____con mol-liaf-fet - ti? Più lu-

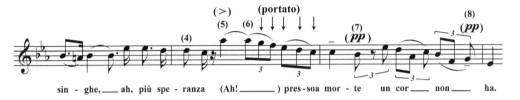

sin - ghe,____ah, più spe - ranza   (Ah!_____) pres-soa mor - te   un cor____ non____ ha.

performance.

BELLINI: *La Sonnambula*. Orchestra of La Scala; Antonino Votto, conductor (1957). EMI.

Here, Callas shines in her vocal prime. The lightness and purity of the sound she produces as Amina in *La Sonnambula* is completely different from that she employs in Puccini's *Madama Butterfly* even though both characters are young girls. Of course, the powerful sounds she produced as *Norma* have no place in *Sonnambula* and they are not to be found.

In the last act she sings the aria "Ah, non credea." The preceding recitative is every bit as involving as the aria. Examine each attack, each interval, each inflection, and one finds so much intelligence and emotion there that the aria, when it finally begins, seems to be an organic outgrowth of the situation in Amina's mind painted by Callas during the recitative. Throughout all this, the sheer beauty of Callas's tone is also worth noting.

The cabaletta that follows ("Ah, non giunge") is stupendous. Here, one is exposed to the fireworks of which Callas was capable. Her firm grounding in the techniques of *bel canto* allowed her to achieve such impeccable virtuosity. She does not aspirate her sixteenth notes as in laughing ("ha, ha, ha"). Many singers do this and they are lauded for their "technique." Callas sang through the pitches, binding them together in a perfect legato.

Her diminuendo on the high E-flat in the cadenza that links the two stanzas of this cabaletta is jaw-dropping. Incredibly, she then descends chromatically for two octaves—each note a pearl—and to

top it off, she then ascends through a series of turns, completing the
entire cadenza in *one* breath.

Example 343

Bellini: La Sonnambula, Act II, scene ii, *"Ah! non giunge"*

Upon the melody's recapitulation she ornaments profusely, ex-
pressing the exultation of the vindicated Amina. These ornaments
are performed as though by a violinist, yet often with the power of a
trumpet. The pitches of her chromatically rising trills at the end of
the final cadenza (performed *pp*) are easily discernible, and she
builds the last one with a magnificent crescendo.

CHERUBINI: *Medea*. Orchestra of La Scala; Tullio Serafin, conductor (1957). EMI.

In this recording, Callas gives vent to the vehemence she was
capable of displaying. Her voice here is completely different from
that of Norma or Amina.

In *Medea*, Callas proves that music of the classical era need not
be played or sung as though one is walking on eggshells. She reminds us that human emotion has always been keenly felt. In this
opera, composed in 1797, there are moments of sheer desperation
and animalistic vitriol, yet Callas never crosses the boundaries of
good taste by utilizing cheap effects such as the squealing and moan-
ing that often pass for drama on the operatic stage.

MAD SCENES. Philharmonia Orchestra; Nicola Rescigno, conductor (1958). EMI.

This recording contains mad scenes from Donizetti's *Anna
Bolena*, Thomas's *Hamlet*, and Bellini's *Il Pirata*. If this were the only
recording Maria Callas had made, she would still deserve her fame.

Her shaping of the "Al dolce guidami" in the *Bolena* scene communicates an overwhelming sense of Anna's longing for simpler times. The final notes of phrases evaporate.

Her note grouping of the triplets in the following examples is different both times they occur. She observes Donizetti's accents to perfection.

Example 344

First time last two triplet notes go to the next beat:

(Andante, in a slow 4)

Example 345

Second time middle triplet note is lifted:

Her echo effects at the end of this reverie are so internalized that one almost feels as if inside the head of the character.

Example 346

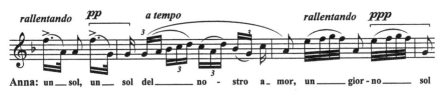

The last note of this arietta is sung at such low volume, coupled with high intensity, that it seems to quiver on the edge of a precipice.

I will say no more about this definitive recording of Maria Callas. However, I will take the liberty of advising the reader to turn out the lights and turn off the telephone while listening to this performance. PONCHIELLI: *La Gioconda*. Orchestra of La Scala; Antonino Votto, conductor (1959). EMI.

This opera perfectly suits Callas's voice and temperament.

The third act contains Callas's profound interpretation of the aria "Suicidio!" The extreme darkness of her low register reflects Gioconda's desperation. In the low-lying phrase "fra le tenebre," she uses a tone and power that suggest a baritone. The depth of her tone at the aria's close, on the word "l'avel" (the grave), is sepulchral. She virtuosically changes tone color on the last few syllables even though the pitch remains the same.

The drama of the entire third act is riveting. The recitatives contain some of the most vivid word painting Callas ever recorded. She was later to say of this portion of this recording: "It's all there for anyone who cares to understand or wishes to know what I was about."[3]

PUCCINI: *Madama Butterfly*. Orchestra of La Scala; Herbert von Karajan, conductor (1955). EMI.

One quality evident in all of Callas's recordings is her intelligent use of vibrato. She keeps it going on the upbeats, which is, unfortunately, extremely rare with singers. Once one is attuned to listening for this, the rightness of it becomes clear. Only in those instances where the character's mental or physical state demands a tired or innocent sound does she purposely "whiten" her tone. There are many examples of her non-use of vibrato throughout this opera, particularly in the first act. Callas's Butterfly begins as an innocent, childlike girl. In the first act, during the final syllables of the phrase "E per farvi contento potrò forse obliar la gente mia," when the teenage Cio-Cio-San renounces the religion of her people, Callas employs just such a non-vibrato sound, emphasizing the simple devotion young Butterfly feels for her American husband.

In the second act aria "Che tua madre dovrà," Callas builds to a searing intensity. The shame Cio-Cio-San feels about her past and her refusal to return to it come churning to the surface in Callas's disquietingly real portrayal. At the end, her cries of "morta" (death) pierce the heart. In this act, there is a noticeable deepening of Callas's voice, which clearly indicates that Butterfly has tragically changed through her endless wait for Pinkerton's return.

Throughout, Callas draws forth a myriad of color within the scaled-down voice she creates for young Cio-Cio-San. Only in the big aria "Un bel di" and in the final pages of the opera where Butterfly completes her transformation from the innocent girl into the woman who willingly sacrifices herself for honor does Callas unfurl her voice to its full size, thus deepening the shattering impact one feels at Butterfly's death.

---

3. Ardoin, *The Callas Legacy*, 154.

VERDI: *ARIAS: Volume I.* Philharmonia Orchestra; Nicola Rescigno, conductor (1958). EMI.

In the sleepwalking scene from *Macbeth* ("Una macchia"), Callas invests each phrase with its own color and mood. As she muses on the murders committed, the vocal line plummets to a low D-flat on the word "fossa" (grave). Through an amazing transformation of her tone, Callas creates the impression that the note is one octave lower than written. Then, changing tone again, the following word (the same pitch) sounds in the proper octave. At the end of the scene, Callas approaches the limits of human possibility with the *fil di voce* ("thread of a voice," as instructed by Verdi) that she produces on the last note—a fiendishly difficult *pianissimo* high D-flat.

This disc also contains the aria "Tu che le vanità" from *Don Carlos*. Callas's line and breath control are impeccable through the extraordinarily long phrases at the beginning and end of this scene. The first time she sings the phrase "S'ancor si piange in cielo, piange sul mio dolore" she sings through the high notes full volume. At its recapitulation she makes striking *pianissimi* on the words "cielo" and "dolore." Just before that recap, Elisabetta has the line "La pace dell'avel!" (The peace of the grave). Here, again, Callas uses the haunting darkness of her chest voice to great effect as she eerily intensifies the final syllable.

VERDI: *ARIAS: Volume II.* Orchestre de la Société des Concerts du Conservatoire; Nicola Rescigno, conductor (1963–64). EMI.

Although in her later recordings from the 1960s Callas often had noticeable difficulty controlling her extreme top register, her communicative musicianship continued to grow. In the Willow Song from Verdi's *Otello*, this problem is, for the most part, kept at bay. The desperate emotions she conveys are unforgettable.

One can examine exactly what Callas does with the repetition of the word "Salce" (willow) and appreciate the results of her intelligent searching. The word is repeated three times, unaccompanied, at four points in the scene. Here are my interpretations of her gradations of volume and intensity on each subsequent repetition, represented in numbers:

Desdemona: "O Salce! Salce! Salce!"

1st time	4	2	1
2nd time	5	4	2
3rd time	5	4	3
4th time	3	2	1

In her master classes at Juilliard, Callas spoke of this recurring figure:

> Each "Salce" needs a different color, and each group must be different from the previous group. For the first time, I would sing the "salce" forte, then piano, then pianissimo, each time draining a bit more color and vibrancy from your tone until the last is like an echo from a great distance. How you plan the other groups is up to you. The second might begin piano and become louder, the third might be a mixture of the first two, and so forth.
>
> The important thing is that they have contrast . . . and there is a tendency you might guard against of letting your support drop as you sing more and more piano.[4]

The "Ave Maria" that follows is profoundly moving. The final syllable of the last "Ave" hovers on the verge of extinction. Callas's control of her fractured voice at this point in her career is almost superhuman. It commands respect.

VERDI: *Aida*. Orchestra of La Scala; Tullio Serafin, conductor (1955). EMI.

In this recording Callas is aided by the extraordinary artistry of baritone Tito Gobbi. The confrontation scene where he sings "Non sei mia figlia! Dei Faraoni tu sei la schiava!" (You are no longer my daughter! You are a slave to the pharaohs!) is the most compelling performance of an operatic duet I have heard on record. Gobbi is magnificent.

In the last act, Callas's phrasing of the melody "O terra addio" is expertly scaled. Note her subtle manipulation of dynamics with caressing *pianissimi* and her approach to the climactic high B-flat. As in all of Callas's singing, the musical line is paramount. Her refined singing provides an educational contrast to the embarrassingly overwrought histrionics of tenor Richard Tucker.

VERDI: *Rigoletto*. Orchestra of La Scala; Tullio Serafin, conductor (1955). EMI.

Callas's duets with Tito Gobbi provide the highlights of this excellent recording. Her scaling of the contrapuntal lines in the many duets with her colleagues is architecturally relevant. The famous aria "Caro nome" is one of the best-recorded examples of the beauty of sound Callas was capable of producing in her all-too-brief vocal prime.

4. Ardoin, *Callas at Juilliard*, 213–214.

Dietrich Fischer-Dieskau, Baritone

German baritone Dietrich Fischer-Dieskau (b. 1925) was a master of German lieder as well as an operatic giant. It is evident that everything is planned to the smallest detail in every recording he made during his long career. Any of his recordings will enlighten and inspire.

RECOMMENDED RECORDING

SCHUBERT: *Die schöne Müllerin.* Gerald Moore, piano (1972). Deutsche Grammophon.

This recording is a fine starting point from which to begin studying Fischer-Dieskau's artistry. In his richly colored conception of Schubert's masterpiece, each song has its own mood.

The very nature of lieder calls for repetition of verses. Listen for the distinct colors and emphases he brings to each verse of every song. His vibrato is also a model to emulate.

One song calls for special mention, *Der Neugierige.* In the phrase beginning "O Bächlein meiner Liebe," which occurs toward the middle of the song, Fischer-Dieskau's control of the line is entrancing.

Dame Janet Baker, Mezzo-Soprano

Dame Janet Baker's (b. 1933) singing had power, clarity of tone, and purpose. She brought an almost spiritual quality to everything she sang.

RECOMMENDED RECORDINGS

BERLIOZ: *Les Nuits d'été.* New Philharmonia Orchestra; Sir John Barbirolli, conductor (1967). EMI.

In this essential recording, Janet Baker displays much character and temperament. Note her phrase endings throughout. They exquisitely taper to nothing with intensity.

Not to detract from her individuality, but in the final song when Baker sings the low-lying phrase "pour mousse un séraphin," there is a fleeting moment where she sounds like Maria Callas in her recording of *Carmen*!

ELGAR: *Sea Pictures.* London Symphony Orchestra; Sir John Barbirolli, conductor (1965). EMI.

Baker's vocal security is phenomenal. She is one of the very few musicians whose concept of musical line was evident in her performances. There is never a hint of ungainly "bulging."

ELGAR: *The Dream of Gerontius.* Hallé Orchestra; Sir John Barbirolli, conductor (1965). EMI.

Dame Janet's portrayal of the Angel's mercy toward the soul of
Gerontius as it descends into purgatory is touching. Hers is a voice
of intelligence and nobility.

Instrumental Recordings

Now to those greats who have so conquered the physical aspects of
playing an instrument that they make the listener forget the instrument itself. They sing.

Fritz Kreisler, Violin

Fritz Kreisler (1875–1962) was perhaps the greatest musician of the
violin ever recorded. The deep humanity of the man is revealed in
his playing of even the simplest salon piece. His singing quality and
the richness of his tone still elicit admiration and inspire awe. In my
opinion, the overriding emotion one feels when listening to him
can only be described as love.

Marcel Tabuteau admired Kreisler immensely and spoke of
him to his students. Laila Storch remembered, "Tabuteau adored
him." John de Lancie recalled, "Tabuteau said he thought
Kreisler's handling of the bow was the greatest of all the great violinists." John Minsker remembered hearing Kreisler: "Kreisler
was marvelous. He was one of these great men who come around
once every generation or once every three or four generations. . . . I did hear Kreisler at the period when he was at his
best, in the 20s and the 30s, and Kreisler was incomparable as a
violinist. He had all those qualities that Tabuteau spoke about."
Describing his tone, Minsker said, "Kreisler had the most beautiful dark sound of any violinist I have ever heard and it's strange
that nobody since him has ever come up with anything approaching that same tone."

Kreisler's recordings made between 1925 and 1930 capture him
at the zenith of his communicative powers. As a composer who performed (he studied music theory early on with Anton Bruckner),
Kreisler's performances never suffered from that debility so common among instrumentalists—not knowing whether one is playing
a dissonant or consonant tone. This simple knowledge informed
Kreisler's phrasing to the point that it became almost impossible for
him to take a musical misstep.

Fritz Kreisler was also a humanitarian. His gentility and musical warmth so endeared him to his public that when he was gravely injured by a truck while crossing the street in New York City in April 1941, the *New York Daily News* headline simply read: *"BELOVED FRITZ KREISLER / . . . Is Badly Hurt in Traffic Accident."*

Listen to Fritz Kreisler—for it is truly he, and not his violin, that you will be hearing.

RECOMMENDED RECORDINGS

BACH: *Adagio from Sonata No. 1 in G Minor.* Unaccompanied (1926). Biddulph.

With this performance, one forgets the dry, stylistically "correct" performances of recent years and seems to meet a newly humanized Bach face to face. Kreisler's refined portamenti (glissandi) reinforce the vocal nature of his playing. This is the only recording of a movement from any of Bach's Sonatas or Partitas for solo violin that Kreisler made without an added piano accompaniment. The result is sublime.

BEETHOVEN: *Concerto for Violin in D Major.* Berlin State Opera Orchestra; Leo Blech, conductor (1926). Biddulph.

Kreisler's first recording of the Beethoven Violin Concerto is still the standard by which all subsequent interpretations of the work must be measured. His magnificently conceived cadenzas are those used by the majority of violinists today. At the climax of the first-movement cadenza, Kreisler's playing of his ingenious *simultaneous* juxtaposition of the first and second themes of the movement is stupefying. The pathos and tenderness he displays in the second movement, and the playful energy he brings to the third, round out a performance that is a sheer joy from beginning to end.

DOHNÁNYI: *Rural Hungarica.* Carl Lamson, piano (1928). Biddulph.

The second movement (*Gypsy Andante*) is the highlight of this work. Kreisler's incredible way with portato and the variety of inflection with which he colors the repeated motifs are gripping. Listen specifically for the incisiveness of his attacks and the accuracy of the intonation in the double stops. In the last part of the movement, Kreisler transports the listener into a dreamlike world, such is the ethereal sweetness of his upper register. Kreisler's effortless virtuosity is admirable—and it is worth remembering that these recordings permitted *no* editing.

DVOŘÁK: *Humoresque.* Franz Rupp, piano (1938). Biddulph.

Kreisler recorded this simple tune by Dvořák many times, but this recording, made when he was sixty-three years old, is the most touching. Kreisler was unsurpassed in his ability to portray a sense of nostalgia. Who else has imbued the famous *Humoresque* with such longing?

DVOŘÁK: *Songs My Mother Taught Me.* Carl Lamson, piano (1928). Biddulph.

The richness of Kreisler's lower register is highlighted during the first statement of this melody. Note his portato "lump-in-the-throat" inflection at the end of the phrase. Immediately afterward, the delicacy of his entrance at the repeat of the melody one octave higher is breathtaking; it floats into existence. One is not aware of an attack. Pay special attention to how he comes away from the downbeats during the triplets in that second statement of the theme. He also gives a light portato inflection to each of the triplet figures and then sustains the long note that follows with great intensity (example 347).

Example 347

Just as with all his phrase endings, the last note of the piece fades away with life and vibrato.

GRIEG: *Sonata for Violin and Piano in C Minor.* Sergei Rachmaninoff, piano (1928). Biddulph.

Both these legendary artists wrench a wealth of color and emotion from this work. During the rising eighths that occur on the downbeats in the theme of the second movement, Kreisler plays with an exactness of rhythm, giving just a bit more weight on the first eighth of each bar and then tapering away. Again, it is Kreisler's vibrato coupled with the amazing finesse of his bow control that make this recording unforgettable.

KREISLER: *Caprice viennois.* Carl Lamson, piano (1926). Biddulph.

This is Kreisler's most biographical composition and his biggest hit. The pensive nostalgia of its main theme is contrasted by its brief scampering central section, a playful remembrance of the good old days of his Viennese childhood.

Jacqueline du Pré, Cello

English cellist Jacqueline du Pré (1945–1987) was a phenomenon. Tremendously gifted and passionately driven, she accomplished in only a few years what other geniuses take a lifetime to approach. Her technical command and flamboyant artistry manifested itself extraordinarily early in life. But tragically, her meteoric rise to public prominence in her teens was mirrored by her sudden disappearance from the concert platform at age twenty-eight. Stricken with multiple sclerosis, she lived another fourteen years as the disease slowly robbed her of movement and finally of life itself.

RECOMMENDED RECORDINGS

CHOPIN: *Sonata in G Minor for Cello and Piano.* Daniel Barenboim, piano (1971). EMI.

One morning in December 1971, after some months of inactivity, Jackie du Pré awoke feeling well (she had for some time been experiencing the symptoms of her then undiagnosed disease). Her husband, Daniel Barenboim, called the EMI studios and found that a space was available to record that day. The result was this recording. Her reading of the third movement is immensely affecting in its simplicity. Barenboim's playing is a model of support and sensitivity.

ELGAR: *Concerto for Cello in E Minor.* Philadelphia Orchestra; Daniel Barenboim, conductor (1970). EMI.

The work with which Jacqueline du Pré will forever be most intimately identified is the Elgar concerto.

In this live recording, not to be confused with her excellent studio recording of five years earlier, du Pré digs into the strings for the opening theme, bringing to life that word Elgar was so fond of writing in his compositions—*nobilmente*. Her ascending scale at the end of the exposition literally explodes with emotion. Contrast this with her gaiety in the second movement and tenderness in the third and there is nothing more to be said, except that in the coda of the last movement, time seems to stand still. (I also urge the reader to seek out her stupendous live 1967 performance of this work with the BBC Symphony conducted by Sir John Barbirolli in Prague on Testament [BBC].)

LALO: *Concerto for Cello in D Minor.* Cleveland Orchestra; Daniel Barenboim, conductor (1973). EMI.

In this live recording, du Pré presents such verve and musical conviction that it is hard to believe she had less than two months before the public left to her. Her rhythmic incisiveness and what she referred to as her "sumptuous" glissandi are in evidence throughout the first movement. The atmospheres of inward placidity and outward turmoil she projects are remarkable in their extremes. There are only the occasionally overly gruff attack and off-center high note that hint at the physical difficulties she was confronting at this time. In the second movement, the bleak sense of despair she communicates early on is set against the almost manic joy with which she invests the Spanish dance sequence that follows. Her jabbing accents perfectly capture its spirit. She begins the last movement with a gypsy-like rendering of the quasi-recitative that leads into the swashbuckling main theme of the finale.

I find myself returning to this recording in order to feel that I am in the same room with her, as if she were playing for me alone. The impression I get from it is not unlike what I feel from most of her recordings—that no instrument could have responded completely to the monumental breadth of her musicianship. Like Maria Callas, she gave everything. One almost feels guilty to receive so much without being able to give her anything in return. But so it is with truth.

Maurice Allard, Bassoon

Maurice Allard (1923–2004) was simply the finest bassoonist of the twentieth century. Allard played first bassoon in the Orchestre du Théâtre National de l'Opéra de Paris (1949–83).

RECOMMENDED RECORDING

VIVALDI: *Five Bassoon Concertos.* I Solisti Veneti; Claudio Scimone, conductor (1974). Erato.

Listen to Allard's groupings and control of the line in these beautiful Vivaldi concertos. The slow movements are sublimely played. The outer movements sparkle with an effortless virtuosity. Every phrase has direction.

The "sleep" movement of the "*La Notte*" concerto is worth singling out as the highlight of this recording. Vivaldi's plain repeated eighths receive the attention they deserve. Through his playing, Allard proves that in the right hands the simplest music can be profoundly moving.

Sol Schoenbach, Bassoon

My teacher, Sol Schoenbach (1915–1999), was known for the educated thought that went into his playing, as well as for his clarity of musical nuance. He was the principal bassoonist of the Philadelphia

Orchestra (1937–57) and became one of the world's most respected woodwind instrumentalists.

RECOMMENDED RECORDINGS

BEETHOVEN: *Quintet for Piano and Winds in E-flat Major.* Rudolf Serkin, piano; John de Lancie, oboe; Anthony Gigliotti, clarinet; Mason Jones, French horn (1953). Sony.

This recording has what I consider to be the single most beautiful phrase by a bassoonist ever captured on disc—the long solo near the beginning of the second movement. The purity of tone, the control of the line, the dynamic contrasts, the clarity of the note groupings, the singing vibrato, and finally the stupendous breath control (all in one breath) add up to a truly exquisite moment in a performance filled with them.

RIMSKY-KORSAKOV: *Scheherazade.* Philadelphia Orchestra; Eugene Ormandy, conductor (1947 and 1953). Columbia Records LP.

Sol Schoenbach captures the cockiness of the Kalander prince in the second phrase of the opening bassoon solo of the second movement by placing a minute pause before the sixteenth note that immediately precedes the accent in the sixth bar (example 348).

Example 348

II - Andantino

Near the end of the solo, a feeling of regret enters his playing as he employs an effective portato on the final triplets (example 349).

Example 349

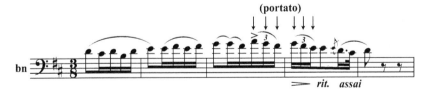

STRAVINSKY: *Rite of Spring* (abridged) from the sound track of the Walt Disney film *Fantasia.* Philadelphia Orchestra; Leopold Stokowski, conductor (1939). Buena Vista Records.

This is one of the earliest, yet probably the most famous, of the recordings of Sol Schoenbach. Made when he was just twenty-four, in 1939, the opening solo is an astounding example of control and limpid phrasing. Schoenbach told me that Stokowski had him play it literally dozens of times until he was satisfied with the result. At a time when most bassoonists struggled their way through this very high, difficult solo, young Schoenbach's committed artistry showed what was possible.

Harold Wright, Clarinet

Harold Wright (1926–1993) was, in my opinion, the greatest musician of his generation on the clarinet. His orchestral recordings as principal clarinetist of the Boston Symphony (1970–93) and his many chamber music recordings with the Boston Symphony Chamber Players and the Marlboro Music Festival attest to his sensitive artistry.

RECOMMENDED RECORDINGS
SCHUBERT: *Shepherd on the Rock*. Benita Valente, soprano; Rudolf Serkin, piano (1960). Sony.

It is almost impossible to imagine a finer interpretation of this work than this recording from the Marlboro Festival. From the first attack, Wright's elegance grabs the ear. Benita Valente also deserves praise. It may seem strange to point out so many details by Valente during an analysis of the recordings of Harold Wright, but her exceptional artistry demands close study.

The middle part of this work, its minor section, ranks with Schubert's most sublime creations. Valente's long phrases here are lessons in breath control. Her line is exemplary. Her subito *piano* illustrated in example 350 is remarkable:

Example 350

Wright says so much with the three concert C's that link the soprano's long phrases, by leaning slightly on the middle one (example 351).

Example 351

Valente builds her musical lines with consummate control, waiting until the high points to use her full power. She starts each
phrase *pp* but with great intensity. In the phrase in example 352 she
makes a remarkable color change over the bar line by lightening her
tone. Wright mirrors this effectively.

Example 352

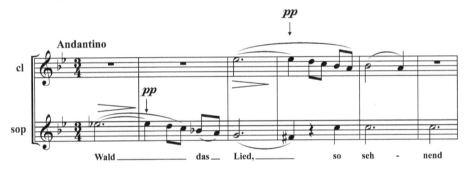

One rarely hears a vocalist achieve this kind of control. It is rare
among instrumentalists as well.

Later in this section of the work, Valente keeps the high B *in* the
line (example 353). Most singers simply allow high notes to stick out
regardless of where the musical line is headed. However, she builds
the line to the following F-sharp appoggiatura as Schubert directs.

Example 353

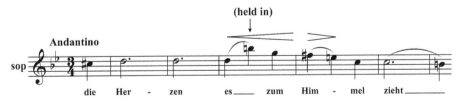

All three artists communicate the jaunty good humor of the
final section. The note groups in the figure shown in example 354

are brought out clearly by Wright. He plays the second group very lightly, creating a shrug-of-the-shoulders inflection.

Example 354

At the end, Wright confidently rushes headlong toward the finish line.

Pianist Rudolf Serkin provides aristocratic poise and rock-solid support throughout without ever becoming overbearing.

WEBER: *Quintet in B-flat Major for Clarinet and Strings.* Vera Beths, violin; Mari Tsumura, violin; Philipp Naegele, viola; Jeffrey Solow, cello (1970). Boston Records.

In this live, *unedited* performance, Wright marries classical reserve with graceful athleticism. Wright was like Kreisler in his way of musical understatement. When confronted with Weber's *fioriture* he avoids ostentatious show, preferring to keep the intricate twists and turns in perspective. His articulation is also crystal clear. Wright achieves an evenness and precision in the passagework that is extraordinary—and it is never rushed. What often seem like meaningless sequences of scales are played here with intense concentration of musical thought. The music achieves a level of profundity that perhaps even Weber may have found surprising.

In the *Fantasia: Adagio*, Wright's playing is suggestive of the ballet, with its supreme balance and delicate control of every physical movement.

The difficult technical passages in the *Menuetto capriccio: Presto* are playfully negotiated. Note how Wright gently resolves the appoggiaturas in the central trio. His high attacks are also without any hint of tongue, yet they begin clearly, cleanly, and on time. Sluggishness of attack in this register is a difficult obstacle for most clarinetists to overcome.

The ebb and flow of Wright's playing is evident throughout the last movement. His virtuosity in the coda astonishes.

John Minsker, English Horn

Known for his magnificent tone and controlled phrasing, John Minsker (1912–2007) was the English hornist of the Philadelphia

Orchestra from 1936 to 1959. He worked closely with Marcel Tabuteau for more than twenty years and came to exemplify the best in the Tabuteau style of playing.

RECOMMENDED RECORDINGS
BACH/STOKOWSKI: *St. John Passion—"Es ist vollbracht."* Philadelphia Orchestra; Leopold Stokowski, conductor (1940). Pearl.

This Stokowski transcription gives long lines to both the English horn and bassoon. Minsker and bassoonist Sol Schoenbach nobly sing this aria. Take notice of Minsker's cadential trill and its appropriate speed.
BORODIN/STOKOWSKI: *Prince Igor—"Dances of the Polovetzki Maidens."* Philadelphia Orchestra; Leopold Stokowski, conductor (1937). Dutton.

Minsker uses a subtle portato at the end of each cadenza-like phrase in the first movement, which Stokowski added to this famous suite of dances. The scaled phrasing of principal flutist William Kincaid, in his alternating phrases with the English horn, is also extraordinary. Kincaid holds in the high note of his phrase each time it occurs, preventing it from jutting out of the line.
MUSSORGSKY/STOKOWSKI: *Pictures at an Exhibition.* Philadelphia Orchestra; Leopold Stokowski, conductor (1939). Dutton.

The playing of John Minsker and Sol Schoenbach is again in the spotlight. Minsker's tone sails. The big tune in *The Old Castle* is given here to the English horn in Stokowski's very Russian transcription of this popular work.
SIBELIUS: *Swan of Tuonela.* Philadelphia Orchestra; Eugene Ormandy, conductor (1940/1950). RCA 78 rpm (1940), Columbia Records LP (1950).

Both of John Minsker's recordings of this work are spectacular. His seriousness of purpose, the flawless line, and the breadth of his tone are astounding. The clear, unforced quality rings. Truly, as Tabuteau taught his students about tone production and projection, Minsker's was "the amplification of a *dolce* tone."

John de Lancie, Oboe
John de Lancie (1921–2002) was Tabuteau's successor as first-chair oboist of the Philadelphia Orchestra (1954–77). He joined as assistant to Tabuteau in 1946 and assumed the principal chair upon Tabuteau's retirement. After leaving the orchestra, he served as the director of the Curtis Institute of Music for eight years. By virtue of his woodwind classes at Curtis, he is *my* Tabuteau.

Listening to any one of his orchestral or chamber music recordings always yields surprising moments of musical illumination. Any solo, no matter how brief, is bound to bear de Lancie's distinctive stamp.

FRANÇAIX: *L'horloge de flore*. London Symphony Orchestra; André Previn, conductor (1966). BMG.

This recording captures the best of de Lancie's playing. The fullness of his tone is beguiling.

In the first movement (*Galant de jour*), listen to de Lancie's line. Each phrase has a focal point. This can be tellingly compared to the French horn solo that follows. The horn player bulges out on each note of the same melody so expertly sustained by de Lancie only moments before.

Take note of de Lancie's subtle use of portato at the ends of some of these opening phrases.

At the beginning of the second movement (*Cupidone bleue*) one is able to tell, through de Lancie's minutely graded inflections, exactly the beat and metrical figure being played, even though the oboe line is unaccompanied. One could take dictation.

Example 355

As with the horn earlier, one can compare de Lancie's metrical, tonal, and articulative precision to the heavy-handed articulation and wayward rhythm of the clarinet solo that follows. John Minsker said that de Lancie not only kept the standard that Tabuteau had set in the Philadelphia Orchestra but that he also built upon it. Minsker also asserted that de Lancie's articulation was unmatched, stating that it may have been even more refined than Tabuteau's.

In *Nyctanthe du Malabar*, de Lancie exudes a debonair nonchalance. Again, the stark contrast between his supple playing and the clumsiness of the clarinet potently illustrates the high level of control de Lancie attained.

Very much a lullaby in everything but name, there is a sublime moment toward the end of the next movement (*Belle-de-nuit*) where the oboe reaches a tied note. The double basses have a pizzicato low C at precisely that moment. Here, de Lancie intensifies his tone and vibrato while taking away the dynamic, giving the impression that the note is momentarily suspended in midair.

Example 356

The chattering woodwinds in the *Géranium triste* movement provide a backdrop for the searching, almost lost quality de Lancie manages to impart. At the end of this section de Lancie magnificently heats up his tone on the long note that joins this to the *Silène noctiflore*, the last movement in this charming work that owes its very existence to de Lancie for his having commissioned it.

MARCELLO: *Oboe Concerto in C Minor.* Philadelphia Orchestra; Eugene Ormandy, conductor (1962). Sony.

This performance was my bible of musical inflections while I was a student at the Curtis Institute. In it, every note is played with purity and purpose. Here, de Lancie lives his definition of phrasing: "*Phrasing is the art of defining—while playing—the grammatical structure of the music.*" He said in his woodwind class many times, "Your phrasing should be painfully clear. If you don't make it clear and understandable, then the whole business of calling music an international language might as well go right out the window." In this recording, de Lancie speaks.

In the first movement, de Lancie's groupings and architecturally relevant playing highlight the structure of each phrase. The note groupings are clearly delineated without being pedantic. Every phrase has an inevitable sense of forward motion.

The second movement is the single most instructive recording of music in my life. At the beginning, de Lancie makes his attack and shows, through its delicacy, just how inappropriate that word— "attack"—is for describing the beginning of his phrases. The notes begin cleanly, but without the "t" sound of the tongue striking the reed. His releases are similarly outstanding. They delicately quiver into nothingness.

Throughout this movement, de Lancie displays his mastery of rubato. The beats are not distorted, yet there is complete freedom within them. There is no rhythmic rigidity, and still there is total discipline—not an easy tightrope to walk.

There is a suspension in bar 24 where de Lancie decreases the dynamic while simultaneously intensifying his tone. Then he resolves delicately on the next note (example 357).

Example 357

Incidentally, this place is one in which bar line phrasing and breathing work perfectly. Here, the harmony resolves at the end of the bar. The next bar is a harmonic surprise that calls for a change of gears. This proves again that there are exceptions to every musical rule, including "Do not breathe on the bar line." De Lancie also appropriately breaks on the bar line between bars 29 and 30 after the harmony resolves.

Example 358

The speed of his cadential trill is perfectly gauged to the mood. It is not like a buzzing doorbell. The last note then miraculously fades to nothing.

The playing in the last movement reflects the upward and downward motion of the sequences. One last gift de Lancie bequeaths to us in this performance is the *lack* of a space before the last note.
MOZART: *Oboe Concerto in C Major.* Philadelphia Orchestra; Eugene Ormandy, conductor (1961). Sony.

De Lancie's expertise is abundantly clear throughout this recording. In the slow movement he achieves total freedom through total control. His lightning trills in the last movement are flawless and his cadenzas fit perfectly into Mozart's style.

STRAUSS: *Oboe Concerto*. Members of the Orpheus Chamber Orchestra; Max Wilcox, conductor (1987). BMG.

This concerto would not exist had de Lancie not planted the seed in Strauss's mind by asking him if he had ever considered writing an oboe concerto.

Recorded in 1987, ten years after his retirement from the Philadelphia Orchestra, de Lancie received permission from the Strauss family to make slight changes to this work in order to provide some much-needed relief for the soloist. Strauss wrote incredibly long lines for the oboe and de Lancie felt that the concerto might be performed more often if the burden the soloist bears were slightly eased by giving a few notes now and then to other wind instruments in the orchestra. He also uses Strauss's original, more compact ending.

A few special moments bear pointing out.

Near the end of the slow movement, at the close of the phrase immediately preceding the cadenza, the line rises to an F and then falls wistfully. The portato inflection de Lancie performs at this point paints a mood of resignation.

Example 359

His trills at the end of the cadenza leading into the final movement are sheer perfection. Their speed, their connections to one another, and the way in which he slows the last one before the turn all seamlessly lead the line to the top of the phrase. De Lancie plays all half-step trills and plays a B-sharp in the turn.

Example 360

At the end of the final cadenza, which leads into the 6/8 coda of the work, the oboe has three quarter-note A's followed by three similar B-flats. De Lancie colors each tone differently, emphasizing the middle note of each group as a focal point. This is simply magnificently imaginative playing.

Example 361

This is a fitting final solo recording from one of the great instrumentalists of the twentieth century.

Alfred Genovese, Oboe
Alfred Genovese (b. 1931) was the principal oboist of the Boston Symphony (1990–99), the assistant principal of the same orchestra (1977–90), and principal of the Metropolitan Opera Orchestra (1960–77). One of Marcel Tabuteau's star pupils, his playing sings.

RECOMMENDED RECORDING
MOZART: *Serenade in B-flat Major for Thirteen Instruments* ("*Gran Partita*"). Marlboro Alumni Ensemble; Marcel Moyse, conductor (1980). Boston Records.
    This performance is my favorite wind ensemble recording. The quality of the music making is on such a high level throughout this all-star group. The entire ensemble rises to the level of Mozart's masterwork, which is, unfortunately, often played as though by a small marching band.
    Genovese's contributions are enormous. Throughout this recording, his playing floats mellifluously. The fullness of his tone is reminiscent of Tabuteau's.
    One inspiring moment stands out above the others. The long note Genovese plays at the beginning of the third movement is, simply put, incredible. He begins *pp* without vibrato, intensifies the tone, takes the vibrato away again, and then after reaching a white-hot intensity lightens up at the last moment before making the delicate descent toward the appoggiatura. On this single note he gives at least five distinct colors. I know of no other note like it on record.
    Genovese manages to play with a subtle rubato at times that all but defies the pulse set by the other instruments. However, he never

plays out of rhythm. This is rare musicianship on the highest level of refinement.

Marc Lifschey, Oboe

Because of the playing of legendary oboist Marc Lifschey (1926–2000), almost any recording of the Cleveland Orchestra made between 1950 and mid-1965 will not disappoint. His playing elicits a pathos that tugs at the heart.

RECOMMENDED RECORDINGS

BACH: *Cantatas No. 56 and No. 82.* Mack Harrell, baritone; RCA Orchestra and Chorus (Cleveland Orchestra and Chorus); Robert Shaw, conductor (1958). RCA LP.

This performance is an excellent example of what the baroque style should be. Lifschey's achingly beautiful playing is the highlight of both of these cantatas. Pay close attention to his groupings and sustained, singing line. His intense vibrato lends an appropriate yearning quality to Bach's music.

In both cantatas take note of the way the cellos and basses play sustained notes in order to create a line, even in faster music of walking eighths, with no loss of clarity. They do not jerkily detach those eighths, as heard in so many contemporary baroque performances. Thanks to Robert Shaw's leadership, this is playing that has not forgotten its vocal roots.

DELIUS: *Prelude to Irmelin.* Cleveland Orchestra; George Szell, conductor (1956). Sony (from a CD titled *Romance* from the *Dinner Classics* line).

Like his teacher Marcel Tabuteau, Lifschey could make the most inconsequential-looking solo of only a few notes into a memorable experience for those listening. At the beginning of this short work, the flute, clarinet, and oboe have similar phrases, one following the other. While the other instrumentalists are superb, Lifschey transports the listener by the way he plays the upward interval in his phrase. He drives with great intensity on the lower note and the upper note floats out, creating a feeling of levitation by its lightness. Listen to this singing interval. Study it. It is extraordinary.

Marcel Tabuteau, Oboe

Marcel Tabuteau (1887–1966) transformed the American musical scene. A graduate of the Paris Conservatoire, he came to the United States in 1905 after being offered the English horn position in the New York Symphony Society by Walter Damrosch. Three years later he accepted Toscanini's invitation to become principal oboe of the Metropolitan Opera. In 1915 Leopold Stokowski hired him as principal oboe of the Philadelphia Orchestra, where he remained until 1954. In 1937 he was awarded France's *Legion d'honneur.*

Tabuteau's influence as a teacher remains unsurpassed in the history of musical life in the United States. The list of his students at the Curtis Institute of Music reads like a "Who's Who" of American oboe playing. Composers, pianists, string, brass, and percussion players, in addition to those he taught in his legendary woodwind classes, gave credit to Tabuteau for opening their eyes and ears to the meaning of music. His legacy exerts a strong hold on the minds of many musicians generations removed from him. Those who remain, who worked with or learned from him—many do not separate the two—say they will never forget the man, his playing, or his teaching.

RECOMMENDED RECORDINGS
As for the hundreds of recordings he made during his tenure with the Philadelphia Orchestra, it is unfortunate that during Tabuteau's prime (c. 1925–45) the art of phonographic recording was not sufficiently developed in order to capture his tone fully. The oboe sound was notoriously difficult to record and reproduce faithfully at that time.

Scott Radio Advertisement.

The radio advertisement of the 1940s, pictured here, bears witness to the difficulty sound engineers had in reproducing the true sound of the oboe. Its text reads in part:

> The OBOE was the despair of a radio engineer's life because he couldn't capture its tone and timbre . . . but have you ever heard it on a Scott? The Oboe is a strange, shy instrument in the orchestra, lending a distinctive "flavor" to fine music with its peculiar moody note. Because its range is so elusive, few radios have been deft enough to capture it truly, to the annoyance and despair of radio technicians. (unidentified oboist)

John Minsker, among others, spoke of how full and varying in color Tabuteau's tone was in person and of what a "catastrophe" it is that his playing was not well preserved: "The fact that the tone didn't pick up fully on the recordings also affected the pick-up of his finesse. So much of what Tabuteau did was with the quality of the tone itself. . . . If anybody had a beautiful tone, it was Tabuteau. He could change the color and intensity of the tone without changing the volume and even *increase* the intensity as he *decreased* the volume. . . . Somehow, those original recordings sounded better on the playback machines of that time." John Mack (1927–2006), principal oboist of the Cleveland Orchestra (1965–2000) and a student of Tabuteau's, also bemoaned the fact that Tabuteau's tone was never fully captured, telling me: "I'd give anything if I could only play for fifteen seconds like Tabuteau for my students."[5]

Fortunately, recording companies are making great strides in restoring and transferring 78-rpm recordings. Consequently, more of what actually occurred on stage can now be heard and appreciated. Nevertheless, whatever their vintage or relation to the reality of Tabuteau's playing, these flawed recordings remain the only documents we have of a unique artist whose flair for telling stories through musical inflection will not soon be forgotten.

BACH: *Concerto for Violin and Oboe in C Minor.* Isaac Stern, violin; Prades Festival Orchestra; Pablo Casals, conductor (1950). Sony.

There are some recordings dating from the last years of Tabuteau's playing career that do give clearer glimpses of his artistry, capturing his tone quality far more faithfully than the old shellac discs had.

This recording of Bach's Concerto for Violin and Oboe is the

---

5. As told to the author.

best representation of what made Marcel Tabuteau stand apart from all the others.

Tabuteau's tonal modulations in the slow movement were captured more completely on this recording than any other I have heard. This is due to the use of magnetic tape as the recording medium and to Tabuteau's close proximity to the microphone.

There are three episodes in the *Adagio*, as the intertwining lines between Isaac Stern's violin and Tabuteau's oboe reach ever greater heights of intensity, in which there are moments when one cannot immediately tell who has the upper line, due to Tabuteau's amazing ability to tonally remake his oboe into a violin. At times, he uncannily intensifies his vibrato to emulate Stern's quality.

Example 362

At the B theme, Tabuteau enters on a low F. Incredibly, at this point it sounds as though a *bassoon* has entered the picture.

Example 363

At the end of this phrase (example 363), Tabuteau lifts the descending eighth notes (1) like a leaf floating down to earth on a gentle breeze. Young Isaac Stern emulates this drawn-out portato inflection and succeeds to a degree, but it is Tabuteau who remains the master here.

Tabuteau's octaves are a model of how to play with a sense of weightlessness. These are truly singing intervals. All the work is done on the lower note. The upper one floats out without any accent (example 364).

Example 364

At the end of the movement Tabuteau expands his tone, seemingly without limit. This illustrates Tabuteau's philosophy of a *forte* being "the amplification of a dolce tone." His tone expands to such an extent that he actually sounds like a trumpet on the last note. The decay he executes on this final note is truly a living diminuendo. The secret of producing this sense of buoyant weightlessness is to think of forward motion to the end of the note and beyond.

HANDEL: *Oboe Concerto in G Minor.* Philadelphia Orchestra; Eugene Ormandy, conductor (1952). Columbia Records LP.

When Tabuteau enters in the first movement of this concerto, for a moment one is not sure if one is hearing a clarinet or an oboe, so open is the quality he produces. The way he plays the second note (1) in example 365 immediately points to this as special playing. This note is lighter, yet not devoid of intensity. Usually, when one hears an inflection of this nature, the lighter note is lacking in support, communicating only a glib flippancy. But Tabuteau creates a sense of lightness and grace coupled with inner intensity. In this way he does not lose the line. The note still functions as an upbeat. The intensity of the next A (2) is also worth noting.

Example 365

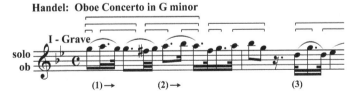

The way Tabuteau slurs the D to the G (3) is practically a glissando due to his legato fingers. The groupings noted are also clearly delineated by his delicate control of the airstream.

Later, note the marvelous groupings and color changes he employs in the phrase contained in example 366. All this is done through manipulation of his breath control under one long slur.

Example 366

The last note in example 367—the rebound, marked (4)—is played so lightly that one almost feels it more than hears it. Incredibly, he still imbues it with a sense of forward motion.

Example 367

Examples 368, 369, 370, and 371 illustrate a few of Tabuteau's note groupings in the second and fourth movements:

Example 368

Example 369

Example 370

Example 371

The pathos he draws from the slow aria movement is remarkable. His upward singing intervals are worth studying. The care with which every note and articulation are approached is evident. It is possible to learn volumes by listening to playing at this lofty level.

In example 372 from the last movement, Tabuteau keeps the half note A moving forward at a *pp* volume (5). In the dotted figure that follows (6) Tabuteau keeps the forward motion floating through the punctuation he makes between the repeated G's, as a skier would glide from one snowdrift to another on the air.

Example 372

Tabuteau was almost sixty-five years old when this recording was made on May 13, 1952, and, although one can occasionally detect some slight finger unevenness in some of the faster passages, this is remarkable playing by any standard.

MOZART: *Divertimento No. 11 in D Major.* Perpignan Festival Orchestra; Pablo Casals, conductor (1951). Sony.

This performance is another, later Tabuteau recording made with Casals at the helm. Tabuteau's rhythmic subtleties and dynamic and tonal colorations easily make the oboe solo in the fourth movement—*Variation I*—the highlight of a delightful rendition of this charming work. The lightness of his articulation makes the line float. He also keeps the highest notes within the line. They do not stick out. They are also kept alive by his subtle use of vibrato. The note groupings reveal his constant mental involvement in the music. On mental engagement John de Lancie said, "If you are intellectualizing, and the goal is perfection, the result cannot help but to be inspiring."[6]

MOZART: *Sinfonia Concertante in E-flat Major for Oboe, Clarinet, Horn, and Bassoon.* Bernard Portnoy, clarinet; Sol Schoenbach, bassoon; Mason Jones, French horn; Philadelphia Orchestra; Leopold Stokowski, conductor (1940). Boston Records (without opening tutti) and Cala (complete).

This is the only solo recording Marcel Tabuteau made with Stokowski, if one does not count his recording of the *Swan of Tuonela* on English horn made in 1929.

6. Master class, Muncie, Indiana, August 16, 1997.

In example 373, Tabuteau makes a breathtaking diminuendo as he rises to the high C's, sustaining them with great intensity while the notes float forward. His shimmering vibrato is quite in evidence here.

Example 373

In example 374, during the cadenza for the four soloists, Tabuteau leans on the middle note of the first and third groups of three eighths, showing those dissonant lower neighbor tones. In the second and fourth groups, he plays the main pitches strongly and then lifts *off* the middle notes—which are simply arpeggiations—thus showing their momentary departure from the downward skeletal spiral (G–F-sharp–F-natural–E-flat–D–D-flat–C), as well as showing that they are consonant pitches.

Example 374

In the second movement, Tabuteau's line is remarkable. Notice the gentle quality of his entrance and how he develops his first phrase. The color change he executes on the dotted eighth at the end of the phrase is typical of his way with tonal manipulation. Tabuteau keeps the last note of that first phrase alive to its extinction. The iron cable of the line, which connects the notes together, is never broken.

Example 375

In the next oboe solo, the line, again, is foremost. Near the end of the phrase Tabuteau places minute bursts of air on the descending eighths, making a beautiful portato inflection:

Example 376

In example 377, notice how Tabuteau ends the fermata note, allowing it to float into the silence that follows. His attack on the E-flat immediately afterward is incredibly gentle, picking up where he had left the previous note. In the next bar he performs another subtle portato on the falling sixteenths.

Example 377

Late in the movement, a similarly affecting portato is heard at the beginning of example 378. This portato is the exception to the rule. Portato normally occurs on descending figures at the end of a line, as shown in example 377. Here, at the beginning of this phrase sequence, on a rising line, it creates a tentative mood.

Example 378

dolce

Note the living quality Tabuteau instills in each note of the theme of the last movement (example 379). His staccatos are not simply pellets of tone hurled at the listener. They live. Each one pulsates with a hint of vibrato and they each have length as well, which creates a line. Even though they are detached from one another, they are not short. This is the living definition of staccato: separated.

Example 379

In the sixteenth-note variation for the oboe, note the floating quality of Tabuteau's articulation. There is no hint here of the country bumpkin staccato so often heard in wind playing. The subtle rubato, the groupings, the intensity of the shimmering high notes, as well as the overall shape of the line amply display Tabuteau's complete control and refined artistry.

SIBELIUS: *Symphony No. 4 in A Minor.* Philadelphia Orchestra; Leopold Stokowski, conductor (1932). Dell'Arte.

Not only is this a magnificent performance, it is also a stunning transfer of these 78-rpm records to compact disc by H. Ward Marston. The oboe playing in the second movement is a highlight. Tabuteau enters with the most delicate of attacks and develops the tone beautifully and, after the descent, he coyly lifts off the tied C in the staff. The triplet at the end of the phrase crackles with energy.

Example 380

His upward intervals shortly afterward are breathtaking. These are singing intervals:

Example 381

Later (example 382), Tabuteau makes an astounding diminuendo. This is exactly the opposite of what Sibelius has marked in the score. Tabuteau was most certainly instructed by Stokowski to make a diminuendo, and this Tabuteau does in no uncertain terms.

Example 382

This recording was made at the height of the Great Depression. Due to financial constraints, the string section was severely reduced. This undoubtedly resulted in Tabuteau being placed closer to the microphone. It is for this reason that I feel his tone and inflections were more fully captured on this orchestral recording than in most made before or after.

MARCEL TABUTEAU EXCERPTS. Philadelphia Orchestra; Leopold Stokowski, conductor (1924–40). Boston Records.

The first forty minutes of this CD consist of excerpts recorded between 1924 and 1940 that, to varying degrees of success, attempt to show Tabuteau's range of expression and tone color. The disc ends with the entire Mozart concertante minus its opening tutti. There is tremendous variance in the quality of these recordings, but some do manage to impart an idea of the greatness of Tabuteau's playing. This recording is, nevertheless, an indispensable reference to Marcel Tabuteau's peak years in the Philadelphia Orchestra under the direction of Leopold Stokowski.

MARCEL TABUTEAU'S LESSONS (formerly *The Art of the Oboe* on LP) (1965–66). Boston Records.

And now for the *pièce de résistance.*

During the last months of his life, Marcel Tabuteau concerned himself with recording his musical ideas. In fact, the last installment for this ongoing project was recorded only the day before he died (January 4, 1966). The previous August, Wayne Rapier, then professor of oboe at the Oberlin Conservatory of Music, presented Tabuteau with a reel-to-reel tape recorder and asked him to record his teaching concepts. Home tape-recording was then in its infancy and Tabuteau, fascinated with Rapier's gift, jumped into this project with his characteristic intensity. The resulting tapes were edited and released on LP as *The Art of the Oboe.* Now re-released on CD, one can easily select a particular lesson and study it many times in order to more fully grasp Tabuteau's often hard-to-digest concepts.

Aside from a television interview filmed in 1959, this is the only known recording of the unforgettable voice of Marcel Tabuteau. In this priceless document, Tabuteau methodically outlines his methods for musical thinking. Through his colorful speaking and playing, Tabuteau explains not only how to play a few orchestral excerpts but also goes into great detail concerning the proper way to execute intervals and long tones, as well as many other basic techniques. By listening to this historic recording it is possible to get a limited sense of what it may have been like to study with him—although here, as many of his students have noted, he seems much more affable than in his days at Curtis!

Marcel Tabuteau's Lessons is his last word to posterity. In these homemade recordings, Tabuteau's imagination and ceaseless search for an ever-expanding range of expression, even in his last days, is inspiring.

Dennis Brain, French Horn

British musician Dennis Brain (1921–1957) was *the* master of the French horn in the 1950s. He died at the age of thirty-six, the result of an auto accident. Fortunately, his recordings do him justice. He made classic recordings of the Mozart, Strauss, and Hindemith concertos as well as orchestral and chamber music recordings.

RECOMMENDED RECORDINGS

MOZART: *Four Concertos for French Horn.* Philharmonia Orchestra; Herbert von Karajan, conductor (1953). EMI.

Brain's beautiful line, the appropriate lightness of his tone and delicacy of attack, and his control and flexible phrasing, all demonstrated here, raised him to a level that sets an example for all.

STRAUSS: *Two Concertos for French Horn.* Philharmonia Orchestra; Wolfgang Sawallisch, conductor (1956). EMI.

The complete authority with which Brain negotiates the many

difficulties in these concertos is remarkable. His outstanding agility was always at the service of the music and never an excuse for mere show. Take note of the tender manipulations of his limpid tone. The liquid connections between the notes in the slow movements lift his playing out of the limited world of instrumentalism and place it onto the higher plane of singing.

Leon Fleisher, Piano
Each of Leon Fleisher's (b. 1928) recordings brings the listener to the realization that a percussion instrument such as the piano need not sound percussive.

RECOMMENDED RECORDINGS
BRAHMS: *Piano Concertos.* Cleveland Orchestra; George Szell, conductor (1958/62). Sony.

Although both these concertos are played excellently throughout, the slow movement of the second is the highlight. Fleisher's playing is filled with inflections and note groupings that keep the music fresh every time one returns to this recording. Likewise, the playing of the Cleveland Orchestra is magnificent. The first and most noticeable orchestral highlight of this movement is the playing of principal cellist Jules Eskin. His line is flawless. Principal oboist Marc Lifschey's contribution is similarly notable. Clarinetists Robert Marcellus and Theodore Johnson poignantly realize the heavenly clarinet duet.

Take special note of the pedal point in the slow movement of the first concerto. Here, Brahms has written simple eighths that, in Fleisher's hands, transcend the page. Each is weighted according to its harmonic meaning. The intensity they generate is incredible.

Daniel Barenboim, Piano
And then there is Daniel Barenboim. All his recordings testify that he has conquered the inherent limitations of the piano's nature as a percussion instrument. The illusion of constant forward motion and the line he creates make one crave his singing sound.

Barenboim communicates the architectural structure of whatever he plays. Far from being a purely intuitive performer, he is able to take wing in a meaningful way because of his educated awareness of the music's structure. Harmonic movement, including the all-important and most often neglected inner passing tones, guides his musical thinking. When listening to his playing one is overcome by the grip it holds over one's emotions while also engaging the mind. This is complete musicianship.

RECOMMENDED RECORDINGS
BACH: *Goldberg Variations* (1989). Teldec.
BACH: *The Well-Tempered Clavier, Books I and II* (2004–2005). Warner Classics.
MOZART: *The Piano Sonatas* (1984–85). EMI.

Orchestral Recordings

Leopold Stokowski, Conductor
All the recordings Leopold Stokowski (1882–1977) made with the Philadelphia Orchestra hold moments of revelation. He was conductor of that great ensemble from 1912 to 1940. Sometimes Stokowski's interpretations crossed the line into excess, but far more often his recordings bring unique insights to some of the best-known orchestral warhorses. He made the old new again. There is a bubbling percolation of energy from each and every member of Stokowski's orchestra. The slides in the strings and Stokowski's insistence on free bowing keep the line going so that one can follow the inner voices much more clearly than in most digital recordings, where the playing is antiseptically clean. The woodwind phrasing is similarly outstanding. The precision of the brass and their proper balance are also testament to Stokowski's fine ear. These early recordings demonstrate that the quality of a performance is more than enough to make up for limited sonic reproduction. After just a few seconds one becomes accustomed to their sound. If only to hint at what the Philadelphia Orchestra sounded like under Stokowski, these recordings are still worthy of study. The commitment of the playing draws one effortlessly into that ever-receding world.

RECOMMENDED RECORDINGS
BACH/STOKOWSKI: *Orchestral Transcriptions.* Philadelphia Orchestra (1927–40). Pearl.
Leopold Stokowski popularized the music of Johann Sebastian Bach at a time when Bach was widely regarded as a dry academic. Stokowski's familiarity with this music stemmed from his early days as an organist. Many feel that Stokowski's concept of sound was formed by the sustaining tone of the pipe organ. One can hear it in these transcriptions.

DEBUSSY: *Prélude à l'après-midi d'un faune.* His Symphony Orchestra (1957). EMI.

This is the most evocative recording of this work I have heard. Flutist Julius Baker's ravishing phrasing and oboist Robert Bloom's control are highlights.

DE FALLA: *El Amor Brujo.* Shirley Verrett, mezzo-soprano; Philadelphia Orchestra (1960). Sony.

Stokowski's reunion recording with his former colleagues after nineteen years away is nothing short of riveting. It is one every serious listener should own. John Minsker mentioned to me how he and John de Lancie looked at each other in amazement after the three mysterious repeated chords at the end of the *Introductión y escena* had first sounded in rehearsal. They felt then that the long-lost Stokowski magic had returned to Philadelphia.

The flexibility of tempo, the coloration and balance of the various sections of the orchestra, and the intensity of the phrasing all testify to Stokowski's mesmerizing hold over the excellent musicians of the Philadelphia Orchestra. The big tune in the *Pantomima* shows what flexibility of tone Stokowski was capable of drawing from his "Fabulous Philadelphians." John de Lancie has exquisite oboe solos throughout and Shirley Verrett shines in her *cante hondo* role.

WAGNER/STOKOWSKI: Love Music from *Tristan und Isolde.* Philadelphia Orchestra (1960). Philadelphia Orchestra Association.

This is another amazing recording made just as Stokowski was reestablishing contact with his old orchestra. He builds his synthesis of melodies from this opera to a towering climax. The way he has the violins slide up to the last note is riveting. The orchestra then sustains that final chord with an inner glow and perfect balance; all the voices can be clearly heard as the note slowly recedes. Stokowski has toyed with Wagner's instrumentation throughout, but if one is willing to forgive this, the rewards to be reaped from study of this recording are immense.

MUSIC FOR STRINGS. Leopold Stokowski Symphony Orchestra (1957–58). EMI.

Although not made with the Philadelphia Orchestra, the tone and phrasing Stokowski conjured from these fine New York players is reminiscent of his heyday in Philadelphia.

With Stokowski conducting, inner voices always have a way of making themselves heard without obliterating the main voice. Take special note of this when listening to these sterling performances.

Others

Seek out recordings of tenor Tito Schipa; baritone Nelson Eddy (movie idol of the 1930s); oboist Richard Woodhams, principal of the Philadelphia Orchestra since 1977; clarinetists Larry Combs, principal, Chicago Symphony Orchestra since 1978, and Robert Marcellus, principal, Cleveland Orchestra (1953–74); flutist Donald Peck, principal, Chicago Symphony (1957–99); violinists Pinchas Zukerman, Oscar Shumsky, Bronislaw Gimpel, and Joseph Silverstein; violist William Primrose; cellists Leonard Rose, Jules Eskin, and Emmanuel Feuermann; the Guarneri String Quartet; the Chamber Symphony of Philadelphia; and the Philadelphia Orchestra under the direction of Eugene Ormandy. All these artists and ensembles instruct and inspire.

Why Listen at All?

There are times when it is hard for one to continue the unwinnable struggle for perfection. It is easy to feel inadequate to the task. It takes a great deal of energy and love of music to stay on the trail of that elusive goal, and there are moments when that energy fails us. The frustration felt can be almost overwhelming at times, but there is something that has always brought me back into line when I have felt down.

When I hear a great artist on a recording or in live performance, exercising care, showing conviction and an understanding of every note, the love of music floods back to rejuvenate the tired mind. I hear, and am inspired by, the results of hard work and probing thought and refuse to believe that this profound emotional communication is brought about by a mindless fluke of nature called "talent." It is communication born of diligent effort, determination, and *intelligence*, which lifts us into the emotional worlds of the composer and performer. When this is achieved, we step beyond ourselves into a greater understanding of life.

Appendix 2. Further Study

Books

John Ardoin, *The Callas Legacy* (Portland, Ore.: Amadeus Press, 1995).

This is a chronology and critique of every known recording of Maria Callas. Ardoin's lucid commentary never flinches from pointing out Callas's flaws, but he offsets this with well-deserved praise and cogent analysis of her supreme musicianship.

Amy Biancolli, *Fritz Kreisler: Love's Sorrow, Love's Joy* (Portland, Ore.: Amadeus Press, 1998).

This long-overdue assessment of Fritz Kreisler's artistry is a worthy tribute. The only other biography of his life, *Fritz Kreisler* (1950), by Louis Lochner, was marred by the censoring hand of Kreisler's wife, Harriet. This book finally puts his immense musical contributions into historical context.

Philip Farkas, *The Art of Musicianship* (Atlanta: Wind Music Publications, 1976).

This concise volume has proven to me the truth in the phrase "Nothing one does or thinks is original." Many of the concepts I naïvely believed to be my own creations are succinctly put forward by this great artist of the French horn, Philip Farkas. Farkas's little masterpiece is testament to his lucid thinking and abiding faith that all can improve their abilities with proper guidance.

John Krell, *Kincaidiana* (Culver City, Calif.: Trio Associates, 1973).

Former piccolo player of the Philadelphia Orchestra, John Krell wrote this compact book as a tribute to his teacher, William Kincaid (1895–1967), principal flutist of the Philadelphia Orchestra (1921–61). The ideas presented are remarkably similar to Tabuteau's and reflect the symbiotic relationship Kincaid and Tabuteau shared.

James Thurmond, *Note Grouping* (Camp Hill, Pa.: JMT Publications, 1982).

Hornist James Thurmond here explains Marcel Tabuteau's number system as he must have used it in his teaching at the Curtis Institute of Music in the 1930s. This is an indispensable guide to the basic

techniques of note grouping from one who was there during the san-
guine days of Tabuteau's early teaching career.

Videos

Callas: A Documentary. A film written by John Ardoin, narrated and
directed by Franco Zeffirelli (1978). Bel Canto Society.

Possibly the best video documentary of Maria Callas's life and
career, made only months after her death, this is Zeffirelli's and Ardoin's love song to her. In it there are many filmed excerpts of her
concert appearances as well as a host of revealing and moving interviews with Callas herself and many of the principal players in her
professional life.

Maria Callas. A Tony Palmer film (1987). Image Entertainment.

A tribute by one of her most devoted admirers, this film supple-
ments the Zeffirelli documentary with revealing interviews and
newsreel footage.

Maria Callas: The Callas Conversations. Interviews with Lord Harewood (1968). EMI.

Lord Harewood was director of the English National Opera.
His passion for opera and the artistry of Maria Callas led him to
film these two fascinating interview programs with her for the BBC.

The Maria Callas Concerts in Hamburg (1959, 1962). EMI.
Maria Callas at Covent Garden (1962, 1964). EMI.
Maria Callas: The Paris Debut (December 19, 1958). EMI.

These incredibly valuable video documents of Maria Callas in
live concert conclusively demonstrate her genius. I am confident they
will set the standard for operatic performance a hundred years hence.

Jacqueline du Pré and the Elgar Cello Concerto. A film by Christopher
Nupen (1982). Teldec.

This film, made when Jacqueline du Pré was only twenty-two
years old in 1967, vividly captures the whirlwind life of this astounding virtuoso and culminates in a shattering performance of
the work with which she will be forever linked in the hearts and
minds of her countless admirers. A young Daniel Barenboim con-
ducts. The world should express gratitude to Christopher Nupen
for having the foresight to capture this vibrant couple in the full
bloom of their youth.

The Unanswered Question. Leonard Bernstein's Harvard University lectures (1973). Kultur.

In these fascinating lecture/demonstrations, Leonard Bernstein covers the origins of music and language as well as music's subsequent development to the mid-twentieth century. In conclusion, he opines that if composers use the "poetry of earth"—namely the "universals" of the overtone series and tonality—serious music will enter a vital new era of "eclecticism."

Recordings

The Art of the Theremin. Clara Rockmore, theremin; Nadia Reisenberg, piano (1987). Delos.

The theremin is an electronic instrument associated primarily with horror film scores. However, with this curious recording we are in the presence of a supremely trained and sensitive musician in the person of Clara Rockmore. Her hands move through the theremin's electrical fields that control volume and pitch to create unforgettable renditions of Rachmaninoff's *Vocalise* and *The Swan* by Saint-Saëns, among other works. With vocal and violinistic grace (she was trained as a violinist), Miss Rockmore tames this unwieldy instrument. At times, the sound produced reminds one of the voice of a young Maria Callas.

Maria Callas in Conversation with Edward Downes (1967). Part of the box set *La Divina* (1995). EMI.

This is a tremendously fascinating radio interview of Callas. In it she explores with fiery intensity her commitment to her art and the reaction of her critics to her unconventional voice and nontraditional operatic portrayals. At times, poor Mr. Downes seems all but unable to get a word in edgewise!

Maria Callas at Juilliard: The Master Classes (1987). EMI.

The famed Juilliard master classes (1971–72), which spawned John Ardoin's book and Terrence McNally's play *Master Class*, are presented here in part, alongside classic recordings of Callas. Paradoxically, it is the "Cortigiani" aria from *Rigoletto* that provides the greatest visceral excitement in this recording. Hearing Callas's piecemeal rendition of this *baritone* aria shows just how convincing a musician and actress she was, even after her voice had all but faded to nothing.

The Unashamed Accompanist. (1999). Testament.

   This is a humorous and enlightening exploration of the art of accompanying in which Gerald Moore speaks and plays through examples from the lieder literature. His dry English wit is a joy. His example from Schubert's *Die schöne Müllerin* is a wonderful study in contrast and a vivid example of how the realization of the piano part can illustrate and reflect the text of a song.

Appendix 3. To Clip or Not to Clip

(A phrasing dilemma in seven chapters)

1. How Should I Play It?

In December of 1992 I played Rossini's overture to *Il Barbiere di Siviglia*, which contains the famous phrase:

Example 383

Oboe, horn, and clarinet have this phrase before the bassoon. In the rehearsal, each player shortened the last quarter of the first and fifth bars, as is tradition, illustrated in example 384. They fully expected the bassoon to follow suit.

Example 384

But when my opportunity came to play the phrase, I purposely played the interpreted quarter note full value, as printed.

Prior to the evening's concert, one of my colleagues turned to address me. Hazarding to predict what he was about to say, I said, "Don't worry, I'll do it your way."

He replied, "It's not *my* way. It's the *Italian style*—Riccardo Muti does it that way."

2. What Is the Italian Style?

Before one can decide whether or not a given phrasing is or is not appropriate to a given national style, the roots of that style must be defined. It is generally agreed that most national styles of composition reflect the characteristics of the native language of the country involved. Nearly every word in Italian ends with a vowel. This attribute provides not only smooth endings to sung phrases but also a seamless linking of phrases.

The works of the leading Italian operatic composers—Bellini, Donizetti, Rossini, Verdi, and Puccini—are known for their *cantabile* melodic writing. The long legato line is a primary characteristic of the Italian School. A connection to the Italian language itself is inescapable. Therefore, in order to justify breaking the legato line of music inherent in the Italian tradition, the reason to do so must be shown to be well-founded.

3. What Is Opera Buffa?

"Opera Buffa" is a substyle of Italian grand opera that literally means "comic opera." A hallmark of this style is the incorporation of comedic elements in the musical content as well as in the plot. Rossini's *Barbiere di Siviglia* is generally considered one of the towering masterpieces of this genre.

In his buffa operas, Rossini frequently utilized a phrase construction consisting of two contrasting characters—one dramatic or legato immediately followed by one comic or staccato in nature, as illustrated in example 385.

Example 385

This juxtaposition of serious and comedic elements is a basic device utilized in theater as well as in music. A mood is first established and then broken through sudden contrast to achieve comic effect. This unpredictability is the source of the humor.

In comedy, the first part of a so-called one-liner sets up a serious situation. The second part then breaks the mood unexpectedly with a humorous rejoinder. The following jokes from comedian W. C. Fields illustrate this point:

Serious set-up
*I was in love with a beautiful
blonde once, dear. She drove
me to drink.*

Comic punch line
That's the one thing I'm indebted to her for.

*During one of my treks through
Afghanistan we lost our
corkscrew . . .*

*. . . and were compelled to live on food and
water, for several days.*

The humor of these quips would be immeasurably dissipated if the set-up were delivered in a flippant way that telegraphed that a punch line was coming.

4. Was Rossini Careful?

Rossini's overture to *Il Barbiere di Siviglia* is filled with examples of his scrupulous craftsmanship. Confining oneself to study of the bassoon part alone provides ample evidence of Rossini's care in selecting note lengths.

Bass line in quarters:

Example 386

Use of staccato eighths:

Example 387

Eighths followed by eighth rests:

Example 388

Sixteenths followed by sixteenth rests:

Example 389

Thirty-seconds followed by dotted eighths (no rests):

Example 390

Tellingly, the musical line at the beginning of the famous "Rossini crescendo" in this overture is motivically related to the bar in question. Here, in example 391, the quarter note at the end of each bar is not traditionally clipped.

Example 391

5. Why Do They Play It That Way?

Before one can accept that the quarter note must be shortened in this troublesome bar, it follows that one has to first accept a few other hypotheses:

1. Rossini did not write exactly what he intended.
2. All subsequent performers of this piece must understand this "Italian Style" of shortening the quarter note here, or else a stylistically incorrect performance will result by playing the printed note value.
3. Present-day Italian sources who espouse this phrasing habit have an absolute understanding of the performance practices of Rossini's day.
4. Rossini himself endorsed this specific performance habit of changing the note's written value.

It seems a stretch to assume all of these preconditions and then, in order to arrive at a stylistically rectified performance, take the active step of altering the only clue Rossini has left us of his intentions, i.e., the score. On reflection, it seems Rossini was fully capable of denoting what length of note he desired (see examples 386 through 390).

6. Why Play the Quarter Note Long?

A Question of Function
What is this quarrelsome quarter note?

It is not only an arpeggiation but also an *anticipation*—an upbeat that immediately precedes another note of the same pitch that occurs on the stronger beat that follows.

Example 392

(anticipation)

Also, the F-sharp that immediately precedes the anticipation is a passing tone—not only to the G immediately following it, but also, and mainly, to the strong G *on the next downbeat*.

Example 393

(passing)

Because of the leading impulses inherent within anticipations and passing tones, both the F-sharp and the G should lead to the next downbeat. This is a double-barreled reason not to make a space at the bar line.

In addition to identifying the function of each note, players must also look for the natural punctuation points in the music they perform. However, punctuating between an anticipation and its arrival note is most certainly the exception in music. When a composer wants this special feeling he or she simply inserts a rest or supplies a staccato marking. Imposing an interpreted rest in this cir-

cumstance must be adequately justified by peripheral considerations
that show the printed note value to be stylistically wrong.

A Question of Character
Clipping the quarter note renders this phrase monochromatic by
establishing a comically drunk character in the first bar. Both halves
of the phrase are then similar in style, i.e., bouncy. This interpo-
lated hiccup destroys the serio-comic, legato-staccato contrast
crafted into this phrase by Rossini.

A Question of Style
To state that one must shorten the quarter note, because it is in the
"Italian Style" to do so, seems to dismiss the following vital clues
that point to a very different conclusion:

  1. The legato musical line exemplified by the "Italian School."
  2. The smooth, singing nature of the Italian language.
  3. The comic element of legato-staccato character contrast in
     "Opera Buffa."
  4. Rossini's meticulous care in selecting note lengths.

7. How Did I Play It?

After arguing a point so completely, it will seem paradoxical that
when it came to the moment in performance, I played the quarter
note short. While I disagree with clipping the note, I realize that
consistency in ensemble performance is paramount. One must
weigh one's personal convictions against the performance of the ensemble as a whole. One may wish to influence and enlighten the
phrasing of other orchestra members through example from time to
time, but the concert is certainly not the moment to undertake such
an endeavor.

   Discussion of this and other phrasing issues within the orchestral workplace results in an opening of minds that frees one from
entrenched dogma. Rational communication allows differences to
be aired and calmly resolved. The ensemble experience then becomes a true collaboration. The meaning of the word ensemble is,
after all, "together." I like to believe that this definition refers not
only to being in the same room playing the same music with other
musicians but also to the bringing together of minds—including the
composer's. This joint mental effort brings all concerned much

closer to the meaning the composer has tried to convey through the flawed medium of written notes.

Over two and a half years after the performance that inspired me to write this essay, I came across a 1945 recording of this Rossini overture by the NBC Symphony conducted by Arturo Toscanini, a very Italian fellow indeed. I was delighted to hear that, in this recording, the quarter note that prompted my dissertation is played as written. I was particularly amused that Toscanini even allowed his bassoonist to stretch the quarter, for a yearning effect.

I have yet to hear a recording of this overture conducted by Riccardo Muti.

Notes

A STYLE IS BORN
1. Videotaped interview with the author, September 5, 1992.
2. Graffman, "Message from the Director."

FUN?
1. Oberlin master class, May 4, 1990.
2. *Callas: A Documentary*, dir. Franco Zeffirelli.
3. Ibid.
4. Interview with Edward Downes, *La Divina*.

FEELING?
1. *Marcel Tabuteau's Lessons.*
2. *200 Years of Woodwinds.*

TALENT?
1. Farkas, *The Art of Musicianship*, 6–7.

SELFLESSNESS?
1. *Leopold Stokowski.*

SOUND WRITING (?)
1. The Suzuki method of learning music is different. Young Suzuki students first learn how to play and then learn how to read music later.

WHAT IS NOTE GROUPING?
1. Drake, Hoffman, and Livingston, "Mairzy Doats."

RHYTHMIC GROUPING
1. As told to the author by John Mack, principal oboe, Cleveland Orchestra (1965–2000).
2. Phrasing numbers are applied to this phrase in Part 6, "Ornaments."

MOTIVIC GROUPING

1. Newman, *Wagner as Man and Artist*, 345.

THE TABUTEAU NUMBER SYSTEM

1. This is a dental mold of Tabuteau's lower teeth. According to John de Lancie, Tabuteau had the protruding tooth in the front of his mouth removed in 1946. Tabuteau told Felix Kraus that he felt he played better without the tooth, calling it "the secret of my embouchure!" In an article in *Musical America* from November 1944, Tabuteau may have shed some light on his state of mind regarding that very tooth: "Of great importance to an oboist are smooth and regular teeth, for he needs them to form a good embouchure."

2. Notice that the accented note in the third bar does not have a higher number than the preceding note. Tabuteau must have forgotten the accent. As Wayne Rapier remembered, by 1965, when Tabuteau recorded his ideas about musical phrasing, he had disposed of most of his music. He played all the excerpts contained in *Marcel Tabuteau's Lessons* from memory. A 5 could be substituted for the 3 Tabuteau places on the accented note.

3. Tabuteau introduces this excerpt as "a little pattern from one of the ballets of Leo Delibes; I *think* it is *Coppelia*"; as mentioned, he had disposed of most of his music by the time he made these recordings.

4. *Marcel Tabuteau's Lessons*.

5. Interview with the author, October 31, 1992.

WHY DOES GROUPING SOUND NATURAL?

1. *Marcel Tabuteau's Lessons*.

SOUND CONNECTION

1. Thurmond, *Note Grouping*, 53.
2. *Marcel Tabuteau's Lessons*.
3. Bach, *Essay on the True Art of Playing Keyboard Instruments*, 60.

TYPE AND FUNCTION

1. Only for those instruments that routinely use vibrato—clarinet and brasses excepted.

SKELETAL STRUCTURE

1. Helmholtz, *On the Sensations of Tone*, 490.
2. Of course, this is not correct vocal technique. This example merely provides an easy way for non-singers to feel the phenomenon of increasing and decreasing vocal vibration.

WHAT IS PHRASING?

1. University of Toronto master class, November 16, 1992.
2. Paraphrase from University of Toronto master class, 1992.
3. Farkas, *The Art of Musicianship*, 12.

REPETITION

1. Farkas, *The Art of Musicianship*, 16.

THE FOUR ELEMENTS OF MUSIC

1. The following four examples were cited by John de Lancie during my last visit with him at a hospital three weeks before he passed away.
2. Quantz, *Essay of a Method for Playing the Transverse Flute*, 254.

THE SINGING INTERVAL

1. *Marcel Tabuteau's Lessons.*

ARTICULATION

1. *Marcel Tabuteau's Lessons.*

TONE

1. Videotaped interview with the author, April 25, 1992.
2. *Marcel Tabuteau's Lessons.*
3. As quoted by oboist John Mack (c. 1994).

INTONATION

1. Pointed out by Leonard Bernstein in his Norton lectures at Harvard (1973).
2. A cent is one one-hundredth of a half step. On the piano all fifths are tuned two cents low.

VIBRATO

1. Mozart, *A Treatise on the Fundamental Principles of Violin Playing*, 203–205.
2. As quoted by Schwarz, *Great Masters of the Violin*, 86.
3. This was effected by trilling a key not crucial to the fingering of the note being played, causing a slight tonal or pitch variation to occur.
4. Bach, *Essay on the True Art of Playing Keyboard Instruments*, 36.
5. Dreyfus, *Bach's Continuo Group*, 109.
6. Glockner, "Stages of Bach's Life and Activities," 53.
7. Many singers today have a wide fluctuation of pitch in their vibrato. Not so long ago the majority of singers utilized a much more concentrated vibrato. There were "nanny-goat" singers but that type of narrow vibrato did not render the pitch a guessing game for the audience.
8. Perhaps this is based on my perspective as a bassoonist. Oboists and flutists routinely use vibrato regardless of whether they double the horns or brass instruments in a chorale. The bassoon is so often coupled with the horns that it seems second nature to me to leave off the vibrato when this type of organ-like writing

occurs. However, in *melodic* lines, one instrument may use vibrato and the other play with a straight tone and still achieve a perfect blend.

9. Of course, leaving off the vibrato on the penultimate note of a phrase is most noticeable only if one uses vibrato the majority of the time. For those who use it sparingly, the penultimate note does not protrude as much if surrounded by other "white" vibrato-less tones.

ORNAMENTS

1. Tromlitz, *The Virtuoso Flute Player*, 241.

2. A note to woodwind players: When trilling, if a choice must be made between fingerings, choose a fingering in which the upper note of the trill is in tune. Ironically, the ear will detect an out-of-tune upper note far more readily than an out-of-tune main note. When a less-than-perfect lower tone results, this is the time when the trill should begin with the normal, in-tune fingering and then change to the trill fingering once the main pitch has been established.

3. Bach, *Essay on the True Art of Playing Keyboard Instruments*, chap. 2, "Embellishments," paragraph 24, p. 85.

4. Ibid., 98.

WAS THERE A BAROQUE STYLE OF PLAYING?

1. Quoted by Mitchell in the introduction to Bach, *Essay on the True Art of Keyboard Playing*, 7–8.

2. Mozart, *A Treatise on the Fundamental Principles of Violin Playing*, 215–216.

3. Quantz, *Essay of a Method for Playing the Transverse Flute*, 205–206.

4. Letter of Bach published in the *Hamburger unpartheiischer Correspondent*, 1773, No. 7 (Jan. 11, 1773), as quoted in his *Essay on the True Art of Playing Keyboard Instruments*, 4.

5. Ibid., 9.

6. Ibid., 31.

7. Ibid., 35.

8. The word "baroque" is derived from the ancient Portuguese word "barroco," which meant "a pearl of irregular shape." The term was first derogatorily applied to visual art of the seventeenth century by art critics of the late-eighteenth and was later appropriated by nineteenth-century music historians to describe music of the period of roughly 1600 to 1750.

9. Helmholtz, *On the Sensations of Tone*, 495–505.

10. Reilly, introduction to Quantz, *Essay of a Method for Playing the Transverse Flute*, xi.

11. Ibid., xxxii.

12. Mitchell, introduction to Bach, *Essay on the True Art of Playing Keyboard Instruments*, 8.

13. Alec Hyatt King, "Note on the 1985 Reprint," in Mozart, *A Treatise on the Fundamental Principles of Violin Playing*, vii.

14. Neumann, *Ornamentation in Baroque and Post-Baroque Music*, 163.

15. Ibid., 30.

16. Ibid., 36.

17. Ibid., 79.

18. Bach, *Essay on the True Art of Playing Keyboard Instruments*, 84–85.

19. Quantz, *Essay of a Method for Playing the Transverse Flute*, xxxiii.

20. Mozart, *A Treatise on the Fundamental Principles of Violin Playing*, 158.
21. Ibid., 101.
22. This "messa di voce" is a special effect that can be used occasionally, but its overuse creates the impression of musical retching.
23. Mozart, *A Treatise on the Fundamental Principles of Violin Playing*, 15.
24. Meaning "lavishly generous."
25. Bach, *Essay on the True Art of Playing Keyboard Instruments*, 81.
26. Mozart, *A Treatise on the Fundamental Principles of Violin Playing*, 51.
27. As quoted by Rochlitz in Mitchell's introduction to Bach, *Essay on the True Art of Playing Keyboard Instruments*, 4.
28. Hart, *Fritz Reiner*, 201.
29. From Bach's autobiography, as quoted by Mitchell in the introduction to *Essay on the True Art of Playing Keyboard Instruments*, 16.
30. Mozart, *A Treatise on the Fundamental Principles of Violin Playing*, 102.
31. Ibid., 51.

PORTATO

1. Farkas, *The Art of Musicianship*, 43.

PRACTICING

1. Applebaum and Applebaum, *The Way They Play*, 95–96.
2. Farkas, *The Art of Musicianship*, 48.

PERFORMING

1. Conversation with the author (c. 1996).
2. Ibid.
3. Videotaped interview with the author, January 21, 1993.
4. Conversation with the author (c. 1996).
5. Mozart, *A Treatise on the Fundament Principles of Violin Playing*, 61.

TEACHING

1. Interview with Edward Downes, *La Divina*.

THE SEARCH

1. Storch, "Marcel Tabuteau," 5–7.
2. *Maria Callas*, dir. Tony Palmer.
3. Schonberg, *The Glorious Ones*, 367.
4. Interview with Lord Harewood, *Maria Callas: The Callas Conversations*.
5. Interview with Edward Downes, *La Divina*.

Bibliography

AUDIOVISUAL MATERIALS

Callas: A Documentary. Directed by Franco Zeffirelli. Written by John Ardoin. Bel Canto Society no. 194, 1978.

La Divina, compact disc 4. Interview of Maria Callas by Edward Downes (1967). EMI 7243-5-65822-4, 1995.

Leopold Stokowski. National Education Television. VHS. 1970.

Marcel Tabuteau's Lessons. 1965–66. Boston Records BR1017CD, 1996.

Maria Callas: The Callas Conversations. Interview with Lord Harewood (April 1968). EMI 4907649 (DVD), 2004.

Maria Callas: La Divina—A Portrait (1987). Directed by Tony Palmer. Image Entertainment ID 5825RA (DVD).

200 Years of Woodwinds. Philadelphia Woodwind Quintet. National Education Television series. 13 episodes. 1959.

PRINTED MATERIALS

Applebaum, Sada, and Samuel Applebaum. *The Way They Play.* Neptune City, N.J.: Paganiniana Publications, 1972.

Ardoin, John. *Callas at Juilliard: The Master Classes.* New York: Knopf, 1987.

————. *The Callas Legacy.* 4th ed. Portland, Ore.: Amadeus Press, 1995.

Arnold, Denis. *The New Oxford Companion to Music.* 2 vols. Oxford: Oxford University Press, 1983.

Bach, C. P. E. *Essay on the True Art of Playing Keyboard Instruments.* Trans. and ed. William J. Mitchell. New York: Norton, 1949.

Baker, Theodore. *Pronouncing Pocket-Manual of Musical Terms.* Revised and augmented ed. New York: G. Schirmer, 1933.

Clarke, Hugh Archibald. *Pronouncing Dictionary of Musical Terms.* Philadelphia: T. Presser, 1896.

Drake, Milton, Al Hoffman, and Jerry Livingston. "Mairzy Doats." New York: Miller Music Corporation, 1943.

Dreyfus, Laurence. *Bach's Continuo Group: Players and Practices in His Vocal Works.* Cambridge, Mass.: Harvard University Press, 1987.

Farkas, Philip. *The Art of Musicianship.* Atlanta: Wind Music Publications, 1976.

Geminiani, Francesco, and David Dodge Boyden. *The Art of Playing on the Violin.* Facsimile ed. London and New York: Oxford University Press, 1900, 1933.

Glockner, Andreas. "Stages of Bach's Life and Activities." In *The World of Bach Cantatas: Early Sacred Cantatas,* ed. Christoph Wolff. New York: Norton, 1997.

Graffman, Gary. "Message from the Director." *Overtones: The Publication of the Curtis Institute of Music.* June 1997.

Grove, Sir George. *Grove Dictionary of Music and Musicians.* Ed. Stanley Sadie. Washington, D.C.: Grove's Dictionaries of Music, 1980.

Hart, Philip. *Fritz Reiner: A Biography.* Evanston, Ill.: Northwestern University Press, 1994.

Helmholtz, Hermann. *On the Sensations of Tone*. 2nd ed. London: Longmans, Green, 1885.

Mozart, Leopold. *A Treatise on the Fundamental Principles of Violin Playing* (1775). 2nd ed. Oxford: Oxford University Press, 1972.

Neumann, Frederick. *Ornamentation in Baroque and Post-Baroque Music*. Princeton, N.J.: Princeton University Press, 1983.

Newman, Ernest. *Wagner as Man and Artist*. New York: Vintage, 1960.

Quantz, Johann Joachim. *On Playing the Flute*. Trans. Edward R. Reilly. New York: G. Schirmer, 1966, 1975.

Schonberg, Harold. *The Glorious Ones*. New York: Times Books, 1985.

Schwarz, Boris. *Great Masters of the Violin*. New York: Simon and Schuster, 1983.

Storch, Laila. "Marcel Tabuteau." *To The World's Oboists* 2, no. 1 (March 1974): 5–7.

Thurmond, James. *Note Grouping*. Camp Hill, Pa.: JMT Publications, 1982.

Tromlitz, Johann George. *The Virtuoso Flute Player*. 1791. Trans. Ardal Powell. New York: Cambridge University Press, 1991.

Index

Grammy Award–winning bassoonist David McGill has been principal bassoonist of the Chicago Symphony Orchestra since 1997, having held the same position in the Cleveland Orchestra, Toronto Symphony, and Tulsa Philharmonic. He has served on the faculties of Indiana University, DePaul University, Roosevelt University, the Cleveland Institute of Music, and the University of Toronto, and he has taught master classes in Finland, Hungary, Canada, and throughout the United States. He is a 1985 graduate of the Curtis Institute of Music in Philadelphia.

CPSIA information can be obtained
at www.ICGtesting.com
Printed in the USA
JSHW041040220522
26242JS00004B/193

9 780253 219268